Swaying
in the
Treetops

*A True Story of Faith
and the Fatherless*

SCOTT AND KATHERINE ROSENOW

Table of Contents

Endorsements

"Swaying in the Treetops will challenge and encourage you. You will find yourself reciting the Rosenows' stories to your friends and family long after you shut the book. It's an inspiration to any of us who have wondered what surrender looks like."

~Beth Guckenberger

Co-Executive Director, Back 2 Back Ministries

"Swaying In The Treetops is an incredible story of courage, love, faithfulness, and family. I found myself thoroughly engaged and inspired, and before long was looking for my own tree to climb."

~Scott Krippayne

Christian Recording Artist

"When Christians seek out and care for the orphan in distress, it makes the Gospel vibrantly visible in both its beauty and its costliness. Nowhere is that more true than with the Rosenow family. Their story weaves an unforgettable journey of faithfulness to God, and along the way reveals God's heart in actions that glow brighter than words alone ever could."

~Jedd Medefind

President, Christian Alliance for Orphans

"God is always doing something bigger than we think or expect . . . more than we could have anticipated! In His desire to be with us, He calls us to 'come out into the deep' with Him. This is the story of God's call to Scott and Kathy Rosenow, and the adventure that ensued. When we set aside our fears and our personal plans to embrace His purposes, Heaven comes down and touches us all. The Rosenows are walking out a God-adventure of epic proportions. Their story will inspire you, touch your heart, challenge your plans, and whet your appetite for a God-adventure of your own! Read at your own risk!"

~Terry Meeuwsen

Co-host, The 700 Club

Director, Orphan's Promise

"An amazing true story of God at work in the lives of an everyday couple as they wrestle with faith, sacrifice, hardship, and triumph while living out the unbelievable call of God on their lives. A captivating book that will be hard to put down."

~Bruce Carroll

Christian Recording Artist

"Scott and Kathy have walked a remarkable journey of faith, and I am humbled and honored that my life story has encouraged them along the way!"

~Joni Eareckson Tada

Joni and Friends International Disability Center

Dedication

We can't even begin to express our gratitude to those who have been a part of this journey with us and who have helped make the writing of this book possible. Our children, first and foremost. They are our heroes, all of them. We thank them for the lessons they have taught us and continue to teach us every day. Their perseverance, their courage, their thirst to drink up love and joy—all of these have taught us to press on and to try harder to see God's handprints in, and to trust Him more fully with, all the details of our lives. Even in the midst of their tremendous struggles to throw off their dark pasts and to learn to let us know and love them, God has used them to shine a penetrating light into our own hearts, revealing there selfishness, our own inability to trust, and our own fear of letting Him truly know and love us. Life with them is making us better people. Without their encouragement, the unselfish willingness of the older ones to care for the younger ones so we could slip away on Fridays and work on the manuscript, their excitement over seeing this project reach completion—without all of this, this book never could've happened.

We are grateful to Kathy's mother, who has been our greatest prayer warrior throughout this whole crazy adoption and faith journey. We thank those who agreed to serve as "test readers," helping us determine whether the stories made sense or were simply confusing. And to those hundreds of you out there who have prayed for our family and for The Shepherd's Crook Orphan Ministry, donated your time and finances to making the dream of this ministry a reality, prepared meals for our children while we had to be away for surgeries or adoptions, helped with fund-raising and letter-writing each time we followed God into another adoption ourselves, you medical professionals who've been so committed to helping the two of us take care of this large and needy family that you have even sometimes donated your services—all of you, we wish there were some way to make you understand what a critical piece of this story you are. We also thank all of the many volunteers who have served and/or are still serving TSC. You have changed hundreds of lives as you poured your hearts into saving orphans.

This book is dedicated to all of you with more love and appreciation than our words could ever speak. But God knows. He has seen every tear you've cried, heard every prayer you've prayed, watched every free minute you've sacrificed, and breathed His blessing on every life you have touched. He knows what our hearts aren't able to say, and someday, He will tell you Himself what an amazing thing you have done.

Preface

Excerpt from E-mail Update by Kathy Rosenow, October 20, 2003:

*One day I asked myself, "**How** did we get here?" I had a clear mental picture of myself climbing a tall, tall tree. I felt like I could remember so clearly what it had been like when God first said, "Come on up – I want you to climb higher in your walk with Me than you have been before." And we started Nathan's adoption. It was great, and He was so faithful to miraculously provide all that we needed to complete that very expensive Bolivian adoption. Then came Meghan, and we climbed a bit higher, still feeling a growing sense of excitement about where God might be leading us as we watched Him again provide all that was needed for her homecoming. Then we started Robyn's and Colin's adoptions. During that period, we scaled this tree at amazing speed, climbing to dizzying heights and feeling pure euphoria as we saw God perform incredible miracles, one after another, to bring those two home and put the pieces into place for the starting of The Shepherd's Crook Orphan Ministry. We felt like we could look* *down and see such beautiful things about God and His plans for His children that we had not been able to see when we were still on the ground or not so high up the tree. And we wanted to yell to the world, "Brothers and sisters in Christ!! Come on up!! You won't believe what it's like up here! Please come and share this with us!" Then we started Carlin's adoption and immediately after that, Aidan's, then Madlin's. And the two years that followed left us exhausted — emotionally, spiritually, and physically. The adoptions were more difficult than our first ones, the answers to prayer didn't come as quickly as they had in the early part of the climb, the heartbreak — especially in Aidan's case — was far more than we had ever dreamed we would experience when we agreed to follow God into this tree. We climbed much more slowly and fearfully during that period. And that day as I asked myself this question and remembered all of these things, I realized that I suddenly felt like I had climbed so far up, that when I looked down I could no longer see any of God's beautiful plans that I had seen earlier. Everything was so far down that it was blurry and I felt like I was so high up that this tree had become as thin as a twig and was suddenly a swaying, crazy, unsafe place to be. I prayed, "God I'm so far up that it's too scary to look down. I can't see anything at all anymore. I'm scared and I don't know what to do!" And as clear as anything, although it wasn't an audible voice, I felt God say to me, "Then stop looking down and look up!" It really is that simple — although not at all easy. I think of that picture and those words often as the climb gets higher and scarier and more difficult.*

We are Scott and Kathy Rosenow. We are the founders of The Shepherd's Crook Orphan Ministry and, at the time of this writing, the parents of twenty-two children, nineteen of whom are still living in our home. When we married in 1977, we had no idea that there would come a time when wheelchairs, prosthetic limbs, anti-seizure medications, Braille, and twenty to forty monthly doctor and therapy appointments would be a part of our daily lives. We could never have dreamed that one day it would take five dozen eggs, a loaf and a half of bread, and three pounds of bacon for a breakfast, or ten pounds of chicken breasts, eight pounds of steamed broccoli, and ten pounds of potatoes for one night's supper. It didn't seem possible that a fifteen-passenger van wouldn't transport our entire family, or that a 2,100-square-foot house could feel so crowded, or that our children's bedrooms would be furnished with not only double-, but triple-bunk beds. And it certainly never even entered our minds that God would allow us the privilege of being a small part of the lives of hundreds of hurting, lonely children from all corners of His world.

This book is the first part of the story of how God changed the two of us: how He molded and shaped our lives and then worked through us to change the futures of many orphans, children all over the world who were born into situations of darkness and hopeless-ness. As God has worked out His plans in and through our lives, we have learned that, although the tree we are climbing seemed terrifyingly high in 2003 (when the e-mail excerpt, above, was written), it goes so much higher still—and we still have so far to go. But as a friend once told us, "If you want to get to the really good fruit, then you have to get out on the branches, where it's shaky and scary." He was right. The fruit is sweeter and richer than we can describe. We thank God that we serve a risen Savior who has promised never to leave us or forsake us as we make this climb, and we continue striving to look up into His loving face as we follow Him into the ever-higher branches.

This story was written by the two of us, Scott and Kathy; however, we have chosen to write it through the voice of a single person, Scott. We did this to avoid confusion and, hopefully, make the book a bit easier to read. We cherished our Friday afternoons at local coffee shops each week, where we would work for several hours alone; every Friday, we searched through old journal entries and e-mails, reliving the excitement, pain, battles, and joy of our adoption journeys, writing together and watching God slowly put this story onto paper for others to read. We will miss those Friday work "dates."

We pray that our story will in some way encourage you in your walk of faith, even if that walk is completely different from ours and has nothing to do with adoption.

Chapter 1

The Building
of a Different House

Imagine yourself as a living house. God comes in to rebuild that house. At first, perhaps, you can understand what He is doing. He is getting the drains right and stopping the leaks in the roof and so on; you knew that those jobs needed doing and so you are not surprised. But presently He starts knocking the house about in a way that hurts abominably and does not seem to make any sense. What on earth is He up to? The explanation is that He is building quite a different house from the one you thought of — throwing out a new wing here, putting on an extra floor there, running up towers, making courtyards. You thought you were being made into a decent little cottage, but He is building a palace. He intends to come and live in it Himself.

C.S. Lewis

Marriage and early years

Some of the most interesting things in life begin unexpectedly. A phone call. An e-mail. A comment from a friend, and suddenly the course you're on changes, and your life changes with it. One such change-of-course happened to us through a series of circumstances which, as a whole, proved to be pivotal. This series of circumstances was many years in the making, as God carefully, meticulously wove the tapestry of our lives into a picture vastly different from the one we imagined at the beginning of our married life.

Kathy and I were both raised in Christian homes and professed faith in Christ while still young. We went to the same high school in the suburbs of Birmingham, Alabama, though I was two years ahead of her. I was, in fact, best friends with Kathy's brother, Gary, and this friendship brought me often into their home. It would be difficult to name just exactly when I began to notice Gary's younger sister Kathy, or when she began to notice me. I believe I noticed her long before she noticed me, but I couldn't prove it. I began to look for ways to "happen to be" over at Gary's house, and in time, both Kathy and I began manufacturing "reasons" for the two of us to end up together. By the fall of 1975, we both realized that we were absolutely crazy about each other. As young as we were, we knew that we wanted to spend the rest of our lives together. In January of 1976, I headed off to begin my tour of duty in the Navy while Kathy was still in high school, and we were forced to conduct our romance long distance, via letters and occasional visits when I could get leave and afford a plane ticket. As 1976 rolled on toward 1977, we made our wedding plans.

We were married almost immediately after Kathy graduated from high school, in June of 1977, while I was serving in the Navy. About a week after our wedding, we loaded up my car and I dragged Kathy nearly eight hundred miles away from the only home she had ever known, where she would begin life as the wife of a sailor stationed at Fort Meade, Maryland, an Army base in a part of the country she had never even visited before. In many ways, this isolated beginning was one of the best things that could've happened to us, because it forced us to learn to fend for ourselves and to depend on one another for almost everything. We were young and hopelessly in love, and poor, and just as happy as we could be. As the years have gone by, our love has grown and deepened through all of the trials, struggles, and victories we've experienced together. And we remain deeply in love and the very best of friends all these years later.

I had two and a half years left to go on my tour of duty when Kathy and I were married. I served out the balance of that time at Ft. Meade, and I never gave the notion of extending or re-enlisting a second thought. I knew that military life was not the life for me, and Kathy felt the same. Upon my separation from the Navy, we moved to Tuscaloosa, Alabama, where, thanks to the provisions of the old GI Bill, I enrolled at the University of Alabama as a mechanical engineering student; Kathy began work as a dental assistant, an opportunity made possible by the training she received while we were living in Maryland. The transition from life on a military base to life on a major university campus was fairly smooth and natural. My school load was not too difficult, and we were having a lot of fun getting used to this new life and looking forward to the future we were envisioning for ourselves. Truthfully, we were not at that time living a life worthy of servants of Christ. We weren't living immorally, but at the same time, church attendance and prayer were not priorities for us, and we were not living the biblical model of the Christian home. We were just happy to be rolling along, mostly on our own, doing occasional lip service to our faith. In the vernacular, we were still baby Christians; we had been born again, but we had not grown at all in spiritual matters. And then came one of those phone calls, one of those unanticipated occurrences that changes the course of your life.

USCGC Blackthorn

Tampa Bay sits nestled on the western side of Florida, about one hundred miles southwest of Orlando. It is a large bay that is home to both Tampa and St. Petersburg, as well as a host of smaller, lesser-known cities. Spanning the bay across its southern end is the Sunshine Skyway Bridge, a five and a half-mile-long structure connecting St. Petersburg on the north with Terra Ceia on the south. The center section of the bridge is high and open, providing a passage for shipping traffic through the Tampa Bay channel, which connects the bay with the Gulf of Mexico. For about three months at the end of 1979 and into January of 1980, the US Coast Guard Cutter *Blackthorn*, a 180-foot buoy tender stationed in Galveston, Texas, had been in dry dock at the Tampa Bay shipyards, being completely overhauled for continued service in the Coast Guard fleet. On the evening of January 28, 1980, *Blackthorn* was finally headed home, making her way out of the bay via the ship channel. As the cutter approached the Skyway Bridge, she had to move over into the center of the channel to make room for the passage of *Kazakhstan*, a brightly lit and fast-moving cruise ship also steaming out of the bay. The seas were calm that evening, with a temperature of 61 degrees and a light breeze from the north. Shortly after *Blackthorn* passed under the Skyway Bridge, with *Kazakhstan's* deck lights blazing ahead of her, *Blackthorn's* officer-in-command noted the approach of a large vessel coming toward them, inbound in the channel. This approaching vessel was *Capricorn*, a 605-foot tanker loaded with 150,000 barrels of fuel oil bound for a power station within the bay area. For reasons that remain somewhat unclear to this day, the ships collided less than a mile west of the bridge. The initial impact rocked *Blackthorn* but appeared to have no significant effect; some of the crewmen were shaken up, but no one was seriously hurt. According to standard procedures, general quarters were sounded and the crew members rushed to their assigned duty stations. Unknown to everyone involved, a fateful consequence of the impact between the two ships was that one of *Capricorn's* two seven-ton anchors had lodged itself in *Blackthorn's* hull. Following the collision, *Capricorn* continued to drift into the bay, and as she did, her slack anchor chain gradually played out—wrapping itself under *Blackthorn's* hull. Once the anchor chain had played out to its full extent, it went instantly taut, and when it did, the drifting tanker jerked the much smaller *Blackthorn* under the surface of the water, pulling her straight to the bottom of the fifty-foot-deep channel. Serving on *Blackthorn* that night was Gary Wayne Crumly, age twenty-three, Quartermaster Second Class—Kathy's only brother.

Early on the morning of January 29, 1980, Kathy and I were awakened by a phone call from Kathy's mother—that life-changing phone call I alluded to above. She was calling to tell us of the wreck of *Blackthorn*. At the time of her call, Gary and twenty-two other crew members were missing and presumed still on board. We jumped into our car and drove the two hours home to Birmingham to be with the family while we waited for news on Gary's status.

The next three weeks are still something of a blur for all of us. After the first few days, Kathy and I returned to Tuscaloosa where Kathy continued to work and I continued attending classes. We would live our seemingly normal life from Monday until Friday, when we would pack up our car and our dog and drive back to Birmingham to be with Kathy's family again—and to hope for some news—until Sunday night, when we would drive back to Tuscaloosa to do it all over again. A liaison officer from the Coast Guard was dispatched to keep the family updated on developments, and there was a regular stream of visitors at Kathy's parents' house, offering prayer support and bringing food for the family.

There were times when we would all sit together and try to make quiet conversation, laughing about funny things Gary had done or said, reliving memories as a family, encouraging each other to hang onto hope that he would be found alive. Other times we each found places of solitude, or we would sit in a silent group, staring at the fire in the fireplace, trying not to let our minds go to the dark places or dwell on the horrific possibilities that seemed to become more likely with each passing day, trying not to lose sight of our belief that God would answer our prayers and bring Gary home to us. And we all spent so much time praying, individually and together, that he might somehow, miraculously, be found alive. We knew that there were stories of survivors of shipwrecks who had found large air pockets within the submerged vessels, and we could imagine that somehow Gary might have found such a pocket and was just waiting for the ship to be raised. Or he might have been swept away by the current and have landed on some strip of land somewhere, and was making his way back to civilization. The details were not of concern to us; we just knew that we were praying, in faith, that God would save Gary in this ordeal.

Day after day, we waited for news that the ship had been raised from the bottom of the channel. After a couple of weeks, Kathy traveled with her mother and father and sister to Galveston, Texas, to spend some time with Gary's young wife, Glenda, who was essentially all alone during this tortuous ordeal. As the days passed while they were all in Galveston, Kathy and her family began to face the growing certainty that hope for Gary's survival was fading. They spent about four days in Galveston before heading back to Alabama.

The weather in Tampa that winter was completely uncooperative, and day after day, we got reports that efforts to raise the ship had been thwarted. For three long weeks we waited, and for three long weeks, we prayed. Finally, late in February, the Coast Guard was able to raise *Blackthorn*, and the last whisperings of hope in our hearts were stilled: Gary's body had been located, still on board. He was found in the chart room, exactly where he should have been at general quarters. He had suffered a blow to the head that, in all probability, had killed him before the ship even sank. A large cabinet had fallen and had struck him on the back of the head. He had been dead the whole time we were waiting and praying for his rescue.

Ultimately, we were left with our terrible grief: Kathy's parents had lost their son; Kathy and her sister had lost their brother; Glenda had lost her husband; I had lost my best friend and my brother-in-law. The pain and sadness and sense of loss that had been building over the previous three weeks now resolved into a deep and abiding grief. We weren't alone in our grieving: in all, twenty-three of the forty-eight crew members on board *Blackthorn* that night were killed in what remains the worst peacetime incident in Coast Guard history. Twenty-two other sons, brothers, husbands, and best friends had died; twenty-five men survived but faced years of battling post-traumatic stress disorder (PTSD) resulting from that horrific night; and all of those families' lives were forever altered, just as ours were.

We have observed, through our own experiences and those of others, that one never gets over the loss of a brother or a child or a spouse, or any dearly loved one; one simply learns to live life differently, with a sort of a hole in the heart. The wound in the heart heals over, but the tender scar remains. I believe God allows us to go through painful experiences for many reasons, and among them is the reality that through these trials, we learn to trust Him even when things don't make sense, even when our prayers are not answered in the ways we think they should be, and even when, like Jacob from the Book of Genesis, we walk with a limp for the rest of our lives because of the trial.[1]

It's difficult to state clearly just how important the accident and Gary's death were for us, how crushing and earth-shaking. Our upbringing had taught us, essentially, that our faith was the critical element in seeing our prayers answered. Kathy and I—and especially Kathy—were convinced that if we prayed with enough faith during the time *Blackthorn* lay at the bottom of the channel, then Gary would miraculously be found alive when they brought the ship up. But when they did finally salvage the vessel and Gary was among those found dead, we were presented with a crisis of faith. This crisis of faith may be summarized as follows: we knew that God, the omnipotent One, could have saved Gary if He had chosen to; we prayed with all of our might and all of our faith, believing that God would, in fact, save Gary; Gary died; so, either God was not really able to do what we asked Him to do, or He chose not to, not to answer our prayers—the prayers we had prayed in faith, claiming the promises we knew from Scripture.

The consequence of this line of reasoning was that God was either not really God, because what kind of God is One who is not omnipotent, or He was a God who didn't care about the prayers of His people. We rejected the former, knowing that it was a logical (and theological) impossibility, and we settled on the latter. The fact that God *could* have saved Gary and chose not to, in our minds made Him guilty of Gary's death. This produced in us—and again, especially in Kathy—the reaction that said, if this is the kind of God He is, then we don't want to have anything to do with Him. Now, there were many who moved in the same spiritual circles we moved in who said that God *allowed* bad things to happen but did not *cause* them. To us, it didn't really matter whether He allowed Gary's death or caused it; the fact that He *could* have prevented it and chose not to, in our minds, made Him responsible.

Again, it would be difficult to state with adequate force the impact of this conclusion for us. Because this was such an emotional issue, our infantile reaction was to turn our backs on this cruel God, whom we had suddenly come to see as if for the first time. We weren't willing to say that it was all untrue, that there was no God and no reason to seek any sort of salvation; but we were willing to remain indifferent. Maybe there was a sovereign God, but we chose to ignore Him.

This state of spiritual rebellion lasted for well over a year, though in retrospect we can see that God's Holy Spirit was working in our hearts and in our lives during that whole time. A few months after Gary's death, while we were still in the throes of our spiritual struggling, Kathy and I decided that we didn't want to wait any longer to start our family. In January of 1981—on the first day of classes of that winter semester—our daughter Kristen was born. We were thrilled. Kristen was beautiful and bright and precocious, and though she was a sober child, we could tell there was a lot going on behind those green eyes. By the time Kristen was about three months old, we came to the realization that as this child grew, we would have to teach her something about God and religion.

We knew that it was time to make up our minds about what we truly believed and who God really was. Ah, the hubris of youth. We smile a bit as we look back at who we were then, with the arrogance to think it was our place to sit in judgment on God. But our God is infinitely patient, kind, and loving, and He never turned His back on us.

Through a series of events, He brought us into contact with the right people in the right circumstances at the right time, and He gently drew us back to Himself. We came to the place where we realized that God's Word is true; not just theoretically true, but existentially true. What God has to say about things really matters. One of the truths that impressed itself upon us through all of this was that our idea of what is "good" is not always the same as God's idea of what is good, but that His definition of good is always the right one. It is difficult—even impossible—to express so weighty a truth as God's beneficent sovereignty in a portion of one little chapter of one little book, and so I will not try. But through all of this we learned that God "causes all things to work together for good to those who love God, to those who are called according to His purpose."[2] We don't have to understand why apparently bad things happen to apparently good people; we simply have to trust—we are privileged to be able to trust—the One who alone is sovereign, who alone is wise and good and just. This marked a turning point for us, and even a beginning. It was the beginning of our learning to trust God, even when things didn't make sense, or didn't seem fair, or didn't turn out the way we thought they should.

It only takes a few sentences to put all of this down on paper, but as I said, the agonizing process actually took more than a year.

In and through all of this spiritual awakening, Kathy and I slipped pretty easily into our new routine as parents, and life was good. Just before Kristen turned two, I graduated with my degree in mechanical engineering, and we were all off on our new life together.

Our introduction to special needs

Three months after I graduated, we welcomed our second child, Erin, into the world, in March of 1983. Erin, like Kristen, was beautiful, but in many ways she was completely different from our first child. While Kristen met all of her developmental milestones naturally and on time, Erin did not. Erin was slow to hold her head up, slow to roll over, slow to sit up, slow to crawl, slow to walk, and slow to talk. Our initial reaction to Erin's lack of age-appropriate progress was one of concern, but we were assured by her pediatrician that she was simply a bit slow in her development, and that there was no cause for alarm.

When Erin was seven months old, we moved to Slidell, Louisiana, where I was starting a new job. Shortly after we got there, Erin developed a mysterious fever that turned out to have been caused by a severe urinary tract infection. After several months and a host of diagnostic procedures, it was determined that she had a condition called bilateral vesicoureteral reflux. This condition means that urine from the bladder back-flows up into the ureters, which are the tubes connecting the kidneys with the bladder. The condition can be so severe that the urine flows all the way back up into the kidneys and can lead to kidney damage. Erin's severe infection, in fact, had resulted in significant damage to her left kidney. We were pleased to learn that her overall kidney function was normal, but the left kidney thereafter was only able to do about twenty-five percent of the total load; the difference was made up completely by the right kidney, which simply increased its capacity in response to the need—a tangible example of the wonder that is the human body as created by God. Erin ultimately, at the age of three and a half, required major reconstructive surgery to re-implant her ureters and correct the reflux. And thus began our sojourn into the world of doctors, medicine, clinicians, and experts. Little did we know that this sojourn would in due time become a way of life for us.

One of the things that Kathy and I came to realize as we were going through all of this with Erin was that we hadn't yet "arrived," spiritually. We still struggled with questions about why. Why would God not answer our prayers for Erin's healing and for her to enjoy "normal" development? And why were we still asking why? The spiritual walk, we were discovering, consists of gains and plateaus. As we would encounter difficulties, and as a consequence of our wrestling with God over those difficulties, we would grow stronger in our faith and in our ability to trust God. But once we would get through those difficulties, we would often level off in our spiritual progress, and more or less coast for a while. Then the next challenge to our faith would come, and we would again have to wrestle with God and ask questions and confront our own complacency.

As we continued our process of growth in and through the struggles we experienced with Erin, Kathy, especially, struggled much with this. Erin would often awaken in the night crying after having a nightmare, but she lacked the verbal skills to explain what had frightened her so badly. After calming Erin each night and getting her back to sleep, Kathy would lie awake in bed, crying silent tears, begging God to heal Erin and allow her to begin talking to us. Kathy often slept fitfully, having a recurring dream in which Erin would walk into our bedroom and describe in full sentences and great detail the nightmares that tormented her. But this dream remained only that—a dream. Erin did not miraculously begin talking, and Kathy was forced, once again, to face her feelings of anger toward this God she continued striving to trust and follow. There was much more soul-searching and wrestling with God as Kathy vigorously fought for years, with all of a mother's love and passion, to open up the locked places that kept this precious daughter isolated from the world around her.

When Erin was just over two years old, in June of 1985, our first baby boy was born to us. Allan, like Kristen, was a perfectly "normal" child. He achieved all of his developmental milestones on time, just as Kristen had done, and we marveled, this time from a position of experience, to see him do this so spontaneously. After watching Erin struggle for every inch of ground developmentally, it was a wonder to us to see Allan so naturally and seemingly effortlessly learn to roll over and sit up and crawl and walk and talk. When Erin was two and a half and still unable to talk, we enrolled her in speech therapy. We had her in speech therapy for twelve and a half years, and to this day she still struggles with all areas of speech and language.

As the kids grew, I changed jobs and we moved back to Alabama, and early in 1989 we found ourselves expecting our fourth child. In June, an ultrasound revealed that this child would be another boy, and that his right hand had not formed. This news was a blow to us, though we were relieved that it wasn't something more serious. We cried and prayed and cried some more, and then began to get ready for our baby boy who would come to us with a birth defect.

We named our little boy Ryan. He was delivered just after midnight, as Wednesday was giving way to Thursday, ushering in Thanksgiving, 1989; our Thanksgiving celebration was especially joyous that year. However, as that day progressed toward evening, Ryan exhibited increasing difficulty with his breathing, and he didn't seem to be perking up as his doctor had hoped he would. Before we went to bed that evening, the doctor moved Ryan into the low-risk Neonatal Intensive Care Unit (NICU) for observation and some supplemental oxygen. When we woke up the next morning, we found that he had been moved to the high-risk NICU during the night, and that there had been a time while we were sleeping when they weren't sure he was going to make it. They later determined that he had contracted an infection during the delivery, probably a Group B strep infection.

He spent his first week in the NICU, while Kathy and I stayed in a hotel attached to the hospital so we could be near him. Over the course of about ten days, Ryan gradually grew stronger, until he was finally healthy and ready to go home with us. On a sunny day in early December, while Kristen and Erin were at school and Allan was with Kathy's parents, we took our newest child home from the hospital. We marveled at the grace of God, so clearly evident to us in the perfect face of this tiny baby. We marveled that we had been allowed to bring him home after such a relatively short time in the hospital, when so many other parents we had met were forced to spend weeks and months at the side of their babies' isolettes, praying that God would spare their children and allow them to take them home, too. What a Mystery is this God we serve, and how unsearchable are His ways.

Once we got through the crisis of Ryan's initial struggles, we began searching for the right approach for his missing hand. The search was difficult and lengthy, but the result was that we found a group of world-class hand surgeons in Louisville, Kentucky, and we took Ryan there for evaluation. The doctors there felt that they could fashion a "helper hand" for Ryan using his own tissue, including bones from some of his toes, and eventually relocating another of his toes to serve as a thumb. The advantages of this approach seemed obvious to us, though we were by no means ignorant of the potential difficulties.

Over the course of the next fifteen years or so, we spent many hours on the road between Alabama and Kentucky, and many hours in Jewish Hospital in Louisville, as Ryan underwent more than twenty-five surgeries and medical procedures. The surgical team did gradually construct a helper hand where Ryan's right hand should have been; however, this helper hand never gave Ryan the function that we hoped it would. After he became an adult, he ultimately decided to take advantage of the advances in prosthetic options that were by then available to him. He had one more surgery to modify this helper hand so he could be fitted with a state-of-the-art myoelectric prosthesis, and he now feels that this provides much of the functionality that the surgical reconstruction did not.

When Ryan was born, Kristen was eight, Erin was six, and Allan was four. While Kristen and Allan both continued doing very well in all areas of development, Erin continued to struggle. We enrolled her in a special pre-school program offered by the public schools when she was five, and when she was six she entered a normal kindergarten classroom. Her kindergarten year was a pretty good one for her, but that was almost exclusively because she had a teacher who was especially sensitive and determined to help Erin succeed. Her subsequent first grade year was not so successful. Academic testing during her kindergarten year had demonstrated that she needed some special assistance and an individualized education plan, or IEP. The IEP was intended to tailor Erin's academic program to address her unique needs while keeping her, as much as possible, within a regular classroom environment. So Erin's first grade year included regular classroom attendance along with some supplemental services in speech/language therapy, reading, and math. She would periodically during each day be taken out of the classroom to attend one or more of her special, or supplemental, sessions. (As a side note, I will mention that this approach looked much better on paper than in actual execution.) As Erin was going through that school year, Kathy and I began to sense that we were losing our special little girl. Her bubbly and animated spirit was dimming, and we could see signs of what we were convinced was the beginning of genuine depression. We were frequently at the school, meeting with the IEP team to try to make the program meet Erin's needs. We took out the last of our meager savings to hire an educational consultant to advise us and advocate for Erin, and we struggled to make it work. But by the time we reached the mid-point of the year, we knew it wasn't working. Erin would often come home from school crying, and her mood more and more of the time was morose or angry. We knew that if we didn't do something to rescue our nearly helpless little girl, we were going to lose her completely.

As Kathy and I wrestled with how best to help Erin, we determined that we had, essentially, only three options: (1) take Erin out of public school and enroll her in a private school more suited to meeting her particular needs; (2) find a different public school that offered better programs for her; or (3) withdraw her from formal school altogether and teach her at home. The last option was the least attractive to us. Home-schooling was still a relatively new concept in the late eighties, and we were convinced that only religious fanatics or outright kooks would take their kids out of school to teach them at home—and that all such lunatics would produce children who were both antisocial and maladjusted. Such were our foolish thoughts when we considered home-schooling. We looked into the possibility of private schooling, but the one or two facilities we found were prohibitively expensive and, in our opinion, would not adequately meet Erin's needs. So, we tried to find a public school system that would be able to offer Erin the things she so desperately needed to thrive. Though we never became convinced that we found a perfectly suitable school, we believed we found something that would come much closer to what we needed, in Huntsville, Alabama, just an hour and a half up the road from where we were living at the time. As we began making plans to relocate to Huntsville, I looked for a job there, to make the move possible. But I didn't find a job, and we drew nearer and nearer the end of the school year, nearer and nearer to the time when we would have to do something definite about the next year. Finally, in desperation and defeat, we decided that we would, in fact, have to pull Erin out of public school and begin teaching her at home. Our decision to begin home-schooling, though we couldn't have known it at the time, was another of those pivotal moments I alluded to in the opening of this chapter.

Our original plan was to school her at home for only one year, to catch her back up with where she should have been and to help heal the damage that had been done during her first grade year. We continued working with the educational consultant, to map out a plan for Erin's year at home. In a move so characteristic of the way God often works, shortly after we made the decision and finalized plans to school Erin at home, I received a job offer from a company in Huntsville. We still believed that we would be better off there—especially in light of the fact that we planned to re-enroll Erin in public school after one year—so I accepted the job offer, even though it meant a cut in pay from what I was then earning. One day, after that awful school year was over but before we moved to Huntsville, Kathy happened to drive past Erin's school. She had missed a turn and pulled into the parking lot at the school, adjacent to the playground. As she was about to turn the car around, she heard Erin in the back seat say something about "that fence." When Kathy probed and managed to piece the whole story together, she learned that Erin would often, during recess at school, go over to the fence, lace her little fingers through the chain link, look out at the road, and cry and pray that Mommy would come and take her away from there, away from the taunting and bullying that she was subjected to nearly every day. Kathy just sat in the car and cried when she heard this. How could we, Erin's parents, have allowed her to be subjected to such hurt without knowing about it, without doing anything to stop it?

Over the course of the years, and through many batteries of tests, we determined that Erin's condition was more comprehensive and more debilitating than we had allowed ourselves to believe all along. When she was old enough for the testing to be conclusive, we were told that she would never be able to live independently, would never be able to drive a car, and that her condition would not improve. This was a devastating revelation, both for us and for Erin. For a long time we once again struggled to hold onto the truths about God's goodness that we had come to cling to in the face of this devastating new reality. God once again carried us through this, and He continues to give us grace to face it whenever the reality of Erin's struggles obtrudes itself into our consciousness again.

God continues to grow our faith

One of the consequences of that experience with Erin and our decision to school her at home was that we resolved that our home would become a safe place for her. In fact, that it would be—must be—a safe place for all of the kids. We knew that Ryan, when he got older, would also fall victim to the cruelty of other children because of his difference. We made the commitment that whenever the kids were in their own home, none of them would ever feel threatened or inferior or strange. Our home was to be a haven, a refuge for all of them. This, too, turned out to be pivotal in preparing us for what God had planned for our future though, again, we didn't know it at the time.

We moved to Huntsville and enrolled Kristen and Allan in public school, and began teaching Erin at home. As I said, we maintained contact with the educational consultant. In January, 1992, we had Erin tested by this consultant. The news was astonishing: within the four months Kathy had been schooling Erin at home, Erin had progressed roughly one and a half years academically! This was mind-boggling to us. More important than her academic progress, though, was that her heart had healed as well. And during those four months, something else was happening. We had begun to realize that people who teach their children at home are not weird and that their children are not antisocial or maladjusted. There are a lot of different reasons people to choose to home-school, and lots of different approaches to it, but by and large the result is exceptional for the kids, both academically and relationally. The truth is, we fell in love with home-schooling. We made the decision to pull Kristen and Allan out of public school, too, and just teach the whole bunch at home. (At the time, we naïvely thought of four kids as "a bunch.") This turned out to be one of the best decisions we ever made, though we jokingly attest to the fact that God had to drag us into home-schooling kicking and screaming.

During 1994 and into 1995, the company I was working for in Huntsville began to experience some financial difficulties, and by the time the calendar showed spring of '95, it was clear to Kathy and me that I needed to find another position, again. This time, in light of the fact that Ryan would be continuing to see his specialists in Louisville for quite a number of years still, we decided to try to find work a little closer to that part of the country — a decision made much easier by the fact that we were now a home-schooling family. After searching for several months, I accepted a position with an engineering firm in the Cincinnati, Ohio area, and we moved there in November 1995.

After we moved to Cincinnati, we both began to feel that God was calling us to be a little bolder in how we lived out our faith. To use an expression that is at risk of becoming trite, we felt that He was leading us out of our comfort zone to be able to move more deeply into our service to Him. The seeds for the path that lay before us, though unknown to either of us, had been sown a little earlier, so I need to back up a bit and cover that period.

Chapter 2

Further In and Further Up

❋

"Come further in! Come further up!" [Aslan] shouted over his shoulder. . .They set out walking westward to follow him.

The Last Battle

C.S. Lewis

God points us toward adoption

Before Kathy and I moved to Cincinnati, while we were still living in Huntsville, Kathy heard a radio broadcast of *Focus on the Family* in which the host, Dr. James Dobson, was interviewing Tim and Christine Burke. The Burkes had recently published a book called *Major League Dad*, which chronicled their remarkable story. Tim had been a Major League Baseball pitcher, and he and Christine had adopted all of their four children, two of whom had significant special needs. The focal point of the book and the interview was that Tim had made the decision in 1993 to quit professional baseball, to devote his time and attention to helping to care for the kids. The story is powerful and the book well worth the read. Kathy was profoundly struck by the concept of adoption and the impact it can have in the life of a child. She felt that our home could be the perfect place for a needy child to find love, acceptance, and the emotional safety we were determined to provide for our children. She quickly became convinced that adoption was the next step in our journey of faith.

As we had been growing spiritually over the many years since Gary's death, we had both found ourselves becoming increasingly convinced that passive Christianity was not the sort of life Jesus had called His followers to live. As stated in the answer to the first question of the Westminster Shorter Catechism, the primary reason man exists is to glorify God and enjoy Him forever. Our lives should be lived so as to glorify God, and not through being well-dressed, well-adjusted, comfortable, smiling, middle-class church-goers, but through serving Him and living for Him and standing for the things that are important to Him. As we studied the lives of Amy Carmichael, Hudson Taylor, Martin Luther, William Tyndale – and many others – we became convicted that living for Christ meant more than observing the status quo. It is true that many examples of such an active faith do live among us today and serve on the mission fields around the world, and we have been privileged to know and observe many of them ourselves. But the thought that we, ordinary American Believers that we were, had been called to live a life of radical obedience and service was revolutionary. We didn't know what our particular calling would be, but we were convinced that God would show us and would lead us, as I said earlier, out of our comfort zone and deeper into our relationship with Himself.

Thus, when Kathy heard the Burkes' interview on *Focus on the Family*, she began to believe that adopting special-needs kids might be our way of serving God in a more tangible and a more committed way. This would definitely be a direction out of our comfort zone, and the aspect of it that appealed to her most was the opportunity to take a child out of a life of despair and poverty, and to place that child within the nurturing environment of a Believing family, where he or she would be exposed to the living truth of the love of Christ. All of our experience and our pain in accepting Erin's and Ryan's disabilities and in learning how to meet their needs seemed to have prepared us for just such a mission as this one. Suddenly, so much of the struggle we had been through made sense. Adopting a child with special needs could be a tangible way for us to work out the Great Commission[3] on a small scale: we would be pulling a child out of the world and "making" him or her a disciple of Christ in a way not possible in any other context.

That evening when I got home from work, Kathy told me about the Burkes' interview, and about her convictions concerning God's calling for our family in this area. We ordered a copy of the program and listened to it together. We even bought a copy of the Burkes' book and read it together. And I agreed that this seemed to be something God was leading us into, and that we needed to begin to investigate the process.

As we looked into the question of international adoption, we learned very quickly that it is very, very expensive, on the order of tens of thousands of dollars. Kathy and I had no savings. No investments, no retirement account, no nest egg. We had depleted our savings and retirement accounts in taking care of Erin's medical and educational needs and Ryan's medical needs, and we had nothing. Once we discovered how shockingly expensive international adoptions could be, we investigated domestic adoption; however, we quickly learned that even these adoptions often cost several thousand dollars, and for us, $3,000 was as impossible as $35,000. It quickly became obvious that though my head was in the clouds, spiritually speaking, my feet were still planted on good ol' *terra firma*. I just knew that there was no way we could ever come up with that kind of money, and thus I just knew that there was no way God was calling us to pursue adoption. And that pretty much closed that chapter, for me at least.

However, around that same time, we came across a flyer at church about a ministry called RockSalt, that brought children from Bolivia here to Cincinnati to receive treatment for severe burns. One of the four Shriners Burn Hospitals is here in Cincinnati, and RockSalt, in conjunction with Healing the Children International, had made arrangements for children from Bolivia to receive treatment there, as needed. The flyer expressed the need for host families for the children, homes in which they could live while here for treatment. The treatment regimen for these kids, we later learned, could be a year at a time, and sometimes even longer. The host families would be responsible for providing care for the children during their time here, including transportation to and from the hospital, all routine needs, and for arranging for other medical care not connected with their burn treatment. I immediately believed that *this* was what God was calling us to do. My reasoning was based on the fact that we could bring a child into our home, provide the care and necessities during his or her time here, and in the process expose him or her to the love of Jesus and the transforming power of the Gospel. Then, we would send that child home to his or her family, and then bring in another child and repeat the process. We could, I reasoned, reach a much larger group of children in need through this ministry than we could through adopting them into our family. I think part of my justification, unconsciously, was that the expense would be manageable and we could still be moving out of our comfort zone in service to our Lord.

Kathy agreed that this seemed like a really good ministry opportunity for our family, and we took the steps required to get us hooked up with RockSalt and approved as a host family. But she also treasured in her heart the conviction that adoption was our ultimate calling and trusted God to handle the financial challenges that would accompany such a step, as well as the timing of it, should He ever lead us in that direction.

A milestone on the road to adoption

After Kathy and I went through the screening and acceptance process with representatives of RockSalt and Healing the Children, we were assigned a little girl from La Paz. Her name was Raiza (ra-EE-suh), and she was seven years old. Raiza had been burned in a tragic accident when she was only five, and though she had received rudimentary burn treatment in Bolivia, she was now in need of significant scar revision. Severe burn scars can develop negatively, resulting in both disfigurement and loss of function, and requiring additional intervention and treatment.

After a wait of several months, we finally welcomed Raiza into our home in July of 1997. This child was a bundle of energy and excitement, and it was amazing to us to see how she experienced the things we had come to take for granted — such as the availability of fresh fruit to eat, indoor bathrooms, and books to look at whenever she wanted. She left behind in La Paz a young mother who was very much pregnant with her second child. Raiza had been born when her mom was only fifteen, and the economic conditions to which she was accustomed were profoundly lower than those of the typical American middle-class family. But the differences between what she experienced in our home and what she was used to were far greater than mere economic considerations. In her past, she had been accustomed to an approach to life in which lying and stealing were not just accepted, but were more or less expected in order to survive. We very quickly discerned her to be sneaky and manipulative, particularly in the emotional sense, and she thought nothing of shading the truth — or telling a barefaced lie — if it suited her purposes. There were many challenges for us all as we assimilated this child into our home and family. We knew all the time that she had her own family waiting for her back in Bolivia, but we found ourselves treating her as, and almost unconsciously thinking of her as, one of our own children. Indeed, to have done otherwise would have made it extremely difficult for us to function as a family in the way to which we were accustomed, and far more difficult for us to offer Raiza the emotional support she would require as she went through her reconstructive surgeries.

In December of that year, Raiza had her first surgery. The doctors removed a thick band of constricted scar tissue from one hip and grafted new skin taken from a donor site on the other hip. The healing regimen was long, slow, and painful, involving daily cleanings of the wounds and the wearing of tight-fitting pressure garments. This factor is the principal reason these children are required to stay with their host families for such a long time. Once Raiza came home from the hospital, we slipped into the routine of pressure garments, dressing changes, stretching exercises, and wound care. It seemed that God was taking us even further into this world of doctors and hospitals. Still, He alone knew where the journey would ultimately take us.

As time moved on, and especially as we worked through all of the pain and trauma of the surgery and rehabilitation, the bond between Raiza and our family strengthened. She became, in most senses of the word, one of our children. She also became more genuinely affectionate, more honest, and more determined to please us. This last item is significant in that it demonstrated the capacity to bond, which is often a problem for children from dysfunctional family situations. Finally, after being in our home for many months, Raiza came to us and told us that she wanted to become a Christian. Our hearts leaped for joy; this was the moment we had prayed for since deciding to participate in the burn program. As we do with all of our own children, we walked her through a process to ascertain how well she understood what she was saying and how genuine was her profession of faith. After several weeks of discussions and questioning, we came to the conclusion that her profession was genuine, and we sat with her on the sofa in our family room as she prayed to ask Christ to forgive her of her sins and to make her one of His own. We were elated that this child, from a land shrouded in spiritual darkness, ignorance, and superstition, was now a child of the Father, now had her name written in the Lamb's Book of Life, was now a new creation in Christ.

A major bend in the road

During that December in 1997, we heard through some friends of ours of a little girl in desperate need. They told us about her because she was in Bolivia and because, through Raiza, we now had a connection with that small, impoverished country.[4] Her name was Lourdes Niña (lor-daise neen-ya), and she was about eighteen months old and living in an orphanage in the city of Oruro. Lourdes had been violently, sexually abused by an orphanage worker when she was only eight months old, to the extent that she had suffered internal injuries and required reconstructive surgery. The authorities were searching, and had been for a long time, for a family to adopt this baby girl. Their search was desperate because, according to what we were told, they were afraid that Lourdes's caregivers would stop caring for her if they found out what had happened to her. We were told that in that culture, the victim (rather than the perpetrator) would be stigmatized for the violence done to her. If the facts were discovered by her immediate caregivers, she would suffer still more injustice and violence through the isolation and neglect that would result. The officials were adamant that they didn't want to see this happen to Lourdes. It was a race against the clock.

This is one of those points in our story where I have to say, simply, that God spoke to me. I didn't hear a voice, I was conscious of no actual words, and I couldn't even really tell you what He "said" — except that I knew, almost instantaneously I knew, that we had to go rescue this child. Having come so quickly to this conclusion, I immediately said to Kathy, "We have to go rescue this little girl." Her very understandable and sensible response was something like, "OK, but I already called the adoption agency and they estimate that the adoption will cost, all told, as much as $35,000." To which I said, "That's God's problem, not ours. We have to obey His leading and go rescue this child; the money is God's problem."

Kathy and I held a family meeting to discuss Lourdes and her situation with our kids, and to ask for their thoughts about our adopting her. Universally and very enthusiastically, they all expressed the desire to be brothers and sisters to this special little girl. This didn't really surprise Kathy and me, since all four of the children had welcomed Raiza with open arms. We then talked and prayed about how we should proceed, not having the funds even to begin. We once again contacted the adoption agency handling Lourdes's adoption and told them of our desire to adopt her, in spite of the fact that we had none of the funds needed to move forward. They gave us some ideas as to how we might proceed, and they also offered to accept donations toward the expenses, providing a tax deduction to the donors. In late January of 1998, Kathy and I composed a letter that we sent out to essentially everyone we knew. We told them of how God had led us to Lourdes and of her plight, and we invited them to partner with us in her rescue by contributing financially. Simultaneously, we began putting together our adoption dossier, which is the compilation of documents required for the process. Each and every one of these documents has some sort of fee attached, and most have multiple fees at various steps in the process. The whole course of compiling a dossier can take as long as a year to complete, though it is desirable to complete it as quickly as possible. The more quickly the dossier is completed, the more quickly the adoption can proceed and the more quickly the child can come home. We were virtually derailed at the beginning stages of this process because we did not have the money necessary to pay the adoption agency their initial fee, nor the home-study agency the fee required to do the home study. At this point, God sent us a little reminder that He was not troubled by our lack of financial resources: a couple who knew us slightly — the wife was a co-worker of mine — had a Christmas bonus that they had as yet not figured out how to spend. They felt that God was leading them to use that money for His work, but they didn't really know where He wanted them to use it. When they learned about our adoption of Lourdes, they immediately felt led to give their considerable bonus, all of it, toward the adoption, to get us moving on the process. When they told us about this, we were just floored. We knew that God would provide the needed funds, but still, to see it beginning to happen in actuality was both humbling and awe-inspiring. This act gave Kathy and me the courage to continue, and the confidence that God would bring this adoption to pass in the power of His benevolent strength and according to His perfect timing.

Unfortunately, not all of the reactions we received about adopting Lourdes were as positive as those of our children. Although there were some in our extended family who were very excited to see what God would do through all of this and were genuinely supportive, there were others who did not conceal their disapproval of our decision. We already had four children at home, ranging in age from eight to seventeen years—and two of these with special needs. According to current American standards, we had a fairly large family and a busy life. These non-supportive family members undoubtedly felt that we would be unable to handle the increased demands of another child and that we had no business trying to bring a baby into an already full household. I think that some, even, could not comprehend our conviction that we were following God's leading in attempting to rescue this needy child, and that we were somehow gratifying something needy within ourselves and attempting to lend credibility to it by covering it with "God talk," or claiming that God had led us to do it. It is difficult to express how hurtful these reactions were. We struggled to understand how someone—anyone—could take anything so beautiful and right as the rescue of a desperate child, and make it into something ugly and selfish. And we struggled with what our response should be. We knew that God is pleased by harmony and mutual respect among family members, and that we would not be honoring His name if we acted disrespectfully toward these family members. But we also knew that we owed our first allegiance to God, and that if it came to a question of honoring God or honoring our family members, our choice was clear. Jesus said, "Anyone who loves his father or mother more than me is not worthy of me; anyone who loves his son or daughter more than me is not worthy of me."[5] We ultimately came to the conclusion that our duty was to follow God's will—to the best of our ability to discern it—and leave the rest to Him. We told our family members that we would love to have their blessing as we pursued this course, but that we would proceed with it or without it. In the decade since we reached that juncture, not all of our family members have come to support our choices or our convictions, but all have accepted and embraced the multitude of children we have made a part of our family, and for this we thank God.

Convinced that adopting Lourdes was what God was calling us to do, Kathy and I—and especially Kathy, who has gifts of organization and administration that I can only envy—threw ourselves into continuing the preparation of our dossier. There were hurdles to overcome, and we had to learn a great deal in a very short time, but within about two months, thanks to the incomprehensible grace of our Lord and the help of another couple who had done an international adoption the year before, we had the dossier completely assembled. Even more remarkable, God had provided *all* of the money necessary for this adoption. There are so many stories comprehended in that simple statement. Stories of absolute strangers sending checks because a friend of theirs had forwarded our letter to them and they felt led to help; of donations arriving at the eleventh hour, just when we reached a point—and there were many throughout the process—at which we could not proceed without additional funds. Kathy clearly remembers one day in particular, as she was doing laundry and praying for God to send the money for the next expense that was due immediately. We had entered one of many periods of silence, times when it seemed as if God had stopped listening to our cries for help. As she moved wet clothes from the washing machine to the dryer, she cried and asked God to hear our prayers for this baby, and to strengthen our faith as we waited on Him to provide. Within an hour, she went to the mailbox and there was a gift for the amount needed to cover that next expense, to permit us to take that next step in the process. We found ourselves praising God, and crying tears of joy, in ways we had not been privileged to do before. Our faith was tested and strengthened multiple times during those two months, and we still marvel at the things God showed us through it all. Staff members at the adoption agency were touched deeply by the overwhelming response to our letter requesting help. There were times when donations poured in so quickly that it was a challenge for their accountant to keep up with them all. They told us that they had never seen anything like it and felt that God's hand was clearly visible throughout the entire process. We felt like we were on the spiritual ride of our lives. Late in March we notified the agency that our dossier was complete and that we were sending it to them—and suddenly, without warning, the bottom fell out.

Chapter 3

Holding His Hand and Walking in the Darkness

I said to the man who stood at the gate of the year,

"Give me a light that I may tread safely into the unknown."

And he replied, "Go into the darkness and

put your hand into the hand of God.

That shall be to you better than light and

safer than a known way!"

God Knows (The Gate of the Year)

Minnie Louise Haskins

Our plans change

On March 19, 1998, we got a phone call from the caseworker at the adoption agency, telling us that Lourdes Niña, the little girl who had changed our lives and ushered us into the world of international adoption, was gone. A couple from Sweden had adopted her. After roughly ten months without any apparent interest shown in this little girl, except for ours, this couple had somehow completed her adoption. We were happy for Lourdes and the family that adopted her, but for ourselves we were devastated. As we wrote in an e-mail message at the time, "The grief is just unbelievable. We have never even seen a picture of her, but in our hearts she was our daughter, and the confusion is staggering." It's somewhat of a mystery, but other adoptive families will be able to testify to the ways in which orphans become sons and daughters from the moment we commit to becoming their parents. Something happens at a heart level that can't really be explained, but the loss of one of these precious children results in genuine pain and emptiness. We did not know what to do, and as we were working through all of the emotions and trying to grasp what we were being told, the agency representative told us about another child, also in desperate need of a family. It was a little boy, seven months old, in La Paz, who had been born without his left foot; would we consider providing a home for him instead? They told us that his future there would be just as bleak as Lourdes's, and that his need was equal to hers. In spite of our grief over this sudden and unexpected loss of little Lourdes, we immediately felt drawn to this child — also orphaned, also worthy of a family and a life that would enable him to reach his full potential. However, we felt a huge sense of responsibility concerning all of the generous people who had given money for the adoption of Lourdes Niña. They had donated their money to save this special little girl; how could we take their money and adopt a completely different child? We decided to contact as many of the donors as possible, tell them exactly what had happened, and ask them their opinion and their desire concerning the money they had donated. We were deeply touched and our hearts were greatly encouraged when, universally, the response we received was on the order of, "We gave that money to God. Let Him decide which child He wants to save."

And so, after much prayer, soul-searching, and discussion, we made the decision to proceed with the adoption of this little boy, whose name was Alberto. This was, incidentally, not as straightforward as it sounds, owing in large part to the fact that Bolivia didn't provide much information to prospective adoptive families. They didn't even allow the families to see pictures of the child ahead of time. And the information that was coming out of Bolivia was confusing, to say the least. With one report, we would be told that this little boy was missing his whole leg, and another would indicate that he was missing only some toes. In the end, we decided to leave it all in God's hands and that we would trust Him with the details of this little guy's disability — and abilities.

Though we had our dossier ready and on its way to Bolivia, we by no means were on the brink of getting on an airplane to fly south. A simple way to introduce the nature of our new set of difficulties would be to say, things just work differently in Bolivia than they do here in the States. Once we got everything sent to Bolivia, the next step, according to what we came to understand, was to get a court date for our initial hearing. This hearing would result in Alberto's being assigned to us and placed in our care, and would mark the "official" beginning of the process in Bolivia. The problem was that we couldn't seem to get that court date set. Our representatives at the adoption agency spent hours on the phone with their contacts in La Paz, and we spent hours on the phone with our adoption agency, and we prayed that the process would move forward. The whole question was complicated by the fact that, back then at least, the entire court system in Bolivia would shut down from mid-June until mid-July. If our process were not finished before the break, it would have to wait until afterward—and no one could really be certain how long this break and its delay would set our process back. Thus, we could end up traveling to La Paz, beginning the adoption process, not completing the adoption before the break, and then having to sit in a hotel doing nothing—other than bonding with our new baby and missing all of our kids back home—until after the end of the break. This was a daunting prospect for us, but at the same time, we felt an urgency to get the adoption completed as quickly as possible, though we couldn't really put into words the reason for this feeling. We did find out, further along in the journey, that our sense of urgency was justified, but that comes later in the story.

As the uncertainty mounted and we still were unable to get a court date, I finally came to the inescapable conviction that it was time for us to travel. The judge in Bolivia who would preside over the adoption was apprised of our story and committed to doing everything in her power to finish the adoption before the judicial break, but there were no guarantees. I felt certain, though, that we would have our court date, and I just knew that we had to go down and get our son. We communicated that to our agency and made our plane reservations and travel plans. I had spoken with my employer, very early in the process, about the need for me to be away from work for an extended period. My boss and his superiors were all very supportive of what Kathy and I were doing, and they gave their overwhelming approval for me to take the five or six weeks of unpaid leave when necessary, without any adverse consequences—so long as I made prior arrangements to have my in-work projects covered during the time I'd be away. And so, all of the pieces were in place for us to head to Bolivia.

Because we needed to have someone take care of our four kids while we were away, and because we knew that we would be gone for at least five weeks, and very possibly longer, we made the decision to take the kids to Birmingham to stay with their grandparents. We also had made arrangements to take Raiza back to Bolivia with us, knowing that she was pretty nearly finished with her post-operative treatment following her reconstructive surgery. The doctors at Shriners were somewhat reluctant to allow her to leave early, but we convinced them that she would be diligent to wear her pressure garments for as long as they instructed her to do so, and that she would comply with their directions in every way. Through representatives of RockSalt in Bolivia, we were able to arrange to spend time with Raiza's mother, once we got to La Paz, to train her in the proper use and care of the pressure garments and the full regimen of post-operative treatment. She agreed to follow these instructions and complete the treatment plan with Raiza, and finally the doctors had given their consent. So we were very excited to be the ones taking Raiza home to her mother after her ten months of living with us—sort of an extra bonus to go along with our trip to get our new son. We drove to Birmingham, said our emotional good-byes to the kids and left them with Kathy's parents, and then my oldest brother drove us to Atlanta, where we caught our flight to La Paz.

La Paz

La Paz was founded in 1548 and sits nestled in a canyon carved into the Bolivian *altiplano*, the high plateau situated between the two primary ridges of the Andes Mountains. At an official altitude of just over 12,000 feet above sea level, this city is the highest capital city of any country in the world. We touched down at the airport, just a few miles southwest of La Paz proper, on May 14, 1998. We landed very early in the morning, when it was still too dark to see the amazing view as our plane approached this airport, which is actually located in the neighboring city of El Alto, at an altitude of nearly 14,000 feet. We were met after coming through security by two new friends: Mike Johnson and his son-in-law, Pablo Molina. Mike and his wife, Kathleen, had graciously extended an invitation for us to stay with them during our time in La Paz. They were living in Bolivia as missionaries and were the founders of RockSalt Ministries, the organization responsible for sending Raiza to us nearly a year earlier. Mike and Pablo were the directors of RockSalt, and Pablo was the pastor of the church Mike and Kathleen had founded years earlier. Mike and Pablo loaded us up in their cars for the drive down through La Paz to the *Zona Sur*, the area in the southeastern part of the city where most of the Americans living in La Paz choose to reside.

As mentioned before, we were able to have Raiza travel back to Bolivia with us for her reunion with her family. Shortly after we got to the Johnsons' house that Friday morning, Raiza's mother, Nolberta, arrived at the Johnson's house with Raiza's new baby sister, Kathleen. Nolberta had named her then-seven-month-old baby after Kathleen Johnson. The first meeting with Nolberta was very moving, very emotional. She was so glad to see Raiza again, and so, so thankful to us—especially Kathy—for everything we had done for Raiza during her time with us. There was some palpable strain in the air during the first day or two, because Raiza had come to think of Kathy and me as her parental figures, and because Nolberta was so naturally meek in every way. Raiza appeared to be confused as to whether Kathy or her mother should be the one to appeal to on questions of authority or discipline. We tried to make the transition a smooth one for both Raiza and her mother, as we continually and gently redirected Raiza back to her mother when she came to us with questions. By the second day things were going much better. Raiza was apprehensive as to what life back at home would look like for her, and she was nervous about leaving the Johnsons' house and going home with her mother. But she was also determined to do everything she could to hold onto what she had learned during her time in America while also blending back into her "real" life in Bolivia as quickly as possible. It was heartbreaking to watch her struggles and realize the burden this eight-year-old child was carrying during this transition.

Alberto

On our second day in Bolivia, Kathy and I, along with Kathleen as interpreter, traveled to the *Hogar de Niños Carlos de Villegas* to meet our son. (The Spanish word *hogar* means home; *hogar de niños*, or "children's home," is the usual name given to orphanages.) Our taxi stopped in front of the *hogar* and we looked at the enclosing wall with its huge, imposing front gate, and we were struck with wonder and apprehension. What would this child look like? Would he accept us or pull away from us? How bad was his disability, really? What would the orphanage workers think of us? Kathleen rang the bell and we soon heard a small voice from the other side call out, "¿Quién es?" meaning, "Who is it?" This was the common call heard when ringing the bell at any gate, to identify the one requesting entry before the gate would be opened. Kathleen explained that we had an appointment, and the gate was opened to us. We passed through a beautiful little front garden and went up the steps and into the building.

Once inside the orphanage, we were greeted by an angular, boisterous woman who, we later learned, was the nun in charge of the orphanage. Her name was Sister Providencia, and we were to see a lot of her over the next week or so. Providencia took us into her office and introduced us to the orphanage's social worker, a much smaller, *mestizo*-looking woman named Rosario. (*Mestizo* is the word used to describe people of mixed European and Native South American descent.) We sat and talked for a few minutes, and then a young orphanage worker walked in with a small bundle in her arms — an eight-month-old baby boy with the most amazing smile on his very round face, and the most amazing mess of hair on his head. We immediately fell in love with this little guy who was actually our newest child, our third son. Alberto was chubby and beautiful. His hair was very nearly black and as coarse as boar's bristle. Kathy took him into her arms and he snuggled right in, very contented. Kathy, of course, was in heaven. We were surprised to see that he was wearing two shoes, and Providencia then encouraged us to take off his left shoe and get a look at his limb deficiency. Development of his left foot was very obviously arrested at some point in utero, but we were pleased to see that he had what appeared to be a fully formed heel and a bit of partially-formed foot beyond. This made it possible for his caregivers to tie a shoe onto the end of his left leg; the shoe would actually stay in place for awhile, although it did nothing to help his function. We were to learn that it was very important in Bolivian culture to make any child with disabilities appear as normal as possible.

Over the course of the next four days, we got to know this new child of ours in the context of his world, the interior of *Carlos de Villegas*. Twice each day we would take a taxi to the *hogar* and spend time holding Alberto, playing with him, and gleaning snippets of information from his caregivers, hampered as we were by their complete inability to speak English and our nearly complete inability to speak Spanish. We would try to be there for two of his feedings each day. The caregivers would allow Kathy or me to feed Alberto, which was a treat for us. The food consisted of some sort of thickened beef broth—not very nutritious, but filling. After his second daily feeding, we would hold him and rock him to sleep.

We did finally get a court date for our initial hearing: the following Thursday, we were to appear in court to learn whether or not we would be allowed to take custody of our new son. The day dawned bright—as it so often does in that beautiful city—but soon began to take a series of ominous turns. Mike was to take us to court and act as interpreter, and he was running late. Kathleen, who had experience with the Bolivian court system and was concerned that everything flow smoothly, anxiously followed us around with her coffee mug in her hand, reminding all of us that if we were even ONE MINUTE late, the judge would refuse to see us. Then Mike went out to start the Jeep and found that it had a flat tire! Changing the tire would be no small—nor brief—endeavor, so Mike came into the house and called a cab. The taxi arrived and Kathleen instructed the driver to get us to the *juzgado* (the court building) in record time. Please note: a taxi ride in La Paz is always an adventure, but a taxi ride in La Paz "in record time" is more of a brush with death. To our surprise and great relief, we arrived at the orphanage only five minutes late. We rushed in, changed Alberto into the special outfit we had brought him for this big day, and made ready to head to court. But then, once again, we bumped up against "the Bolivian way." Our in-country contact person, Clementina, was to meet us at the orphanage and accompany us to the *juzgado*. She had told us what time she would meet us at the orphanage and admonished us not to be late. As I said, when we arrived at the orphanage, we were five minutes late; finally, she showed up ready to go, thirty-five minutes late. We were sweating bullets while waiting for her, Kathleen's warning still ringing in our ears. In the end, we arrived at the court building only ten minutes after our appointment time, and we then discovered that the *fiscal*, or public prosecutor, was herself forty-five minutes late. Thus, they were just beginning the case before ours when we got there, and we were able to relax for a half-hour or so.

When our turn came, we walked into the judge's chambers and found, already seated and waiting for us, the judge, the *fiscal*, a representative of their Children's Services Department, and Rosario, the orphanage's social worker. No one was smiling. We were seated and introductions were made. We had been warned previously that the officials might try to intimidate us, and we were aware that a large anti-American sentiment was common in much of La Paz. And so we steeled ourselves for what was to come. Each of the officials made a bit of a speech, but they were talking too fast and too determinedly for Mike to be able to translate on the fly. Kathy and I did our best to infer their meaning from the little bit of Spanish we could understand and from their body language. Truthfully, though, our meager Spanish did not help us at all, and the body language we perceived left us with the impression that we were horrible people and that the last thing any of them was recommending was for us to be allowed to take our baby with us. At the end of all of the declarations, the judge issued a statement — which Mike was able to translate for us — to the effect that we were being granted permission to take Alberto into our custody and that the adoption process would now officially begin. At this, and much to our surprise, there were smiles all around. Then we all left. Kathy and I kept our burning questions to ourselves, in spite of our almost unbearable curiosity, until we were away from everyone else and out of the building.

Once we were alone, Mike explained to us that Rosario, in spite of what we erroneously thought she was saying, had spent her time telling the judge that she had observed us during our times spent with Alberto, and that we were wonderful and really loved the baby, and all about his missing foot, and that she highly recommended that the court allow us to adopt this baby. The *fiscal*, whom we were convinced really couldn't stand us, spent her time talking about what great people she thought we were because we would choose to adopt "a child of lesser value," and how grateful the country of Bolivia was for our doing that. What a funny thing it is to try to read someone's meaning who is from a different culture, speaking a different language! Though we were saddened that anyone would refer to our precious jewel as "a child of lesser value," we were tremendously relieved that this step was now behind us and that we had our baby with us at last.

We decided to rename our son Nathaniel Jeremiah Rosenow. We wrestled with whether or not we should retain any of the name he had been given at the orphanage, but we decided that it simply didn't represent any meaningful connection for him. It was what they referred to as a *nombre convencional*, a sort of "standard" name selected at random. Choosing such a name is common for abandoned babies at orphanages all over the world. The name we selected, Nathaniel, means "gift of God," or, more literally, "given to me by God." We really felt that this little boy was a gift to all of us directly from God. We chose Jeremiah for his middle name because of the Bible verse, Jeremiah 1:5, which reads, "Before I formed you in the womb I knew you, before you were born I set you apart." This was a significant verse for us as we pondered the sobering truth that, even before we ever dreamed of entering the world of adoption—before this little boy had even been conceived—God had chosen him for our family and set him apart for as-yet-unknown service in His name. We firmly believe and always tell all of our children that before the beginning of time, God planned for each of them to be Rosenows, and that He simply had different paths for bringing each of them to us. Our first four kids came to us through the normal biological process; Nathan, our first adopted child and like all of the children adopted after him, came to us through a more circuitous route, but one no less ordained by God.

The next several weeks are something of a blur to us now, filled as they were with periods of relatively little to do on the adoption front, punctuated by moments of intense, almost frenetic activity. Most of the time was spent getting to know our new son, whom we were now calling Nathan; beginning to bond with him, enjoying him immensely—and vicariously living the life of missionaries in Bolivia.

A real scare

A couple of weeks after bringing Nathan to the Johnsons' home to live with us, we noticed that there was a small lesion—a swollen lump—on top of his right shoulder. We had found a spider in our bed one morning and assumed that Nathan's lesion was a spider bite. Rather than improving with time, however, as would have been expected had it been a bite, it seemed to grow worse. One evening, Kathy and I went with Kathleen to the Children's Hospital in La Paz to meet Beto (BEH-toe), the pediatrician who helped with the burn program. We were going to tour the hospital, and Kathleen wanted to visit one of the babies there whom Beto was treating. Beto asked Kathy and me to bring Nathan along so he could look at Nathan's shoulder. Beto was a native Bolivian who had trained in the United States and was quite a gifted pediatrician.

Beto examined Nathan's shoulder. He quickly determined that the lesion was potentially very serious and that Nathan needed to begin oral antibiotics immediately. He explained that the lesion was cellulitis, probably caused by a staph infection, and that it was a very aggressive infection. In fact, if it did not respond quickly to the oral antibiotics, he would have to begin IV antibiotics. Beto was so concerned, in fact, that he walked us out of the hospital and to the nearest pharmacy, helped us buy the right antibiotic, and then walked to a nearby *tienda,* a sort of convenience store, to buy bottled water for mixing the antibiotic. (Prescriptions are almost never required for medications, and those that come in the form of a liquid suspension have to be mixed by the consumers.) He did not leave us until he was satisfied that Nathan had taken his first dose and that Kathy and I understood exactly what we needed to do to care for him.

A couple of days later, Beto came to the Johnsons' house and checked Nathan again. He said that the lesion looked a bit better and seemed to be improving, but that it needed to be drained, right then and there. This sounded pretty reasonable to us, until we saw preparations under way for the draining process. Beto had Kathleen find a sewing needle, which he cleaned first with a match flame and then with alcohol. He also cleaned Nathan's shoulder with the alcohol, and then he had us restrain our eight-month-old baby so that he couldn't move. Beto lanced the lesion with the needle and then squeezed out the contents, the amount of which shocked and surprised us — right there in the living room! Nathan screamed and screamed as we held him still for the torturous ordeal.

After we brought Nathan home to America, our doctors confirmed Beto's diagnosis and let us know that Nathan could actually have lost his arm had he not gotten treatment when he did. We also learned that Nathan probably contracted the infection when he was inoculated for tuberculosis at the orphanage: the shot was given in his shoulder, right where the infection later occurred. Even with Beto's early and aggressive treatment, Nathan had to have surgery on his shoulder about two months after we brought him home, to clean out the wound and make sure that all traces of the infection were gone. This served as confirmation to us that we could not have waited any longer than we did, and certainly not until after the judicial break, to go to Bolivia to get our son. God's prompting us to travel to Bolivia when we did, saved Nathan's arm and probably his life.

We turn the corner

After roughly four weeks of experiencing life in Bolivia and bonding with our new son, Kathy and I recognized that we were growing restless, eager to return home — and we desperately missed our children. It seemed like an eternity since we had been able to talk to them or look at their faces. We longed to be reunited with them and begin our life with Nathan now a part of our family. Fortunately, the process itself was drawing to its close, though the Enemy would not give up this special child and allow us to leave without a bit of a fight. Had we known what lay ahead as we entered that final week or so in South America, we would certainly have shuddered with dread and apprehension.

Chapter 4

Victory is the Lord's

The LORD said to Gideon, "The people with you are too many for
me to give the Midianites into their hand, lest Israel boast over
me, saying, 'My own hand has saved me.'"
And he sent all the rest of Israel every man to his tent,
but retained the 300 men.

Judges 7:2, 8

Nearing the end

As the month of May gave way to June, we began to feel a
growing uneasiness about the final steps in the adoption
process, and especially about whether we would be able to be done
before the national judicial break in mid-June. We repeatedly tried
to pin down Clementina as to what final steps were required and
how we could most expeditiously complete them. She was evasive.
One of the things we noticed among Bolivians, as a general rule,
is their cultural desire to please: they would rather tell a lie—say
what they think you want to hear—than give disappointing news.

This tendency often left us confused and frustrated as we tried repeatedly to figure out what the rest of the process would look like. Clementina, in turn, tried to calm our anxiety and assure us that she had things under control, that we didn't need to worry about it, and that she would make sure everything got done on time. These assurances did little to assuage our concern, since we had more than once seen evidence that she was not competent, not able to get things done without a lot of prompting and urging from us, and was perfectly comfortable lying to us on virtually any subject.

During this time, we had some occasional contact with Raiza, and we were saddened to see that things were not as well with her as we had hoped they would be. Her mom's live-in boyfriend, and the father of Raiza's baby sister, did not like Raiza, and he was often verbally abusive to her and her mother. We were also greatly disappointed to learn that Raiza's mother was not keeping her promise to continue Raiza's post-operative care. Soon after Raiza and her mother returned home, the daily massages were stopped and the burn garments were tossed aside. One of the most distressing things we learned was that, in spite of her mother's promises to take her, Raiza had not been allowed to go to church since returning to her family.

When Raiza would visit us at the Johnsons', the three of us would go up on the roof of the house together to talk. Many of the houses in Bolivia have an accessible, flat roof with a parapet or low wall around the perimeter. The families use these rooftop areas as patios where they gather with friends, or have a cook-out, or hang out the laundry, or gaze at the stars in the evening—or all of the above. In this small outdoor sanctuary, Kathy and I would hold Raiza while she cried and unburdened her heart to us. We ached for her and the pain she was experiencing, and we were appalled at the thought of having to leave her behind when we went home. At the conclusion of Nathan's adoption process, that was exactly what we had to do, and we cried bitter tears at our final meeting with her and the subsequent parting. Our only consolation was the knowledge that we were leaving her and her future in the hands of the One who formed her in the womb, the One who brought her to us in the first place, and we held onto the hope that she would be returning to our home for more surgeries in the future. We prayed that God would help her hold onto the things we had taught her and remind her of the truth that she belonged to Him and was loved by Him and by us.

The second court appearance

We received notice during the first week in June that our court appearance would not be until a few days before the judicial break. We also learned that the required steps following that court appearance would take about five days to complete, and we were told that these steps, too, had to be done before the break. We sent an urgent plea for prayer to everyone who was following our adoption saga, and we began making preparations for me to return to the States while Kathy remained behind with Nathan for at least another month. Then, against our expectations, we had our court date a few days earlier than they had said it would be. It was on Monday, June 8, 1998. The actual court appearance was pretty quick and not nearly as big a deal as we expected it to be. We went into the judge's chambers and sat down, the judge read a brief statement, and it was done. The whole thing lasted about five minutes.

As we left the *juzgado*, it began to dawn on us that the adoption was now official. Nathan was our son. He was the same beautiful brown little baby we had walked into the building with, and he had been our son in our hearts from the moment our agency told us about him after Lourdes disappeared. But now, as we exited the building with him in our arms, the knowledge that he was officially a Rosenow caused our hearts to sing. It is impossible to describe the joy we felt, the ways in which this official step caused us to praise God with all of our being. Regardless of the difficulties still ahead before we could leave Bolivia, the path that had been Alberto's life had been irreversibly replaced by an entirely new path, one for Nathaniel Jeremiah Rosenow. We went out to a Mexican restaurant that night to celebrate with most of the Johnson family, and we remember this as one of the high points of our time in Bolivia.

Following the hearing, the attorney assigned to our case told us that everything was done and official and that we didn't have to worry about the judicial break any longer. This was quite surprising to us in light of what we had been told only a week earlier, and though we wanted more than anything to believe what our attorney was now telling us, we remained guarded. And we knew we weren't out of the woods yet, in any case. Our airline reservations were less than a week and a half away, and even though the adoption was complete, there were several steps remaining before we could get Nathan's immigrant visa so we could bring him home to the States. We determined that we would do everything possible to complete those steps one by one, and in record time. I guess we forgot that we were in Bolivia.

Tiahuanacu

Our final court hearing, as I said, was Monday morning, June 8. Our discouragement and sense of urgency began to mount as Tuesday and Wednesday passed with nothing but silence on the adoption front. Not one bit of progress was made toward completing the remaining steps, and we could almost see the sand slipping through the hourglass as we keenly felt the loss of those precious days. On Thursday, to help us relax and take our minds off of everything for a while, Mike and Pablo and Mike's daughters took us on a sightseeing tour of some famous pre-Columbian ruins. These ruins, situated roughly fifteen miles southeast of the shores of Lake Titicaca, are called Tiahuanacu and date back to a time before the Incas conquered that part of South America.

Nathan spent the day riding in a snuggly-carrier with Kathy, and he seemed perfectly content. By this time he had become comfortable and happy with us as his parents. We loved to see him laugh and jabber, even when total strangers would talk to him—as long as one of us was holding him so he could feel safe and secure.

When we returned to the Johnsons' after our day of touring, we were surprised to see that Kathleen had put together a birthday party for Kathy, who turned thirty-nine that very day. Kathy was deeply touched that Kathleen, with all the demands on her time and energy, would go to the trouble to recognize this special day.

We had a wonderful evening of celebration and laughter, and the party provided a much-needed break from the stress of trying to get everything done so we could head home on time the next week.

Later that evening, Pablo told us that he knew a guy who might be able to get the birth certificate for us in a hurry. Pablo was going to meet this friend the next morning, and if he said that he could help, Pablo was going to call us at the house and tell us to get down to the friend's office right away. We went to bed still worried about getting out on time, but hopeful that maybe this new connection would get things moving again.

The next morning, Friday, Pablo headed out to meet with his friend. After an hour or so, he called to tell us that the friend would try to help, but that the best he could hope for was to have the birth certificate ready on Monday — though he would make no promises. Even having the birth certificate on Monday meant that we would have only two days to complete everything, since our flight out of Bolivia was on Wednesday. This sort of clinched it, making it clear to us that we were going to have to reschedule our flight home. We were no longer living in fear of the judicial break, but we still did not want to have to incur the extra expense of changing tickets. In fact, one of the tickets was given to us through donated frequent-flyer miles, and we weren't even certain we'd be able to change that one. And on top of everything, we were aching to get home and see our other kids. That day, far away in Alabama, Allan had turned thirteen. We were feeling weary and almost overcome with sadness that we were missing this very special day with our son. We wanted to go home.

That afternoon, after we had gotten the bad news from Pablo, Kathy and I went out for a while with Nathan, just to walk, get some fresh air, and get away from everything for a time. As we walked and talked, we were wondering how long we might end up stuck in Bolivia. Needless to say, we were feeling pretty down about everything. Kathy then reminded me about an analogy Kristen had used while we were struggling frantically to get things in place to be able to travel to Bolivia. She had compared what was happening in our struggle with what God did with Gideon when he was preparing to attack the Midianite army.

In the face of the terrible oppression the Israelites were enduring at the hands of the Midianites, Gideon assembled the army of Israel, a force of 32,000 warriors, to go and face the Midianite army. But God chose to make sure that everyone would know without doubt that it was He, the God of Israel, who had delivered His people from the hands of their enemies. So He commanded Gideon to instruct all the men of Israel's army who were afraid, to return to their homes. Twenty-two thousand men heeded the admonition and departed from Mount Gilead, leaving an army of 10,000 to face the Midianites. But God was not satisfied: there were still too many. So He had Gideon separate the army according to the manner in which they drank from the stream. After this test, the men who remained, the army of Israel, were only 300. God chose to whittle the army down from 32,000 to 300, just to make sure that no one would be mistaken as to who had delivered Israel on that day. We are told that the army of the Midianites "lay along the valley like locusts in abundance, and their camels were without number, as the sand that is on the seashore in abundance."[6] Only the Lord God could deliver victory to the Israelites under such odds. And He did. The army of Israel utterly defeated the Midianites and won a great victory on that day, and the glory was the Lord's.

As we talked about that, Kathy said, "I think God just took out our last soldier when He took out Pablo's friend." And we agreed that that was entirely plausible, that God had determined to demonstrate that He alone was going to take things from that point on. There would be no confusion as to who was moving mountains, should He decide to move those mountains. That evening, Kathy went with Kathleen to visit another missionary in the area. While they were gone, Clementina called. This in itself was somewhat surprising, since she almost never called, and especially not in the evening. But I was even more surprised when I learned she was calling to let us know that she had Nathan's birth certificate and that we needed to get downtown right away to try to get the *carnet*. Apparently the person Pablo had met with that morning had managed to get the birth certificate in a matter of a few hours after our request for help, in spite of the fact that he hadn't even been sure if he'd be able to have it by Monday. We were amazed! We praised God for making this happen, and for so clearly demon-strating that it was He who had done it. And we were once again hopeful that we might be able to get out on time the next week. Pablo rushed us downtown to meet our contact person, and as so often happens, especially in Bolivia, we got there fifteen minutes too late. We couldn't start the process to get the *carnet* because we got to the office too late. This whole day had been one of ups and downs—really high ups, and really low downs.

Things get rather complicated from here, but Pablo had another friend who thought he could help us get the *carnet*, someone who had formerly been a police officer but was now a pastor. He called this friend and arranged for him to meet us at the police station. We stood around outside of the police station—which is where you have to go to get the *carnet*—Nathan resting comfortably in Kathy's arms, all of us waiting for Pablo's friend to show up. We waited for an hour and a half, and it got dark and cold outside. The head of the police station saw us huddled on the sidewalk and told us to come inside where it was warm, for the baby. Pablo explained to him why we were out there waiting after everything had closed. This man, whose rank in the police department was Major, seemed interested in our story, especially after he noticed Nathan's missing foot. He was very touched by this Bolivian baby's special need and the fact that he had been adopted and was on his way to a new life.

We were struck over and over again, during our time there, by how obviously all of the nationals recognized that there was no hope for a one-footed baby in a country as poor as Bolivia. The only future for him there, after growing up in an orphanage, would be living on the streets, surviving as best he could as a beggar. Often as we walked the crowded streets and sidewalks of La Paz, we saw numbers of disabled Bolivians, their faces void of any hope and their spirits destroyed by the ridicule and abuse they suffered as people "of lesser value." In spite of the fact that we observed anti-American sentiment all around La Paz, almost everyone who came in contact with us and our son recognized the hope we were bringing to one little disabled Bolivian boy. Somehow this recognition seemed to instill in them hope. Many of them desired to help in some way, as we fought our way through the confusion of the Bolivian legal system.

The Major made a few phone calls and then said to us, "If you will be here at 8:30 Monday morning, I will personally do your son's identification card, and I will guarantee that it will be done by 10:00." It was, by then, late Friday evening. We still had our plane reservations for the following Wednesday, and we still had many steps to complete before we could step on that plane with our baby. But we were filled with such excitement, such gratitude — first of all, to this kind man who had taken an interest in our story and volunteered to help us. Even more, we were grateful to our God, who had so obviously heard our many petitions and was still moving in our adoption story. We praised this God we serve, and we headed back to the Johnsons' for the weekend.

And then Monday morning came. We were up bright and early, and headed to the city in plenty of time. Kathleen accompanied Kathy and me to act as guide and interpreter. We arrived at the police station fifteen minutes before they opened, and we were second in line waiting to get in. The Major remembered us from Friday evening and was ready to get things started. But Clementina was late, as usual, and she had all of Nathan's original documents with her. We couldn't start without those documents, so we had to wait for her. She finally showed up about ten minutes after the office opened, and from that point everything should've been smooth sailing. Obviously, the fact that I said "should've been" indicates that things did not sail so smoothly. Clementina had her own connections at the police station and disdained the help offered us by the Major. We didn't know what, exactly, was going on at the time because of the language barrier—Kathleen couldn't really translate while it was unfolding—but Clementina was clearly being belligerent toward the Major. In spite of that, the Major assigned a junior officer to help us through the process. This junior officer took us around to get all of the paperwork done, shunting us to the front of long lines and making everything happen very quickly. At one point, the underling took us to another official sitting behind a desk, to have some other step in the process completed. This official, though, simply turned his back on us, as if to say, "I will not help you in any way." Clementina began to get very nasty once again, but Kathleen stepped up and very nicely explained our whole situation—that we had adopted this little baby who had a birth defect, that he needed to get to the States quickly for a medical evaluation, that our plane tickets were for that Wednesday and that it would be very difficult, if not impossible, to change them. The official then did a full one-eighty and became very nice and very helpful. He gathered up our papers and said that he would take them to someone who would finish us quickly.

At that point, we were surprised and taken aback when Clementina literally grabbed the papers out of the man's hands and said that she had her own connections at the *carnet* office, that she would use her connections and not his. Kathy and I did not know what was going on because it was all being conducted in

Spanish, so in spite of a growing sense of uneasiness, we followed along as Clementina took us to her own contact. This person told us that he would have the *carnet* ready by noon. This, of course, was maddening to us, since the Major had promised to have it done by 10:00, and every minute was precious to us. Clementina would not listen to a word we said as we argued with her about what she was doing; finally, in frustration and mounting despair, we gave up the argument. They filled out some forms and took Nathan's footprints—and wasn't that just a circus! They were almost beside themselves with trying to figure out what to do with a baby that had only one foot. After that, they told us we would have to wait to have the baby's picture taken, and so we sat down to wait.

We were still sitting on that bench an hour later, at 11:00 AM. The Major happened to walk by and see us, and he asked why we were sitting there. We explained as tactfully as we could what was going on; he then did some ordering and yelling, and within a few minutes we were having Nathan's picture snapped while he cried his head off. This had already been a very long day for him, and none of us knew that it was really just getting started. Clementina apparently realized that she had been trumped, and she simply followed along from that point forward.

After we left the police station—with Nathan's precious *carnet* in our hands—we had to take some of our documents to the US Embassy to try to get an appointment for the visa interview and make things move more smoothly when the time came. After waiting an hour and a half to see someone, we met the immigrant visa liaison officer. He was very rude and almost offensive to us, but we later learned that his animosity was directed at Clementina, whom he knew well from previous experience. By this time, Kathy had been holding Nathan or carrying him on her hip for five hours, and they were both exhausted. Once the liaison officer saw that our documents were in order, he calmed down a bit and told us he would see us at 8:30 the next morning, Tuesday, *if* we had a passport for the baby. He told us not to bother coming if we didn't have the passport, and he obviously thought that getting the passport by then was a pretty remote possibility.

After we left the Embassy we headed to the Child Welfare offices to request a *salida de viaje*, travel authorization for Nathan. No one is allowed to take a child out of the country without this authorization, not even Bolivians themselves. Even if only going from one province to another, the parents would have to obtain this *salida* from Child Welfare services to be permitted to do so. As was so often the case during the documents phase of this adoption, Kathy and I pretty much sat on the curb outside of the offices while Clementina ran around getting the documents, having them signed, having them notarized, etc. After about two and a half hours, I went to find Clementina to ask what was going on and how much longer we should expect to be sitting there. Clementina explained that the doctor who was supposed to sign our papers had refused to do so, but that the social worker there had said that she would do it. The social worker, however, was at that time having tea and couldn't be bothered until she was finished with her tea. I found Clementina outside of the office where the social worker, along with other staffers, was having her tea. The social worker apparently saw me come up and talk to Clementina, and she immediately came out and smiled — and signed the documents for us. We received no explanation for why she interrupted her tea time to do this, but once again we thanked God for completing this next step for us. After that, the documents had to be signed by a judge. All of the judges in the country were on holiday then, except for one: one judge remains on duty just to sign papers during the break. Clementina said that she would go and have the judge sign the documents and that we should go to the immigration offices and wait for her, that she would meet us there in twenty minutes. In spite of our firm conviction that she would not show up, we did as we were told and took a taxi to *migración*, the national emigration/immigration offices. We waited at *migración* for an hour and a half without any sign of Clementina, and finally we went home to the Johnsons'. She called later that evening to tell us that it had taken her until 6:45 to get the papers signed and notarized, and that we should meet her at *migración* at 8:30 in the morning. She was confident we would be able to get the passport the next day, even though it normally takes as long as three days. We managed to contact the liaison officer at the embassy, and he agreed to change our appointment to 8:30 Wednesday morning, rather than Tuesday. We also planned to go to the Delta Airlines office the next day, Tuesday, and see if there would be any way to change our tickets to a Friday flight, just to buy us that additional time we would undoubtedly require.

Another Bolivian complication

Bolivians are notorious for conducting job actions, or strikes, to protest virtually any real or imagined problem. The strikes are widespread and often violent. Many experts characterize the labor unions in Bolivia as some of the strongest and most influential in Latin America. Whenever the workers have a complaint against the government or its policies, they will stop work, blockade roads, conduct semi-organized marches, and even vandalize indiscriminately, all to make their protests heard and felt. These strikes can take place on a regional or, more often, a national level. The major urban centers of La Paz, Santa Cruz, and Cochabamba are hardest hit by these strikes, to the extent that it would not be considered safe to venture into town while one of these strikes is going on. Public transportation shuts down, taxis refuse to run, and most businesses, public and private, simply close up until the strike is over. In response to the unrest, the police move in with their big trucks and their tear gas, and the whole thing very often gets out of control. It is not uncommon for people to be killed in these major strikes.

Kathy and I did not sleep well Monday night. We were anxious about the remaining steps and how we would get them done in time to catch our flight, worried that we might not be able to change Kathy's ticket, worried about our kids back at home, and just tired of being in Bolivia, so far away from everything we knew. When we woke up Tuesday morning, sleep-deprived but ready to go into the city and get Nathan's passport as quickly as possible, we were greeted by the disturbing news that a strike was underway and that we would not be able to head downtown. No taxis would take us, for fear of the striking workers. We were supposed to meet Clementina at the passport office at 8:30, and we couldn't even venture into the city. We called Clementina and let her know that we were not able to come, and she said that she lived near *migración* and would go on ahead and start on the paperwork. She told us to get to the office as quickly as we could.

We called the airline office and found, to our surprise, that they were open. They agreed to let us change our tickets from the Wednesday flight to the corresponding Thursday flight, but they said that it would not be possible to change them to Friday. That made it even more imperative for us to get our passport that day, Tuesday. After fretting about the strike for an hour or so, we decided to start walking, praying that God would protect us from the demonstrators, and see if we could catch a taxi somewhere along the way. One of the RockSalt volunteers, Luciano (loo-see-AH-no), went with us to act as interpreter and guide. After a few blocks, a taxi driver picked us up and agreed to take us as far as he could toward the *migración* office. Unexpectedly — miraculously — we made it all the way to the office, arriving around noon. To our great surprise, we found that Clementina had in fact begun the paperwork, and we were quickly able to complete it. Following that, we had to meet with the director of *migración* to ask him to agree to give us the passport that same day. As he looked over all of our paperwork, he told Kathy and me, through Luciano, that our passports had incorrect visa stamps from the Bolivian Consulate in the States. We had had to get those stamps before we traveled, and apparently the purpose of our visit should have been listed as adoption but wasn't. Because of this discrepancy, the director said that he would have to review the entire court transcript of Nathan's adoption before deciding whether or not to grant the passport application. He instructed us to return to the office at 6:30 that evening, when he would let us know his decision. We were concerned, but we tried to be guardedly optimistic that we would have the passport by the end of the day and be good to go for our visa appointment the next morning.

Because of the morning's labor strike, most of the businesses in La Paz had opened late that day. This is very common; so common, in fact, that the government has developed a means for dealing with it. The Ministry of Labor declares the day to be a special work day, because of the late start, and all businesses work straight through the normal lunch hour and then close up for the day at 3:00 PM. That is exactly what happened that fateful Tuesday. We arrived back at the Johnsons' in the early afternoon and made plans to return to *migración* at 6:30, as we had been instructed. But about the time we were settling in and enjoying a late lunch, Pablo told us of the Labor Minister's declaration of a special work day. We would thus not be able to go back to *migración* that evening; we would not be able to pick up the passport that day; and there was no way we would be able to have our visa appointment at the US Embassy without that passport. Kathy and I were devastated. This probably constituted our lowest point on that whole trip. Late that afternoon, I sent an e-mail back to our prayer supporters in the States, asking for prayer for our situation. The subject line of that e-mail was "God

Said No"; I was in a foul mood, and I didn't exercise any great pains to conceal the fact.

The God we serve, though, is a God of grace. He met me in my foul mood, and He spoke to me through His word. That Tuesday evening I was thinking and praying, and I read again the story of Joseph from the book of Genesis. Joseph was a godly man who did his best to live consistently with the requirements of the LORD, to serve Him and live according to His commandments. The recompense Joseph received for his faithfulness was to be sold into slavery by his own jealous brothers, to be sold again into bondage to an official in the foreign nation of Egypt, and ultimately to be wrongly accused of a crime and to be thrown into prison. This honest and upright man spent two years in prison, praying to God, serving Him faithfully, and waiting for his deliverance. In the end, God not only delivered Joseph from prison and bondage, but He elevated him to a position of prominence, second only to Pharaoh in all of Egypt. And Joseph, because of his position in the Egyptian government, proved to be the savior of his whole family when famine threatened all of the Middle East and much of North Africa. At the crucial point in the story, when Joseph was revealed to his brothers as their deliverer, he said to them, "I am your brother, Joseph, whom you sold into Egypt. And now do not be distressed or angry with yourselves because you sold me here, for God sent me before you to preserve life. For the famine has been in the land these two years, and there are yet five years in which there will be neither plowing nor harvest. And God sent me before you to preserve for you a remnant on earth, and to keep alive for you many survivors."[7] Later on Joseph said to his brothers, "Do not fear, for am I in the place of God? As for you, you meant evil against me, but God meant it for good, to bring it about that many people should be kept alive, as they are today."[8] Joseph acknowledged that God sovereignly ordained that he, Joseph, would not only suffer for Him, but that he would rise up to become a deliverer of God's people. This is a beautiful picture on many levels, but for me on that day, it served to remind me that the circumstances we find ourselves in, whether good or bad, are not necessarily an indication of God's favor or disfavor toward us. God works things out according to His unsearchable wisdom and always in His own perfect timing, always out of the infinite abundance of His goodness and love. I realized that if God had ordained that we should remain in Bolivia for another week—or even another three weeks—then that was good, and it should be the only thing we desired. I talked through all of this with Kathy, and we prayed together. Then we went to bed, trusting God to work out His plans for our time there in Bolivia and to help us accept those plans, whatever they might be. We slept peacefully that night, perhaps more peacefully than we had done in a week.

The next morning, Wednesday, we headed back to *migración* and arrived as they were opening. We were ushered in to speak to the director. He was very angry because, in spite of the declaration of the special work day, he had gone to the office to meet us at 6:30 the previous evening, as we had agreed, and we had not shown up. After ranting and raving for a full ten minutes—in Spanish—he reluctantly agreed to give us the passport. We later found out from

Pablo, who had accompanied us that morning, that the director told Clementina that he was giving us the passport for our benefit, and the baby's, but not for hers. As respectfully as we could manage, we grabbed the passport from him and bolted for the door. It was nearly 8:30, and we had to get in line at the embassy by then or we would not be allowed to apply for our visa that day. But of course, there was a complication: we didn't have the completed medical form necessary for the visa.

All adopted children applying for immigrant visas to the United States are required to undergo a medical exam performed by a physician approved by the US Consulate in that country. The physician has to fill out a form, provided by the Consulate, which then becomes part of the application packet. The Consulate cannot approve the visa application without, among other things, that medical form. A few days before our experience with the director of *migración*, we had taken Nathan to a Consulate-approved physician and had the medical exam performed, but the doctor hadn't completed the required form. We were trying to make arrangements to get the form picked up so we could still do the visa interview, as scheduled. While Kathy and Clementina went to the Embassy to get in line for the visa interview, Pablo and I went to the doctor's office to pick up the form. When we got to the office, however, we found that it was closed. Apparently the doctor was away and had closed the office during his absence. Providentially, though, Pablo knew someone who knew the doctor's receptionist, and with a few phone calls we learned where she lived. We grabbed another taxi and headed off in search of her home.

Another thing I learned about Bolivia that morning: addresses are rather arbitrary and only loosely connected with physical buildings. We quickly found the neighborhood, but then we had trouble finding the street. The taxi driver told us he knew where it was, but he didn't. We stopped a few people on the street, asking for directions; they each said they knew where the house was, but they didn't. After a maddening interval of about fifteen minutes of near-frantic searching, we found the house. Pablo did a beautiful job of explaining the situation to the startled young woman, and she agreed to accompany us to the doctor's office and get the form for us. What a morning that was. We raced back to the doctor's office, got the form, put the receptionist into a taxi to take her home, and then raced back to the Embassy, where Pablo dropped me off to go in and find Kathy, while he, tired but pleased with his morning's work, headed home. I will admit that I was forty years old when we arrived in La Paz to adopt Nathan, but I have no idea how much older I was when I finally got to the Embassy that morning.

The remainder of that day is somewhat lost in mist. We walked through all of the paperwork with the liaison officer and then had the exit interview, and then the liaison officer told us that our visa petition had been granted and we could come back at 3:00 to pick up the visa. We were happy, but once again guarded. We got back to the Embassy that afternoon and, after a wait of about two hours, were handed the visa packet for Nathan. After the most intense and stressful and emotional week and a half we had ever been through, it was over. Nathan was officially our son, and now the US government had told us that we could bring him home to America with us, to meet his brothers and sisters and grandparents and extended family and a host of friends, all waiting to welcome him. We went back to the Johnsons' house and had a "sho-nuff"[9] celebration! A number of friends dropped by—dear friends we had never even met just five weeks earlier—and we had music and singing and laughter. After the party was over and all of the guests had gone home, Kathy and I went upstairs to pack. We finished around 2:30 in the morning, knowing that we had to get up at 4:00 to head to the airport and that we would probably be exhausted all the way home—and not caring in the least. We were going home!

Kathy and I, with our new son, boarded the plane in La Paz, Bolivia, on June 18, 1998, which also happened to be our twenty-first wedding anniversary. Neither of us could have imagined a better anniversary present than to be heading home. The flight to the US was pretty uneventful, though very long. Once we landed in Miami, we got off the plane and headed to the immigration check-point at the airport. Incoming US citizens generally have no problem getting through immigration, but when you are bringing an adopted child home, you have to submit his or her visa packet to the immigration services officer for processing. The time required for this processing varies, depending on the airport, the time of day, the mood of the immigration officers—and perhaps the color of the shirt the baby is wearing that day. That time it took several hours for the processing. Once we finally got through immigration, we picked up our bags and went through customs, and headed out to find a taxi. The flight schedules had necessitated that we spend a night in Miami before heading home the next day. We checked into our wonderful American hotel near the airport, and we spent an absolutely amazing evening enjoying the hot shower and the ability to drink water from the tap and countless other small amenities most of us take for granted. The hotel was modest by typical American standards, but after our five weeks in Bolivia, it felt like the Ritz.

On the morning of June 19, we headed back to the airport for our flight to Atlanta. This flight should have been under an hour long, but bad weather forced our plane to circle for a time near Atlanta, and then the air traffic controllers diverted our plane to Daytona Beach, Florida, to wait out the storms in Atlanta. We sat on the tarmac in Daytona Beach, trying to amuse and comfort our nine-month-old baby, without any idea of how long we would be there or how long till we would get home to our kids.

The struggle to adopt a child from another country into a Christian home is more than just a fight to finish paperwork and raise money and work through the bureaucratic mess that is the adoption process. It is a struggle against the Enemy of our faith, who is loath to let a single soul pass out of his control and into the Lord's camp. That day in Bolivia when the labor strike made it impossible to get into the city to pick up Nathan's passport, when I wrote that gloomy e-mail to our friends in the States, we got a really encouraging response from a family friend. He wrote:

These struggles you are going through are to be expected. You are changing the eternal destiny of Nathan. You have taken a child which nobody wanted, who, apart from your love, more than likely would have spent his life firmly in Satan's grasp. Satan is going to oppose what you are doing, and now that it is almost over, his opposition is going to intensify. The battle you are in is a spiritual battle. Remember, your Father will not leave you or forsake you. Do not let the attack of the Enemy cause you to doubt. As you go through the trials and the pain to complete the adoption, it will help you and your family to more fully understand what it means to be adopted as children of the Father. Remember the pain that Christ endured so that your adoption could be completed. Use this as a chance to draw closer to Christ and to identify with Him.

We have seen, time and time again, that Satan fights against us whenever we strive to rescue a needy child. We are still sometimes discouraged when the battle is intense, but we are no longer surprised. The Bible tells us, "For we do not wrestle against flesh and blood, but against the rulers, against the authorities, against the cosmic powers over this present darkness, against the spiritual forces of evil in the heavenly places."[10] God has taught us that the fight must go on, but that we have to fight using the weapons He has given us—prayer, the Scriptures, and the fellowship and encouragement of other Believers. We have to look to Him for the energy to continue to wield our swords, and we have to trust Him for the victory. His Word is clear: the battle is His. Our part is to be willing to follow Him into the battle, to be His instruments in fighting the fight, and to give glory to Him for every victory along the way. Sometimes that means being persecuted for our faith, sometimes it means fighting against ruthless or evil men to be able to do what is right, and sometimes it means resisting the devil while he throws corrupt officials and bad weather and irritation upon irritation in our path to try to dissuade us from doing what God has called us to do.

After sitting in Daytona Beach for two and a half hours, we flew back up to Atlanta. Once in the terminal, we began looking for my brother, who was supposed to meet us there to drive us home to Birmingham. The fact that we were about five hours later than scheduled caused us to wonder if he would even still be there. He was; he had been waiting in his car most of the afternoon, popping back in to the terminal from time to time to see when our flight was expected to land.

The drive back to Birmingham was torture, since we were exhausted and strained, and dying to see our other kids. Also, a series of traffic jams along the route transformed this normally two-hour drive into a four-hour ordeal. We finally got to Kathy's parents' house late that evening. We will never forget the looks on our children's faces as they poured out of the house, dashed past us, and scrambled into the car to get their hands on their new little brother, this child they had been reading about in e-mails for the past five weeks and praying for over the past few months. We were overwhelmed by the outpouring of genuine love they almost smothered him with before we could even get him out of his car seat. Nathan was so tired that he cried whenever anyone looked at him, but even that was enough to elicit, "Oh, look how cute he is when he does that!" from all of his brothers and sisters. What a grand first meeting for our children—all five of them now—and what a glorious reunion for our entire family!

Two days later, after making sure that all of the extended family in Birmingham had been able to meet our new son, Kathy and I and our five kids climbed into our loaded mini-van and drove back to Cincinnati. As we drove, and as we began to settle back into our routine at home, we marveled at the adventure God had privileged us to be a part of, the thrill ride He had taken us on over the past six months. God often takes us through experiences to change us, to make us more into the people He wants us to be, more conformed to the image of Christ. And sometimes, in addition to that, these experiences are intended to prepare us for what lies ahead. Our time in Bolivia, the love we developed for the people there, and especially our adoption of Nathan, definitely changed us and, without our realizing it, began to prepare us for what lay ahead. Rescuing a needy child and being a part of transforming his life is a little bit like surviving a serious car accident. You begin to look at almost everything differently than you did before. In many ways, we were as changed as Nathan was through our adoption of him, and God opened up doors to us that we never even knew were there before. The first of those doors was Meghan.

Chapter 5

Forever Changed,
And No Looking Back

I am not what I ought to be;

I am not what I want to be;

I am not what I hope to be;

but by the grace of God, I am not what I was.

John Newton

(Paraphrased)

Tien Yue

Liaoning is a province in northeastern China bordered by North Korea on the east and Inner Mongolia on the west. In the central plains of Liaoning, not far from the shores of the Bohai Sea, sits the small city of Gaizhou. Sometime in mid-March 1996, a baby girl was abandoned at the city shelter for the homeless in Gaizhou City. The baby was about two days old and had congenital deformities of both hands and both feet. This tiny baby was transferred to the orphanage in Gaizhou, where she was cared for along with the many other children housed there. At some point while she was still a baby, the orphanage arranged for corrective surgery for this child, whom they were calling Gao Jing Mei. The surgery removed the extra big toes and extra thumbs she had been born with, leaving large scars on both hands and both feet. There were other problems associated with Jing Mei's hands and feet, but the corrective procedures for those would have to wait. When Jing Mei was somewhere between two and three years old, the orphanage she was living in ran out of money and was forced to close. Jing Mei was then transferred to the Changchun Children's Welfare Institute (CWI), three hundred miles away in the neighboring province of Jilin. The caretakers at the Changchun CWI began calling her Tien Yue. Late in 1998, Tien Yue was noticed by the Chinese representative of an American adoption agency, and this agency began the search for a family for this special little girl.

Changed

Kathy and I brought Nathan home in June 1998, and as I mentioned a bit earlier, we came home changed. We had rescued our precious baby boy from life at an orphanage and what would follow when he grew up, but we could not get away from the knowledge that we had left about five hundred children behind at *Hogar de Niños Carlos de Villegas*. And that was just one orphanage; one orphanage . . . in one city . . . in one small country. How overwhelmingly the need impressed itself upon us then! We didn't yet know anything about the actual numbers of orphans worldwide — the statistical magnitude of this problem of children not having homes and families—but a little mental math told us that the problem was huge. The faces of dozens of Bolivian children haunted us, reminding us that, while we had brought Nathan home and were settling back into middle-class life in the most affluent nation on Earth, little boys and little girls and babies in Bolivia were going to sleep every night longing for the comforts and peace and security of a real home. How could we simply go back to life as we had known it before, as if we had not been changed by our experiences? We could not.

Nathan was only nine months old when we brought him home, and it is so easy to love a cute little baby. The other four kids thought he was the best thing that had ever happened to our family, and Nathan almost immediately accepted all of them as a necessary and hugely beneficial part of his life. Kathy and I sometimes found ourselves tiptoeing into Nathan's room at night, just to look at him while he slept. As we did so, we were often overcome with the emotion that came with the realization of what God had done in this little boy's life. He had pulled him out of an orphanage in an impoverished country where he had no hope of a future, and very little likelihood of ever being exposed to the Gospel, and He had transported him into a family and the fulfillment of the promise found in Jeremiah: "For I know the plans I have for you, declares the LORD, plans for welfare and not for evil, to give you a future and a hope."[11] We were seeing the reality of the here-and-now portion of that promise[12] working out in our little boy's life.

As the months rolled by, and as we returned to these thoughts over and over again, and as we watched this little boy bloom in the environment of this family God had created, we began to wonder if we might not be able to do the same thing again. In spite of the fact that we were concerned about the cost of another adoption and that I might have difficulty requesting the time off work again, only six months after taking time off for Nathan's adoption, we committed to praying about it and waiting to see how God would lead. We wondered if God might be leading us once more to pursue adoption, to provide a safe and loving and nurturing environment for another needy child.

As we examined this calling to provide a home for another child—this new, clear calling that was so much more compelling after our five weeks in Bolivia—we looked at which special needs we felt we could "handle." We both knew that we were equipped to accommodate a variety of physical limitations, such as missing or deformed limbs or cleft palate or the like, but we were also convinced that we were not able to take on any sort of mental handicap. In retrospect, we think God must have smiled indulgently to Himself as we came to this conclusion, since He knew His plans for us before the world began. But I'm getting ahead of myself: the explanation for that comes much later in this book. Our desire was to provide a home and opportunity for a child who would be overlooked by the majority of adoptive parents, and we felt strongly that our calling was to reach out to these least of the least in God's name. Kathy, being much more action-oriented than I am, began searching for a child needing a home, one with a physical handicap that would make it more difficult for him or her to find a home.

This search ultimately led to International Assistance and Adoption Project (IAAP). The director of this agency, Dick Graham, described a little girl in need of a home: she was three or four years old, in China, and had been born with extra big toes on both feet and extra thumbs on both hands. Her name was Tien Yue. Dick explained that the little girl's birth defects would possibly be seen as an evil omen in the part of China where she was living, and that she would likely be shunned her entire life because of them. Along the way, as we were praying and seeking God's leading, we learned that China requires only one parent to travel, not both, and that the time in-country is only two weeks. Further, Dick told us that he was waiving all agency fees associated with this adoption in an effort to find a family for this little girl.

In the end, we felt that God clearly was leading us to pursue the adoption of Tien Yue, whom we decided to name Meghan Alyssa, which means "pearl of great happiness." We decided that Kathy would travel without me, so that I could stay home and keep the children. We again dove into the paperwork and began raising money. As in the case of Nathan's adoption, we had no money available to begin the adoption process. We trusted that God would provide, as He had done before, and we wrote letters and e-mails to everyone we knew, to tell them of our new adventure and to invite them to partner with us in rescuing another child. Our position, once again, was that we didn't want to try to coerce anyone into helping, either because of guilt or simply because of their love and concern for us; rather, we asked people to pray, to ask God if He might be leading them to help financially in the rescue of this little girl. Having done that, we prayed, we waited, we prayed some more, and we left the outcome in God's hands.

Our year of 1999 was a busy one, with all of the usual activity associated with a family of five children, but we also had Kristen's high school graduation, an out-of-town reconstructive hand surgery for Ryan, an unexpected knee surgery for Kristen, and all of the paperwork and stress that go along with an international adoption. Along the way, a friend from our church, Sally Alspaugh, agreed to travel to China with Kathy to help her with all she would have to deal with over there, and to help take care of Meghan on the long trip home. This was a real blessing to us, and it helped both Kathy and me relax a bit about how the trip would go.

Our dossier was finished and in China by the beginning of June, and then we waited. Through the generosity of IAAP and the kindness of so many of our friends — and a number of complete strangers — God provided all of the funds needed to cover the adoption and travel expenses. We finally got word that Kathy would be traveling in October to get Meghan. Because of a conflict with the timing of the trip, Sally wasn't going to be able to accompany Kathy on the trip over, but would join her near the end of the first week. We worked our way through the remainder of the summer, and in September we took Kristen to Beaver Falls, Pennsylvania, where she would be attending Geneva College, majoring in Linguistics.

China

In early October, it was time for Kathy to travel. Because I would be at work all day each day, and because Kristen was now away at college, Kathy's parents and sister traveled to Cincinnati to stay in our home and care for the children during the day. On Friday, October 8, 1999, Kathy said her good-byes to all of the children, and I took her to the airport for her to begin the long trek to China. She first flew to Los Angeles, California, and then from L.A. to Seoul, South Korea. Finally, she flew from Seoul to Beijing, China, arriving on October 9, local. Her introduction to the most populous nation in the world was hectic and blurred: she had been awake for roughly thirty-six hours by the time she arrived in Beijing. There was another couple adopting a child through IAAP who were traveling with Kathy. David and Kim Brown were there to adopt a fourteen-month-old girl, whom they were going to name Erin. The Browns and Kathy met up with Dick's in-country contact when they arrived in Beijing. This Chinese woman's anglicized name was Hannah, and she was to serve as travel guide, adoption resource, translator, and advisor during their stay in China. Over the course of the next day or so, Hannah took the American trio on a whirlwind tour of the high points of Beijing, including Tiananmen Square, the Forbidden City, and the Great Wall.

The differences between Kathy's experience in China and our earlier experience in Bolivia were many, and some were profound. For example, the hotels in China that host international adoptive families are beautiful, very Western, and often luxurious. They have resplendent lobbies—sometimes with live piano music playing at certain hours—and all of the modern conveniences of a first class international hotel. They usually feature sumptuous breakfast buffets with a full spread of American, European, and Chinese foods, and the hotel staff often speak passable, if not perfect, English. Other differences were noted on the streets. To Kathy, a wide-eyed, small-town American, these streets felt very foreign, with their constantly crowded sidewalks, more bicycles than could be imagined in one city, and very Spartan-looking, Communist-era buildings.[13] Once she came off of these streets, though, and into her hotel, she could almost forget that she wasn't in America — were it not for the ceaseless flow of Chinese speech all around her, the uniformed bellmen, and the bowing hotel staff.

The adoption process in China, too, is dramatically different than what we experienced in Bolivia. Each year there are more than four thousand adoptions to the US from China,[14] and the peak year, 2004, saw nearly eight thousand. By contrast, the peak year for adoptions from Bolivia during the previous ten years was the year we brought Nathan home, 1998, in which there were seventy-three adoptions to the US. This multitude of annual adoptions has, undoubtedly, helped the Chinese hone their system into one that is both smooth and efficient. The trip to China is approximately two weeks long, and entire adoption system, unlike the labyrinthine semi-chaos of a Bolivian adoption, functions in most cases like a well-oiled machine.

Meghan

The next morning, Monday, it was time to receive the girls. Hannah met Kathy and the Browns in the hotel lobby, and after a little while, some orphanage officials came in with Meghan and Erin. Kathy squatted down and held her arms out to Meghan, who

101

was much tinier than we had expected. Meghan instantly ran up to Kathy and threw her little arms around Kathy's neck. After holding tightly for a moment, Meghan pulled away a bit and looked straight into Kathy's eyes. She then pressed her body against Kathy's and held on tightly again. Kathy was moved to tears at the thought that this lost little child was now her daughter, and very surprised at this affectionate and enthusiastic greeting. She was soon to learn that Meghan greeted everyone in this way. Meghan had somehow learned to smile, hug, kiss, and show all signs of affection, both for people she knew and for complete strangers, with absolutely no real meaning behind these actions.

Kathy also soon saw that when Meghan was not in this mode of automatically showing affection, she often scowled and looked angry.[15] After a few minutes of greeting, Hannah told Kathy and Kim to take their respective daughters up to their rooms and change their clothes, and to be back down in the lobby in twenty minutes. Meghan allowed Kathy to undress her and put on one of the dresses and a pair of tights she had brought for her, although Meghan was a blur of hyperactive energy and motion. In spite of the fact that she desperately needed a bath and had her "angry face" on, she looked very cute as they dashed back down to the hotel lobby.

Next, it was time for the whole group to travel to the registrar's office for the paperwork. It quickly became apparent that this precious little girl had come with quite a lot of personality. Almost as soon as the group left the hotel, Meghan began to test the boundaries. She continually tried to pull away from Kathy and dash into the busy streets, and she resisted when Kathy told her "no," although she clearly understood what was meant by this English word. She grew more and more aggressive in her challenges. It was obvious that someone had explained to Meghan beforehand that a strange-looking woman would come and get her, and that this woman would be her new mother. This apparently had left her confused, or perhaps a bit conflicted. She would do something she knew to be wrong, and while doing so she would constantly watch Kathy to see what her reaction would be. She seemed to be pushing as hard as she could to show Kathy that she was her own boss, that Kathy could not make her behave. But she also wanted to have Kathy near her at all times. As she became more comfortable with Kathy, she also pushed harder against the boundaries, more aggressively forcing Kathy to respond to her misbehavior.

Kathy, on the other hand, felt hampered in her ability to respond to Meghan's challenges. She was continually under a spotlight, knowing that many of the officials would be watching to see how she, like any other adoptive parent, responded to her new child. She was afraid that too much leniency would be interpreted as not being able to control her child, and that too much severity would be interpreted as lack of affection, or worse. Kathy and I have always functioned as a team in matters of parenting, as in all others, and for her to have to face the challenges of this unmanageable child without the support, encouragement, and advice of her life's companion was particularly difficult.

After the session at the registrar's office, Kathy and Meghan and the Browns, led by Hannah, went to a restaurant for some food. After Meghan finished eating, Kathy took her to an indoor playground at the restaurant while the others finished their meals. An employee at the restaurant shouted instructions to Meghan in Chinese to help her learn to propel herself on a swing, and after a while Meghan actually got it. She loved it and was so excited at her success, and she smiled broadly at Kathy, who captured the event on our video camera. But then it was time to leave. Kathy tried to call Meghan to come to her. Meghan refused. Kathy reached out and managed to get hold of Meghan's hand. In response, Meghan went limp and refused to comply, and she laughed a triumphant, you-can't-make-me-do-what-I-don't-want-to-do sort of laugh. Finally, Hannah stepped in and grabbed Meghan's hand and ordered her, in Chinese of course, to walk. Meghan turned her back on Kathy and begged Hannah to carry her; Hannah refused, saying that no one would be carrying Meghan thereafter. And away the two of them marched, leaving Kathy to follow along. This incident was both humiliating and demoralizing to Kathy. How was she going to survive two weeks in this country that was so strange to her, with this out-of-control child?

Over the years, we've learned that all of these behaviors are common among institutionalized children, and especially those who are a little older. Thankfully, there are resources available now, that weren't available back when we adopted Meghan, for helping adoptive parents prepare for and respond to these behaviors and their underlying causes.[16]

On Tuesday, Kathy and company went to the notary's office to complete the adoption paperwork for both Meghan and Erin. This day, like its predecessor, was trying and emotionally draining for

Kathy. For some reason, the notary official seemed unable to complete his work. After about three hours, he told the party to go have lunch and return afterward. Meghan was difficult during the meal, actually climbing up onto the table several times to take food from other plates, and throwing a fit every time Kathy tried to correct her behavior. Meghan then began crying — clearly an angry cry and not a sad one — and Kathy decided to ignore her. The more Meghan was ignored, the more loudly she cried. Finally, to keep from disturbing the other patrons at the restaurant, Kathy picked her up, carried her out of the building, plunked her down on one of the steps, and then sat down beside her. Kathy just sat there, not paying any attention to Meghan's behavior and pretending to be oblivious to the many stares from passers-by. The spectacle of a Caucasian woman doing something, whatever it was, to cause a Chinese child to wail in distress brought many curious and disapproving stares from onlookers. After a while of this, Meghan, who had become surprisingly adept at communicating with Kathy through mime and a few words of English, must have decided that she wasn't going to win, because she let Kathy know that she was ready to eat and be a good girl. Kathy took her by the hand and the two of them walked, calmly and quietly, back into the restaurant. Kathy felt that she might have just won the first victory in the power struggle with our small but mighty daughter.

They finished the meal with relatively few additional problems, and then the group returned to the notary's office. Once the notary finished his paperwork, the adoption was final. Gao Jing Mei (aka Tien Yue) was, as of October 12, 1999, officially and irrevocably

Meghan Alyssa Rosenow. The elation we felt upon this momentous occasion was, admittedly, quite a bit less than what we felt at the same point in Nathan's process. It is not that we were not thrilled, nor that we thanked God any less for this blessing; but the process itself was so much quicker, so much less dramatic than it had been in Bolivia, and the child herself was not a lovable, cuddly baby, but a prickly, pouty, difficult three-year-old who didn't seem to want to be Meghan Alyssa Rosenow. In spite of these differences, though, we were indeed thrilled and excited, and all of us at home, once Kathy relayed the news, had a joyful mini-celebration of the event. (The full celebration would have to wait till Kathy and Meghan came home.)

Three more days were required in Changchun, waiting for Meghan's and Erin's passports, before the group could travel to Guangzhou, where the US Immigration portion of the adoption would be completed. During those three days, Kathy spent time getting to know this beautiful, difficult child who was now ours. At times, Meghan could be so cute and endearing. At other times, she would revert to her manipulative and moody alter ego.

There were moments of warmth and tenderness, too. The long afternoons in the hotel were spent playing together as mother and daughter with the doll Kathy had brought for Meghan, teaching her little songs — which Meghan picked up amazingly quickly — or showing her how to cut with scissors. By far, though, Meghan's favorite activity with her mommy was looking through the photo book Kathy had made for her, to introduce Meghan to her new family waiting for her in Ohio. Her curiosity about this new family was almost insatiable, and she was very insistent about doing her best to learn everyone's names. Every day ended with a time of snuggling in Meghan's bed, looking through this book together and repeating the names of each sibling and each pet before Meghan fell asleep.

Little by little, as one day rolled into the next, Kathy began to notice that she was making progress in the battle to win Meghan's heart, as evidenced by Meghan's increasing willingness to obey Kathy. This was a gradual increase, and it felt tenuous at best during that first week, but even these small steps were encouraging and gave Kathy hope.

Often in the evening, after getting Meghan settled into bed, Kathy would call home to talk to me about the challenges, triumphs, and frustrations of her unfolding adventure. China is twelve hours ahead of Ohio time, so evening for her was morning for me. She would explain what Meghan had done that day, what difficulties she had faced, and we would talk about the best way for her to handle such situations, the best way for her to survive the ordeal of Meghan's adoption.

Meghan's passport was delivered to Kathy on Friday afternoon. On Saturday, Sally arrived in Changchun to provide reinforcement and back-up for Kathy with Meghan. On Sunday morning, the whole group headed to Guangzhou for the completion of the process.

Kathy found the atmosphere in Guangzhou completely different than in Changchun. There was more obvious Western influence, as well as a general air of ease and relaxation. Up until late-2005, the visa processing unit of the US Consulate was located on the Shamian Island, and so it was a necessary stop for Americans adopting from China. Most adopting families found it convenient to stay in one of the island's western-style hotels during their stay there, and the abundance of other Americans has always been an attractive feature of this part of Guangzhou.

The few days that Kathy and the others spent in Guangzhou were refreshing after the stress and climate of Changchun. They left northern China on October 17, and the weather was already turning cold and harsh. When they stepped out into the street in Guangzhou, they were surprised at the dramatic change in temperature. Even in late October, Guangzhou is typically warm and pleasant. As they strolled leisurely about Shamian Island, they saw many retirement-age nationals, often practicing Tai Chi, playing badminton, or vigorously discussing some topic of apparent importance. Meghan's behavior, too, was improved in Guangzhou. She thrived on the outside air and exercise, and it seemed that the change of location and climate, the taking away of everything that was familiar, brought her to a greater dependence on Kathy. This increased dependence took away much of Meghan's reckless defiance.

The day after they arrived in southern China, Martin—the in-country agent in Guangzhou—took the group to a clinic on the island for the girls' required medical examinations. This was a terrifying experience for Meghan, and she screamed in fear throughout the entire exam. We learned, years later, that when children undergo surgery in China (as in many developing nations) they are rarely, if ever, given any sort of post-operative pain medication. Hospital stays and medical procedures there are traumatic and excruciatingly painful experiences. It took Meghan a long time to get past her fear of doctors in the US because of the memories of her hospital stays in China. It still breaks our hearts to think of what she must've gone through during those times as a lonely little girl with no mommy or daddy to comfort and hold her. And it breaks our hearts to think of the millions of children around the world still subjected to these ordeals every day, as they long for a family to advocate for them and protect them.

During those last few days of Kathy's trip to China, I received word from our contacts in Bolivia that Raiza would be returning to the States for additional treatment. The urgency of her condition, in fact, required that she come immediately. She would be arriving about a week after Kathy returned from China with Meghan. This was very good news for all of us, as we had been longing to see Raiza again after a separation of more than a year. I told Kathy, during one of our phone conversations, of the news about Raiza's return, and she was overjoyed.

The interview at the Consular Section for Meghan's visa was set for Tuesday morning, and when Kathy went to bed on Monday she was struck by the contrast between Meghan's adoption process in China and Nathan's in Bolivia. None of the turmoil, conflict, randomness, and confusion that had characterized the process in Bolivia had been evident in China. Her final step would be completed the next day, and they would board the airplane for home on Thursday. This time the whole adoption had gone smoothly — essentially without a hitch. Kathy went to sleep peaceful and contented, knowing that soon she would be home, soon able to see and hold her other children and introduce them to their new sister. But then came Tuesday, and along with the new day, another of those dramatic moments that stand forever in our memories.

Chapter 6

A Glimpse of the Master's Plan

I would not, if I could, turn back now,
because I believe that God is going to reveal Himself
in a wonderful way.

Gladys Aylward

Tuesday in Guangzhou

Excerpt from Kathy's China journal, Tuesday evening, October 19, 1999:

It was supposed to be over today. It is for all the other people who were packed into that room at the Consulate.

In the shower at 5:45 this morning, breakfast at 7:30, some packing, then in the lobby waiting for Martin by 9:30. We leave with Martin and walk to the Consulate, stopping next door first to have the girls' visa pictures taken. Into the Consulate and walk upstairs into a crowded room with about fifteen other adoptive couples. There are a lot of little Chinese children and toys, and

Meghan is showing signs of stress. Quiet, very watchful, with-drawn. As time goes on, she becomes angry, kind of wild – banging on toys with a toy hammer, whining . . . Couples are being called up to one of four desks and asked questions, turning in forms. After about fifteen minutes, each couple walks away smiling, kisses each other and says, "It's over. We're going home!" Finally my name is called. Sally watches Meghan for me – a huge job today. (WHAT would I have done without Sally?) Right away, there is trouble. Some of our forms from Changchun are handwritten and not typed, and my name spelling is inconsistent throughout the documents. One of those forms is the wrong form altogether. On one, November is abbreviated as NO. instead of Nov. The interviewer tells me to sit and wait, and someone will call me back up with a decision. David and Kim have all of the same problems and Martin is telling us not to worry, it will all be fine. David and Kim are called back to the desk where they all work out a way around the problems with the documents. They have to agree to have the document with the November abbreviation re-translated by tomorrow morning, but they are finished and all is fine. My turn. These document problems, it turns out, are very minor. Big problem is that on the I-864, Scott, the petitioner on the I-600A and the person responsible for the household income, is listed as Meghan's sponsor – just as we were told to do it by Martin. This is apparently a huge problem. The person in China to bring Meghan home must be the sponsor, and since that is me and I have no income, they need a new I-864A, signed by Scott in the pres-ence of an INS officer!!! Difficult, since he's in the USA and I'm

112

here. If I can get this done by tomorrow morning, the interviewer tells me, I can still leave with Kim and David on Thursday. If not, I'm stuck in China. I couldn't believe my ears!!! I thought I would die on the spot. How could this be???!! The interviewer, unlike our interviewer in Bolivia, was so kind, and I thanked her for that. She thanked me for being so calm and said that other women came unglued when this kind of thing happened. I was surprised that she couldn't tell how unglued I was inside — just how much I wanted to fall apart, how I had to shut off all emotions in order to keep things moving along. I walked back to the hotel with Kim, David, and Sally, and thanked Sally for caring for Meghan, who whined and pouted all the way back. I didn't scold her. I sensed that she was emotionally exhausted and I wished so much that I could get inside her little head. I fixed her some noodle soup in the room and while she ate, I called Scott and woke him again, trying to hold myself together over the phone. It was just after midnight in Ohio.

So began Kathy's Tuesday in China, the day that was supposed to have been one of the happiest of her whole time there, the capping off of a successful adoption trip. When she called me, she sounded fairly calm, but knowing her as well as I do, I could tell how upset she was. We talked for about half an hour — long enough for me to understand what had happened and what I needed to do to make sure she could finish the process and get on the plane with David and Kim on Thursday. I did my best to comfort her and assure her that I would do everything that could be done, but she was still quite upset at the end of the conversation.

After we talked, I wearily climbed back into bed and tried to turn my brain off so that I could get a few more hours of sleep, since I couldn't do anything else till morning anyway. That was easier said than done. I was faced with an almost impossible task, and my beautiful wife and new daughter were depending on me to get them out of China—from seven thousand miles away. I started Tuesday morning very early, as I finally gave up on sleep and got out of bed to begin the process of running down the forms and people needed to get Kathy and Meghan home.

The race at home

What I was being asked to do was to get a Form I-864A (*Contract Between Sponsor and Household Member*) and fill it out, then take it down to the INS office in Cincinnati and sign it in the presence of an INS officer, and then ask the INS office to fax the form directly to the INS field office in Guangzhou. My window of opportunity was fairly narrow, though, because the completed form would have to be waiting in the Guangzhou INS office when they opened the next morning—meaning, I would have to have it done by the end of my day on Tuesday. I had one shot to get it done. These days, all immigration forms are available for download via the Internet, but that wasn't the case back in 1999, and I didn't have a blank I-864A. So, after my phone conversation with Kathy, Sally got a copy of the form from the INS office in China, and while I was trying to catch a few hours sleep at home, she faxed the form from the business office in the hotel in Guangzhou to her office in Cincinnati. (We didn't have a fax machine at home.) I would, first thing Tuesday morning, drive to Sally's office and pick up the blank form, and then head downtown with it. The whole matter was complicated by the fact that Ryan, then nine years old, had been running a high fever for several days and had an appointment with his doctor the next morning, too.

As soon as it was light on Tuesday morning in Cincinnati, I began the day by putting together a quick e-mail to send to all of the people following our adoption journey, urging them to pray for Kathy and the speedy resolution of this bump in the road. I then drove out to Sally's office and picked up the Form I-864A she had faxed to me. I also called my office while driving and explained why I needed to take the day off on such short notice. Just as they had been during our trip to Bolivia for Nathan's adoption, they were very supportive and told me to take whatever time I needed to straighten out the problem. I then headed downtown to the INS office, praying that I would be able to find someone who would talk to me there. It is impossible to get in to see anyone at INS without an appointment. Fortunately, a friend had given us the name and phone number of a supervisor at the INS office, and I was hoping I would be able to talk to her and get the help I needed. I found a place to park, walked over to the J. W. Peck Federal Building, and started calling on my cell phone from the sidewalk in front of the building. How did anyone ever do this sort of thing before cell phones! While I was working on this, Kristen — who happened to be home that week on fall break — was taking Ryan to the doctor to be checked out because of his fever, while Kathy's parents and sister took care of our other children at home. Ryan's appointment was at 10:00, and Kristen was due to head back to school that afternoon; thus, the stress on her was significant, too.

I called the number I had for the supervisor, and I was told that she wasn't in and that they weren't allowed to tell me when, or if, she would be in. They also told me that they had never heard of faxing any form to an embassy anywhere, and that they didn't see how they could help me. I felt the panic rise within me as I talked with this person. Kathy called me on my cell phone at about 8:15 (Tuesday morning where I was, Tuesday evening where she was) to see how it was going, and I had to tell her what I had found out. But I also, once again, promised her that I would keep trying, all day if I had to.

After a couple of these unsuccessful attempts, I was finally able to speak to the supervisor and explain our situation to her. She initially seemed to think that there was nothing they could do, but I persisted, being completely desperate, and she finally told me to come up to the INS offices and that someone would help me. I practically ran to the fourth floor of the Federal Building. I gave my Form I-864A to the person assigned to help me, answered a few questions, signed the form in front of her, and made her promise — promise! — that she would fax it to China immediately. I now had assurances that Kathy would be able to complete the process in Guangzhou and head home as scheduled.

On the way back to the house, I had to meet Kristen at the pharmacy to get a prescription filled for an antibiotic for Ryan. It turned out that he had strep-induced tonsillitis and was a very sick little boy. Later that day, after lunch, I drove Kristen about three hours north to meet up with a friend from school, who would take her the rest of the way back to the campus. By the end of the day, I was both exhausted and relieved. We all praised God that He had, in spite of intimidating obstacles, made it possible for me to complete the necessary steps at my end for Kathy and Meghan to be able to come home to us on Thursday. But I also anxiously waited for confirmation that the form had actually made it to the Consulate, while still-fresh memories of broken promises and thwarted efforts in Nathan's adoption process whirled around in my head.

Kathy returned to the Consulate on Wednesday and was immensely relieved to be told that the form from the States had indeed arrived, that everything was in order, and that she would be granted a visa for Meghan. There was, needless to say, great rejoicing in China and, later, when we heard about it, in Ohio. Sally and Kathy, along with Kim and David Brown and the two adopted girls, headed to the airport in Guangzhou on Thursday morning, full of expectations of being safe and sound in America within the next twenty-four hours. While they were in line at the airport, waiting to get their boarding passes, Martin asked them if they had confirmed their airline reservations for the return flight. Though this step is unheard of here in the States, it is quite important when traveling abroad. Even with paid tickets, passengers are routinely bumped from flights if reservations are not confirmed within about seventy-two hours before scheduled departure. Both Kathy and the Browns said no, they hadn't, because they had just assumed, quite logically, that Martin would take care of that step for them, mostly because Hannah had taken care of this step for them while they were up north. Bad assumption. When they got to the head of the line, they found that their reservations had been canceled and they had been bumped from the flight. Once again, it was as if Satan shook his fist at Kathy and me and said, "You may have rescued this child from a future of hopelessness and despair, but I will not let you take her easily!" After the elation of obtaining Meghan's visa, Kathy was now faced with the reality that they had no plane tickets for the flight home.

Kathy and the others were put on stand-by status, and they sat down to wait. As they waited, they listened as one stand-by passenger after another was called up to the desk and then permitted to board the plane. After what seemed like an eternity, they finally heard Kathy's and Sally's names over the intercom—but they were the last ones called. David and Kim did not make it onto the flight. At first Kathy refused to leave without them, but Sally took over and convinced Kathy that the right thing to do was to get on that plane and get out of town. Even though Kathy had only known the Browns for about two weeks, the trials and tribulations of international adoption had drawn them close together, and she hated to leave them behind in uncertainty and disappointment. Kathy, Meghan, and Sally arrived in Los Angeles late in the day on Thursday. As soon as they arrived, Kathy called Dick Graham to check on the Browns. Dick told her that they had managed to catch a bus to Hong Kong and had quite enjoyed their long ride through the countryside, observing aspects of daily life in China they had not been able to experience during their time in the cities. Dick and Cheryl had arranged for them to catch a flight from Hong Kong the next day, and they were scheduled to arrive in L.A. on Friday, only slightly behind their original plans.

Kathy, Meghan, and Sally spent Thursday night in a hotel in L.A., and on Friday they completed the final leg of the very long and difficult trip. When we picked them up at the airport Friday evening, our reunion was indescribably sweet and joyful. Meghan hugged her new daddy and all of her new brothers and sisters, and we all headed home to begin our new life together.

Normal life, again

Seven days after Kathy brought Meghan home from China, we drove again to the airport to pick up Raiza, back to stay with us while in Ohio for more burn treatments. We waited eagerly for her to come down the ped-way, hoping to see the same little girl we had left in La Paz a little more than a year earlier. We were disappointed. The girl who greeted us at the airport that day did look very much like our Raiza, but she now, at the age of ten, seemed to be a sullen pre-teen, angry and distant. In spite of her altered appearance and demeanor, we were glad to see her again and glad to have her home with us, even if only for a while. We tried, more or less, to pick things up where they had left off the previous summer, and she did her best to play her part. But she was not the same child. She had changed in the intervening months since we last saw her. There was a hardening within her that we could sense the moment she walked off of the plane.

It quickly became evident that she had returned to her old ways of thinking and interacting. The lies and deception were very much a part of her life again, but because she was an older child now, they were of an uglier and more damaging nature than the lies of the little girl who had come to us nearly two years earlier. We discerned soon after she was back in our home that she was almost overwhelmed with a sense of hopelessness because of her bleak and dysfunctional home life waiting for her back in Bolivia. She told us time and time again that she wanted to be adopted by our family, but she knew that this wasn't a possibility because she already had a family in La Paz. The knowledge that this was a dream that could never be realized caused a smoldering bitterness to take root in her aching heart, and almost from the first night of her return to our home, we fought a spiritual battle to reach her and to help her free herself from the anger that held her prisoner. It was to be the beginning of a very long two-year period in our lives—one marked with frustration and pain and tears beyond counting.

There were amazingly beautiful moments, though, in the midst of our struggles to reach Raiza's heart and to make Meghan our own daughter. Moments which, even now, take our breath away as we remember them. About four months after Meghan came home to us, on a Sunday morning as we were getting ready for church, Kathy noticed Meghan sitting on her bed, singing to herself. As Kathy recognized the tune and began to understand the words—through Meghan's still-strong Chinese accent—her eyes filled with tears. "I'm so happy, so very happy, I've got the love of Jesus in my heart." Kathy told me about it later, and we cried together. We both knew that Meghan was not yet a Christian, but she was singing about the love of Jesus, and she was regularly being exposed to the outworking of that love in her own life. We resolved between ourselves, then and there, that no matter how hard it might get, as long as we had breath and as long as we could still stand up, we would keep taking in as many children as God chose to send us.

Later that month, during a phone conversation with Dick Graham about some post-adoption paperwork, Dick told Kathy about a two-year-old girl in China, one with birth defects very similar to Meghan's, although less severe. We wrestled with whether or not this child was sufficiently disabled—whether her special needs were "special" enough—for us to adopt her. We felt called to rescue those children who would be overlooked by the typical adoptive family, and we weren't at all sure that this little girl fit that description. Dick assured us that she did, and that her chances of being adopted were almost non-existent, partially because she was located in a province in Northern China where adoptions were rare. Few people would ever even know about her, and those who did hear about her would have many healthy baby girls to choose from, rather than this little girl—who was not an infant and had been born with a disability, albeit mild. As usual, we prayed. After about a week of soul-searching and prayer, we came to the conclusion that God was leading us to another little girl in China, and that our responsibility was to go and get her. We committed to this adoption, and we decided to name this daughter Robyn Isabella, which means "consecrated to God." We began raising funds, and by the end of March, even though we had a long way to go on the financial end, our dossier for Robyn was on its way to China.

As we waited for developments in Robyn's adoption, life went on at the Rosenow house. In March, we traveled to Louisville for surgery for both Ryan and Meghan. Ryan had an Ilizarov, a bone-lengthening device pioneered by the Russians, attached to his right arm. He had to wear the device for three months, and four times every day we turned the four lengthening screws that would "stretch" his forearm bones a total of one millimeter per day. Meghan had corrective surgery on her left hand and left foot. She wore casts on her arm and leg for about a month. Then in April, Raiza went into the Shriners Hospital here in Cincinnati for some additional scar revision surgery. She stayed in the hospital for a little over a week and, as before, came home to the routine of cleanings, pressure garments, and stretching exercises.

We achieved a significant milestone in April. Meghan had been home from China for roughly six months, and it was at about this point that we sensed that we were at a critical point in the bonding process. Meghan's behavior became increasingly independent, in the sense of choosing to do what she wanted rather than what we required of her in a given situation. Kathy would firmly tell her that she must obey our rules, and would stand her in the corner and admonish her to accept our authority as her parents. Her response to Kathy, in her somewhat broken English, was, "You not the boss; I the boss." Kathy would explain to Meghan — in terms that Meghan could understand — that, in spite of her desire to be the boss, God had placed her under our authority for her own good, and that we were not going to shirk the responsibility God had given us simply because she didn't like it.

There was a period of about two weeks in which Meghan would go to the corner for disobedience every day, and every day she would repeat her determination to be "the boss." Finally, one day at the end of that two-week period, she suddenly and unexpectedly turned to Kathy with tears in her eyes and said, "I ready be your little girl now." Her choice of wording struck us as highly significant and touched our hearts deeply. Though there have been many smaller battles over the years, this marked a turning point in Meghan's bonding, and we never again faced the rebellious determination that had characterized her behavior to that point. What an amazing thing it is to watch a child who does not have our genes in her cells or our blood coursing through her veins—a child who was born years before we even knew about her—truly become our child every bit as much as the children who grew in Kathy's womb.

Around the middle of May we learned that we wouldn't be traveling to China in the summer, as we had thought, and that it would be at least September before we could go get Robyn. The reason for this delay, we were told, was that China would not allow us to complete Robyn's adoption until at least a year after Meghan's, which had been in October. We had not been told of this requirement before, and it came as an unsettling surprise. But we adjusted our thinking and continued with our planning for the trip.

Two providential paths converge

Early in June, through a circuitous and providential series of events, we learned of a baby boy in Bolivia living in the same orphanage Nathan had come from, *Carlos de Villegas*. This little guy was nearly two years old and had been born very prematurely, at only twenty-six weeks gestation. He had developed a number of complications due to his premature birth, including almost-total blindness in both eyes. *Carlos de Villegas* could only keep boys until the age of two, after which they were transferred to other institutions. The orphanage had been notified by the authorities that this little boy, whom they had named Reynaldo (ray-NAL-doh), was soon to be transferred to a state institution for the mentally disabled — simply because of his blindness. Sister Providencia and her staff were very worried about Reynaldo and his future, being familiar with the quality of life available at the mental institution to which he was destined to be transferred. They managed to send word to us about Reynaldo in the hope that we might come and rescue him, too.

When we heard the news about this special little boy, our hearts were immediately drawn to him and his plight, but we recognized that our ability to help him was limited. We were, after all, in the midst of an international adoption from China, and the thought of doing two adoptions at the same time, in two different countries, was daunting. We knew that we would have to raise at least another $30,000, in addition to what we were already trying to raise to complete Robyn's adoption. On top of everything else, the agency we had used for Nathan's adoption was no longer working in Bolivia, and we didn't know of any other agencies doing Bolivian adoptions. The mountain of impossibilities was a large one, but we agreed to look into it and see if there was anything we could do. And we committed to praying about this little boy. We truthfully couldn't bear the thought of his ending up in a state mental institution simply because he was blind.

Initially, our supposition that another adoption from Bolivia lay outside the realm of the possible seemed to be valid. We could not find an agency willing to help us, and we couldn't get any additional information on Reynaldo. After about a week, though, things began to change. We found an agency still doing adoptions from Bolivia, and we were able to communicate with their Bolivia case manager—who just "happened" to be in Bolivia at the time. She visited *Carlos de Villegas* and actually got to see Reynaldo. Suddenly, we found ourselves in the midst of another adoption. Our heads were spinning. The logistics of conducting two adoptions simultaneously were almost overwhelming, especially since in neither case could we get firm answers as to when we might expect to travel. We began raising funds for Reynaldo's adoption—while still working feverishly to raise the money for Robyn's—and we entered into a whole new dimension of prayer and reliance on God.

It was at this point that our hearts received a painful and surprising blow. For the first time, we were made fully aware of the fact that many people—even many who identified themselves as Christians—were not ready to follow us into the tree we had been called to climb. Many, in fact, were harshly critical of our intention to remain obedient to this calling. After we notified our e-mail list of prayer supporters that we would be moving forward with Reynaldo's adoption, we actually got a few responses that stated that we had "gone too far now." Some said that they "no longer wanted to be a part of" our journey. It's hard to describe how much this hurt, but we have learned as the years have passed that this is, very sadly, not at all uncommon. We now know of many adoptive couples who have faced ridicule and even persecution from members of their own church congregations. This must grieve our Father's heart deeply.

Kathy and I held a family meeting after receiving these hurtful responses and discussed everything openly with the children. We all agreed to commit as a family to continue moving forward, accepting the fact that we might very well end up marching on with no one but each other to link arms with. Frankly, we had entered a place where things were getting much more difficult—requiring much more faith on our part. We knew that, with the addition of little Reynaldo to our family, we would reach a point where my paycheck would no longer cover all of our family's monthly expenses. We would have to learn to depend daily on God in ways we never had before. We didn't need negative voices pulling our focus away from our calling. We wrote to our full update list to ask our supporters whether or not they would like to continue receiving our e-mail updates. About half of our list responded that they would like to do so. Those faithful friends who chose to continue the journey with us remained a beautiful source of encouragement and strength to us as our adoptions progressed. And as our family has grown over the years and that climb has become more difficult, rather than finding ourselves alone in the journey, we have watched as God has brought overwhelming support and love to us through many, many fellow Believers who have joined us along the way. We have never lost sight of what a blessing this is.

We decided to call our second Bolivian son Colin Zachary, which means "young one the Lord hath remembered." We were certain that God had not forgotten this little one, in spite of the fact that he was hidden away in a small, impoverished South American country, and that many people didn't seem to care about his plight. We believed that God would bring Colin home to us in His own perfect timing.

Our plans for this trip were complicated by the fact that our family composition was different than it had been in 1998, when Kathy and I traveled to Bolivia for five weeks to adopt Nathan. We recognized that Nathan was still very little, at not quite three years old, and that our being away for five or six weeks would be traumatizing for him. Further, Meghan had only been home for about seven months, and her bonding with us, though progressing beautifully, was still very much a work in progress. We feared that an interruption of more than a month would cause serious harm to that process. So, we concluded that we would have to find a way to take these two little ones with us. Immediately, though, we thought of a snag: there would be times—meetings and appointments—when we could not be accompanied by two small children. We couldn't very well leave them alone in the hotel room during such times.

Our solution was to have Kristen go with us, to take care of the babies when we had to be out. But that left us with a problem at this end, because Kristen was supposed to take care of Erin, Allan, Raiza, and Ryan while we were gone. Thus, our final plan was to take all of the children with us — except for Raiza, whose visa would not allow her to leave the US and then return. We would have to find a family for her to stay with. We began praying that God would make it possible for us to travel as a family, in spite of the added airfare and the additional food and lodging costs in Bolivia.

The Shepherd's Crook

As Kathy and I entered into this monumental period in the summer of 2000, we began to consider the long-term picture for our family. We were convinced that God had called us into the ministry of adoption, but as we thought about the number of orphanages around the world and the number of children in each orphanage, we realized how small our contribution to the solution would ultimately turn out to be. Not that our efforts were meaningless, but that they would barely constitute a drop in comparison with the overwhelming ocean of need. Even if we continued adopting for as long as God gave us strength and resources to do so, we could not reach more than a couple dozen children — at most. As we considered all of this, we began to feel that God might be calling us to found a ministry devoted to helping more of these children find their forever families.

We soon came to the conclusion that beginning a ministry was what we were being called to do. We held a family meeting about it, and all of the kids were supportive and enthusiastic. Allan, our techno-artist and multimedia talent, went to work creating the logo for our new ministry. We talked together as a family and came up with a name for the ministry: The Shepherd's Crook. The image of the shepherd's crook, or staff, was powerful and packed with meaning in the context of the ministry we were forming. Its primary meaning for us, though, was that the crook, in the hands of the shepherd, was used to help the shepherd care for his sheep. We envisaged our ministry as a tool to be used by *The* Shepherd, Jesus Christ, to help care for the neediest and lowliest of His flock—the needy and destitute orphans of the world.

So, in the midst of our plans to adopt Robyn from China, and now Colin from Bolivia, we also set to work establishing The Shepherd's Crook Orphan Ministry. We chose Ezekiel 34:16 as our banner verse: "I will seek what was lost and bring back what was driven away, bind up the broken and strengthen what was sick." This seemed to capture precisely what we felt called to do, and the ways in which we felt called to minister to God's needy ones. God at this time sent us a palpable confirmation that He was the Author of this new plan when we were fortunate enough to be introduced to the founder and president of another ministry in our town that had a similar heart and focus for the orphan. This man, Jeff Greer, became convinced that our vision was compatible with theirs and suggested that, until we could become stable on our own, we start our organization as a sub-ministry of his—which we thought was a great idea and very generous. So we became The Shepherd's Crook, a ministry of Back 2 Back Ministries in Cincinnati, Ohio.

Life goes on, and then some

In mid-June, Kathy and I squeezed in some additional surgeries for Ryan and Meghan in Louisville, and we juggled the demands of everyday life with a large and growing family. As the summer wore on, we were amazed time and time again as God answered our prayers and provided the money for our two ongoing adoptions. At one point, not long after we committed to adopting Colin, we were short of the funds needed to send to INS to get that portion of the process moving. We had about half of the fees, but we couldn't send in the paperwork until we had all of the money. One day, while Kathy was praying and crying out to God to provide for this adoption—knowing that time was precious and every day we lost was a critical day for him—the phone rang. It was a friend from California, calling to say that she was putting a check in the mail for us and asking where she should send it. The amount of her gift was exactly the balance we needed to be able to send in our paperwork to INS.

We experienced a series of ups and downs as we drew nearer to the time for us to travel to pick up Robyn and Colin. We would think we were OK with the funding, and then we would discover an additional area of need, and we'd once again be petitioning God to provide. Just when we'd think we were not going to make it in time, God would provide, almost miraculously. It would require an entire book just to relate all of the ways in which God blessed us during those months. One such story, though, has to be told.

Late in the summer, after we had committed to pursuing Colin's adoption and were frantically trying to raise funds, a woman at our church approached us with an idea for raising funds. She wanted to hold a massive yard sale and to advertise that it was to raise funds for two adoptions; she thought she could bring in quite a bit of money. She and her mom worked tirelessly to pull the whole thing together, and we were amazed and humbled at the way the members of our church rallied to make this event a success. Several women volunteered to sort and price the mountain of donated items, and they worked late into the night before the sale.

The day of the sale was packed with heartwarming moments and amazing financial blessings, as God moved in miraculous ways through the efforts of these committed volunteers. One man who came to the sale said that he had been saving his money for Lasik surgery on his eyes. He said that he felt convicted that Colin's eyes were more important than his own, and he donated all the money he had saved, $2,000, toward the adoption. In all, the sale brought in nearly $8,000. At the end of the day, we were filled with such gratitude for the labor of love this event represented, and we were greatly encouraged to continue trusting God to provide for all of our needs.

After initially thinking we would be traveling before September, we ultimately settled into the reality that we would not be traveling till later in the fall. We would be heading to China in mid-October, and then we would turn right around and leave for Bolivia in early November. Because this year promised to be so arduous for the whole family, Kristen decided to take the year off from school, to permit her to help with the children while we were gone to China and to travel to Bolivia with us.

Finally, the day came when it was time for us to travel to China to meet and bring home our new little daughter, who was now two and a half years old. Kathy and I took off from Dayton International Airport on Wednesday, October 18, 2000. We arrived in Shenyang, China on Friday morning (local), exhausted after going thirty-six hours without sleep. We thought we would have the weekend to rest up and get our bearings before meeting Robyn, but that was not to be. We found out shortly after our arrival at the hotel that we would be meeting Robyn within the hour. We scrambled to get checked in and cleaned up a bit, and we were ready for her when she got there.

Our initial meeting with Robyn was very different from Nathan's or Meghan's. There were no smiles, no hugs. She was clearly terrified and very subdued—until we took her into our arms, where she immediately began to scream and fight like a trapped animal. We were told to take her up to our hotel room and change her clothes as quickly as possible, because we had an appointment that afternoon at the civil affairs office and then at the notary, to finalize the adoption documents. Kathy and I took Robyn upstairs to our room. That elevator ride up to our hotel room is seared into our memory. Robyn continued to kick, scream, and fight desperately to be released. It took both of us together to restrain her as we rode the elevator upstairs. It was heartbreaking to see such fear in this little child. We got her into our room and, working together, we were able to strip off her old, worn-out clothes and get her into one of her new outfits. She was considerably larger than we expected, and she barely fit into the clothes we had brought for her.

How can I describe this newest Rosenow? She was portly, to say the least, well on her way to being obese. We had been told that Robyn's abandonment, at the age of approximately eighteen months, had been particularly traumatic. Witnesses had seen an elderly woman intentionally leave Robyn standing by herself on a busy street corner, where she waited and cried for hours before someone finally called the police to come and take her to the local orphanage. This betrayal had left deep scars in this very tender child's heart. She was timid and fearful, and whenever she was anxious or uneasy, she would shake almost uncontrollably. Kathy and I instantly fell in love with her eyes, and we knew that we were privileged by God to be able to take this frightened, damaged little child home and immerse her in the love and healing of our family — and that she would unfold and open up like a flower. We almost couldn't wait.

Our trip to China to adopt Robyn was, in most ways, as different from Kathy's trip to adopt Meghan as exhilaration is from melancholy. Although Robyn remained terrified of new situations or being taken outside, she very quickly began attaching to Kathy and me. We were able daily to see glimpses of her transformation from a sullen, fearful little girl into a more peaceful, and sometimes even happy child, and it brought tears to our eyes each time we saw her shy smile. She was soon holding our hands as we walked through the corridors of the hotel. She would play little hand games with us whenever we had to sit for a time, such as at a restaurant waiting for our food, and she wanted to know we were near at all times. By the end of that first week, when it was time for us to travel to Guangzhou to complete the process, we felt that we had made dramatic progress toward seeing her become a Rosenow.

Our week in the south was uneventful and serene. We took strolls around the island, shopped in the local shops for souvenirs, ate at many of the restaurants on Shamian Island, and had some wonderful bonding moments with Robyn, as she continued to blossom before our eyes, albeit very slowly.

On Thursday, November 2, 2000, we left Guangzhou bound for home. The very long flight back was surprisingly pleasant, with Robyn sleeping the majority of the time, at least on the longer legs of the journey. The family reunion at the airport in Dayton was predictably sweet. Robyn very quickly settled into the new family she had joined, even though she would revert to her fearful, severe trembling in any new situation, and she refused to speak above a whisper for many months. Her brothers and sisters fell instantly in love with this sweet and timid child. We were to be home for only about five days before heading to Bolivia with the whole family. No time for jet lag!

On Tuesday, November 7, we put Raiza on a plane for Jackson, Mississippi, where she would be staying with dear friends that she knew and loved, during our trip to Bolivia. Then, later that day, Kathy and I voted in the 2000 national election. All night that night, Kathy and I stayed up packing for the trip. As we packed, we watched the election coverage on TV. The next morning, very early, we boarded our plane bound for La Paz, and the nation still had no officially elected President. Over the course of the next five weeks, while the country learned about chads and obscure election rules, we were four thousand miles from home and experiencing one of the greatest adventures of our lives.

Chapter 7

Reaching for the Upper Air

❋

Too many Christians, meant for the eagle-life,

content themselves with a barnyard existence.

Now and then they feel something stirring within them,

but they are too indolent to make the effort necessary

to take their place in the upper air and among the mountain crags.

So they spend all their days down in the dust,

among earthly things, never waking up to their God-given

potentials.

J.R. Miller

Welcome to Bolivia, Again

Two parents, seven children, twelve checked bags, and eighteen carry-on items, including two strollers. Six American passports, two Chinese passports, and one Bolivian passport. Such was the Rosenow family as we descended upon the Dayton International Airport on Wednesday, November 8, 2000. This motley group boarded a small plane in Dayton, bound for Miami en route to La Paz. When we landed in Miami that evening, we grabbed something for the kids to eat in the main terminal, and then began wandering around to find where we were supposed to catch our next flight, scheduled to leave in the wee hours of the morning. As I mentioned in the last chapter, Kathy and I had spent the whole night before we left town packing for the trip and watching election results on TV. We didn't get any sleep at all, and our lack of sleep made the bizarre flight to Bolivia seem even stranger, bordering on surreal.

When we landed in La Paz on Thursday afternoon, Kathy and I had both been awake and active for about fifty hours, and the toll on both of us was beginning to show. Though we were foggy-headed and apt to stumble a bit, we knew we had to make sure we didn't lose any of our children along the way and keep pressing on until we could get to our hotel, get our family settled a bit — and then crash. Our in-country liaison and translator for this trip, Carola, met us at the airport. Carola had made arrangements for us to stay in a small apartment in the Hotel Calacoto. Calacoto is one of the neighborhoods in the *Zona Sur*, the region in southeastern La Paz that is home to most westerners living there.

We found the hotel to be beautiful and charming, and the owner was kind and gracious. We checked into the small, two-bedroom apartment that was to be our home for at least the next five weeks. We were very cramped, but we were together, and we knew that we could find a way to make it work. We had a brief meeting with the hotel owner, to discuss our room rate and terms, and then it was time to get the kids something to eat. We were completely exhausted, and we just didn't know what we were going to do. About that time, Pablo Molina and his wife, Christy, showed up to welcome us back to Bolivia[17] and to ask if there were anything we needed.

Our most pressing need at that moment was the feeding of our kids. Pablo and Christy could see how exhausted Kathy and I were, so they went out and bought some roasted chicken and fixin's for our whole crew and brought it back to the hotel. I honestly don't know if I've ever tasted better roasted chicken. And then, after having seen to our needs and making sure we had everything in order, Pablo and Christy left. By the time we all fell into bed that evening, Kathy and I had been awake for about sixty hours, and all of us were tired to the bone. We all slept for a full thirteen hours that night, and it was absolutely wonderful.

We spent the next two days unpacking and settling into our little apartment, and we even ventured out to a local grocery store to get some food and supplies. It was exhilarating for Kathy and me to be back in La Paz, and the feeling was enhanced for both of us as we witnessed the wonder in the eyes of our children. How God blessed us in being able to take the whole family on this adventure!

Reynaldo

The nuns at *Carlos de Villegas* had requested that we, all of us, come to the orphanage to meet Reynaldo on Sunday, just three days after we arrived in La Paz. They wanted Reynaldo to begin getting to know his new brothers and sisters, as well as his parents, right away. So on Sunday afternoon, we squeezed into two small taxis and drove to the orphanage, where the nuns greeted us almost like royalty. They all remembered Nathan, who was now a bubbly three-year-old, and they were ecstatic to see him again. He performed like a little champ, showing them his prosthesis and demonstrating how well he could walk and run. Sister Providencia, the orphanage director, had huge tears in her kind eyes as she hugged our little boy and saw how really well he was doing with his new family.

And then, almost as in a play, a hush fell over the group. We looked up, and there across the courtyard we saw another nun coming toward us with a small bundle in her arms. The bundle was actually a little boy — our new son. She placed him on his feet and he began walking, very tentatively, in our direction, as she held his hand and encouraged him. This nun was *Hermana* Caridad (car-ee-DAHD). She had taken Reynaldo under her wing and cared for him tenderly during his time at the orphanage whenever she was on duty, and she, too, had tears in her eyes as Kathy squatted in front of Reynaldo and said, "Hola Bébe." Reynaldo reached up, cupped Kathy's face in his very small hands, lifted his sightless eyes toward the sky, and said, "Hola Mamá." There were very few dry eyes watching this introduction unfold.

Under Kathy's direction, Kristen explained to the nuns that we had decided to change Reynaldo's name to Colin Zachary and that the meaning of this new name was "young one the LORD hath remembered." She said that, although his life had been hard so far, God had been caring for him, guarding him, and preparing our family for him. Caridad literally dropped her face into her hands and then, through more tears, explained to us that she had prayed over and over again that God would move someone's heart to make this child their son. She said that the actual words of her prayer had been, "God, please don't forget this child." What a huge God we serve—One who hears prayers from every corner of the earth and whose touch reaches across oceans and brings lives together to fulfill His plans.

Our first day at the orphanage was very emotional, and the nuns and staff made us feel so welcome. When after two hours we decided it was time to head back to the hotel, they seemed almost like they hated to see us go. All of our kids loved being there, playing and interacting with the children and babies. We hated to leave Colin behind, and we were very worried about his eyes. They seemed to be irritated, especially his left one. He poked at it constantly and it was very red.

Before traveling to Bolivia, we had arranged some doctor appointments for Colin, and one of them was with a nationally known pediatric ophthalmologist in Cincinnati on December 20. We were even more concerned now that we get the adoption completed as quickly as possible, to be able to get home in time for Colin to make that appointment. But our first *audiencia*, or court appearance, wasn't scheduled until November 21, which didn't seem to give us enough time to finish everything and still be home by December 20.

We received a bit of good news when we got back to the hotel that day. The owner of the Hotel Calacoto had been touched by our family and the reason we had come to Bolivia a second time. Carola had filled her in on our story at some point, and we had had a number of interactions with her over the course of our first few days there. She came to us that Sunday evening to tell us that she was moving our family into a much larger apartment, and that she was going to keep our daily room rate the same as it had been for the smaller apartment. We were grateful beyond words, and we were also very glad to move into the larger place. Though it was still only two bedrooms, it had a large living room with two sofas for more sleeping space, a dining room large enough for all of us to eat at the table together, and a full-sized kitchen, making it possible for us to prepare our own meals. This little gesture also confirmed for us, once again, that God was concerned about the small details of our trip as well as the big ones, and we thanked Him heartily for His provision.

The Bolivian roller coaster

We first met Colin at *Carlos de Villegas* on Sunday, November 12. The following Thursday we got news that our first *audiencia* still wasn't scheduled until the following Tuesday, November 21; however, completely against convention, the nuns decided that they were going to let Colin go live with us at the apartment while we waited for the *audiencia*. This was exciting news for us, since we felt that the bonding with Colin couldn't begin in earnest until he was living with us. When we got to the orphanage to pick Colin up, we got some more good news: normally, the process in Bolivia entails three *audiencias*. At the first, the court grants permission for the parents to visit the child at his or her orphanage; the second grants permission for the child to live with the parents while the adoption proceeds; and the third is when the court grants the adoption petition and declares everything final. The nuns told us that the court had decided to waive the first *audiencia* — just as the judge had done in Nathan's case — and thus the one scheduled for the following Tuesday would actually be the second. This truncation of the process was very good news for us, as every day was precious.

We took Colin back to the apartment and began to settle in to what would become our daily routine for the next several weeks. Because we home-school the children, we had taken along with us enough materials and books to be able to continue their schooling while we were in Bolivia. Every morning, Kristen and Allan would run down to the street to purchase amazing Bolivian bread, baked in little outdoor ovens right there on the streets, and we would begin each day with a family breakfast and Bible time. Breakfast was followed by school for the younger kids; for the older kids, it was chores first, and then school. We enjoyed a lunch together at midday, often outside in the back garden just behind our apartment. This garden was where the hotel booked many of its outdoor events, and it included a playground area. The seasons in the southern hemisphere are essentially opposite to those here in the States, and so even though it was November, Bolivia was nearing the end of spring and moving toward summer. The beautiful weather, combined with the convenience of the outside garden, provided the opportunity for our children to enjoy fresh air and exercise almost every day — when we didn't have other obligations or appointments that prevented our doing so.

After lunch, we would put the youngest four down for naps, and while the older kids continued their schoolwork, overseen by Kristen, Kathy and I would often walk to the nearby Internet café for some e-mail correspondence. Most days, after naps and school, we would all walk as a family to the new supermarket, called *Supermercado Ketal* (kay-TAHL), where we could purchase all of the ingredients for the next day's meals. Our evenings were quiet and private, as we cuddled our four little ones until their bedtimes and then ended each day with hot cocoa and reading time aloud with the older kids. We were reading through *The Chronicles of Narnia* with them. These memories still warm our hearts today, years later.

Battling for a little heart

We quickly learned that this blind two-year-old was more of a handful than might have been suggested by his tiny size. He obviously had become accustomed to having his own way, and he made it clear that he was not about to take orders from a couple of gringos who sounded funny, smelled funny, and couldn't even speak Spanish.

Very soon after Colin came to live with us, we discerned a deep and intense anger in his little heart. He often refused to eat, holding food in his mouth for surprising lengths of time. He wouldn't drink at all, just letting the liquid run out of his mouth. Although we were initially alarmed and worried about what we thought was an inability to eat and drink, it quickly became clear to us that refusing to eat or drink was his way of manipulating and controlling his new life. He wasn't combative over these things, or any other areas in which he refused to obey. He was just silently, but very clearly, rebellious. He would completely zone out and act like he couldn't hear us and just refuse to do what he knew we wanted him to do. We didn't know it at the time, but this was the beginning of a long adjustment. It was to be a full two years before Colin finally surrendered his heart to us and accepted us as his family. He seemed especially resistant to bonding with Kathy—but when it finally happened, it was beautiful and it was deep.

We saw almost immediately that he was an extremely intelligent little boy. We felt certain that much of his anger was due to the fact that he desired so much more than his dark world had allowed him to have. He was frustrated and longed for stimulation, and right away began to respond to activities that would challenge him mentally. He was brave and curious and would wander through the apartment, memorizing where the furniture was placed and where each step or door was located. We were amazed as we watched him explore his new world, and we ached to be allowed to be a part of it with him. Thankfully, he did allow us to snuggle him, but it was more like he tolerated it, rather than embracing it and desiring it the way Robyn did.

Colin initially hated his baths and would scream throughout the entire ordeal each night. This didn't seem to be out of anger or a desire to control, however. Rather, he seemed genuinely terrified of the bath. Once the traumatic bath time was behind us, though, our evenings were the most restful and peaceful times we had with him, and we looked forward to them each day. As I mentioned earlier, we would always spend some good "connect and snuggle" time with the four little ones before putting them to bed. We would all gather in the family room, and after playing a few games of "Memory" with Nathan and Meghan, we would snuggle Robyn and Colin in our laps and sing songs, teaching the hand motions to children's favorites like "Twinkle, Twinkle Little Star" and "Itsy Bitsy Spider." This was the one setting when we would see Colin actually come to life. He would smile and softly join in the singing.

Whenever a new child joins our family, we always choose a specific song to be that child's "special song." The choosing of these songs pretty quickly became an important family tradition and always involved much family discussion. We had chosen "What a Wonderful World" for Colin's song, and from the very beginning, he loved it and would listen each night as we sang it to him, his face a picture of focused but peaceful concentration. He quickly learned all of the words to his song, and we were very excited to hear that he had an amazing singing voice. He seemed to have perfect pitch, and a great sense of rhythm, too.

Yes, we had our hands very full and a long road ahead, as we searched for ways to work through Colin's anger issues. But what a jewel we had found hidden away in that Bolivian orphanage! We were struck many times by the thought that the world would've missed knowing about this incredible child, had he been locked away in the mental institution as planned. These thoughts, and the certainty that God had brought this child to us as our son, helped us to persevere in our struggles to reach Colin and draw him into our world, where we could love him and truly get to know him.

Dean and Linda

When Kathy was young, she and her family attended a church in the suburbs of Birmingham, Alabama. There was a young couple attending the same church, whose names were Dean and Linda Self. In fact, Kathy and her brother, Gary, had attended a weekly Bible study led by Dean during the early 70s. Dean was a former police officer who later left all of that behind to become a missionary to South America. When Kathy and I traveled to Bolivia for Nathan's adoption, Dean and Linda were associated with South America Missions (SAM) and working in the Bolivian city of Santa Cruz—and so we had been unable to see them. But this time they were living in El Alto, the city adjacent to La Paz a bit higher on the *altiplano*. Shortly after we got settled into our apartment at Hotel Calacoto, they came to visit us and catch up on some old times. They were very excited about the new work they were doing, which was to minister to the Aymara (ī-MAR-ah), the indigenous people of the *altiplano*. We didn't know it at that first meeting, but Dean and Linda were to become an integral part of our second adoption journey in Bolivia, and almost all of our recollections of Colin's adoption are imbued with memories of time spent with them. They had lived in La Paz during previous missionary assignments, and they knew the city and its people and ways very well.

The Audiencia

On Tuesday, November 21, we had our *audiencia* with the judge. This was a fairly formal affair, attended by Kathy and me, along with Colin, Carola, our attorney, the *fiscal*, the ex-ONAMFA official, the orphanage social worker, and the judge. Once the legal details were taken care of, the judge asked the orphanage social worker to take Colin and officially hand him to Kathy. She, the judge, then instructed Kathy to hand Colin to me, and she formally charged us, under law and before God, to take good care of this baby and to raise him as our own. By this time, pretty much everyone in the room was in tears. All of the officials thanked us profusely for providing a home for this special child. It was an emotional experience, but it made for a very good day. They did count this appearance as Colin's second *audiencia*, so the adoption could now begin in earnest.

Thanksgiving

Two days later, our whole family had the enormous privilege of celebrating a true American Thanksgiving in La Paz, Bolivia, in the home of Dean and Linda. What a special and memorable day that was for all of us. We knew ahead of time that we would be celebrating this holiday far from home, but we had no idea that it would turn out to be so wonderful. Linda prepared a Thanksgiving feast, including roast chicken, mashed potatoes with gravy, sweet potatoes, and stuffing. Dean and Linda further delighted us by presenting a birthday cake and gifts to Ryan and me. Ryan's birthday was on Thanksgiving Day that year, and mine was two days after. Though we were far from home and most things familiar, we still remember that as one of the best Thanksgivings of our lives.

A Desperately Low Point

The next day, we all were supposed to be at Colin's orphanage by 9:00 a.m. to meet with the orphanage social worker, the psychologist, the orphanage director, and the medical doctor. This was all a routine part of the process, and now that Colin had had his second *audiencia,* we could proceed with these steps.

Following our meeting at the orphanage, we took all of the children back to the apartment. After lunch, we put the younger ones down for their naps, and Kathy and I headed back to the orphanage. We had to deliver a letter to the social worker that she was going to take to the judge, to try to get Colin's case moving more quickly. The letter was from our Children's Hospital, explaining the need for Colin to get to the States in time for his appointment on December 20. We delivered the letter as planned, and the two of us then headed back to the hotel. When we got there, we stopped in front of a little *tienda,* or shop, and hopped out to pick up a couple of things needed for dinner. Kathy got out on one side, while I paid the driver and got out on the other. We watched the taxi drive away, and then a dramatic and terrible truth dawned on us. We had left our black bag in the car. The black bag was a little satchel we used for carrying all of our important documents. All of our important documents!

In that small black bag, we carried all of the papers we would need when we applied for Colin's visa at the US Consulate, once his adoption was complete and we were getting ready to come home. The bag also held our original adoption papers for Nathan, Meghan, and Robyn, along with Nathan's and Meghan's green cards.[18] The paralyzing panic we both felt at that moment was substantial, very much like we had witnessed a crime or seen a horrific accident. Many of the documents contained in that bag were irreplaceable. I carried them with me because I didn't feel comfortable leaving them in the room or in the hotel safe.

We ran to our hotel and explained to the front desk clerk what had happened. A complicating factor was that we had not noticed the cab number or even the company the driver worked for, so we had nowhere to begin our search. Everyone in the hotel immediately jumped into action to try to help us. One employee ran around the corner to a taxi stand to have them get on all of the dispatch lines, to see if they could locate the taxi. Another employee called the local radio stations to ask them to advertise our plight, and we offered a reward for the return of the bag and all of the papers. At this point, we didn't know how on earth we were going to be able to finish Colin's adoption without those papers, and we also wondered how we were going to be able to get Nathan and Meghan back into the States without their green cards.

This misadventure represented the very lowest point on our adoption journey to Bolivia up to then, and we wrote to all of our friends and supporters stateside to ask for their prayers on our behalf. We never did recover those lost documents, but we did manage to work around the difficulties their absence presented. The vice-Consul at the US Consulate, when he heard our story of what had happened to the documents, kindly offered to draft letters for Nathan and Meghan, to permit them to enter the States again when it was time to go home. He also agreed to accept faxed copies of our documents for processing the visa, even though they usually require originals, and he assured us that everything would be fine. Thankfully, Kathy tends to be somewhat obsessive about such things and had made multiple copies of everything before we traveled. These copies, however, were all back in the US at our home.

So one of our dear friends in Ohio went to our house—fortunately we had left a key with her—and rummaged through our papers to find copies of the documents we needed to complete Colin's adoption. She then went through the torturous process of faxing, via a 1950s-vintage Bolivian phone system, all of those documents to us at our hotel. Through all of this we learned, in a fresh and poignant way, to trust God in areas that are completely beyond our control.

Lago Titicaca

On Monday, November 27, Dean and Linda took all of us on an excursion to Lake Titicaca, the highest navigable lake in the world. We had a great time, and I just couldn't believe how clear and cold the water of the lake was, how completely free of pollution. The sun was shining brightly, and we could see straight through the water to the bottom. In our boat as we traveled back across the lake, having spent some time on the other side, we were accompanied by a local rural family—and their new lamb, which all of our kids got to pet, to their utter delight. We then drove back toward La Paz, stopping for a lunch of fresh lake trout at a thoroughly authentic Bolivian café.

As we headed the rest of the way back across the *altiplano* after lunch, we noticed the air temperature dropping quite dramatically. Suddenly we found ourselves in the midst of a hailstorm. We were traveling in a pickup truck, and several of the kids were in the open truck bed. Dean stopped the truck and we piled as many as we could into the cab, ending up with eight people in a space meant for five, but that left four still in the bed. We covered them with heavy woolen blankets for protection and continued toward home. The storm only lasted fifteen minutes, and actually the kids in the bed of the truck had the time of their lives.

A call to arms

Woven within and among all of these times, in which we and our children were privileged to experience the people and beauty and culture and sadness of Bolivia, were weeks of mounting frustrations over the adoption process. Some of these frustrations were of a different nature than those we had encountered during Nathan's adoption, but the result was the same: longer than necessary delays and a system that appeared to have no rhyme or reason—and certainly no concern for a two-year-old orphan's vision problems.

A few days after our trip to Lake Titicaca, we were still just plodding along, waiting for things to happen. Our documents had not been found, and we still didn't have a scheduled date for our final *audiencia*. There seemed to be nothing we could do to make things move more quickly. It is difficult to explain what was going through our minds, now that we had entered the month of December, now that our scheduled departure date was looming nearer and nearer without any likelihood of finishing the adoption in time. As we watched one day roll into the next, we felt a growing sense of uneasiness, which eventually welled into a state of near panic.

Kathy and I awoke on the morning of Saturday, December 2, in a deep despair. Everything looked black and impossible. We were convinced that we weren't going to make it home in time for Colin's appointment. We had already heard from the airline that it would be highly unlikely, if we had to change our return flight, that we could get tickets for all of us before the first of the year, and probably it would be later in January. It all just seemed so senseless to me: more and more weeks of just sitting and waiting while every passing day would undoubtedly mean additional damage to Colin's eyes! The only reason we were going to be stuck there, and the reason Colin's vision would undoubtedly suffer, was that "the system" in Bolivia couldn't get itself moving. It seemed that everyone involved in the process took at least five times longer than necessary to complete each step along the way.

Later that day, I wrote an e-mail to our friends and supporters back home. The subject line was "A Call to Arms." I explained my mindset and invited all of them to join us in praying that God would overrule the inadequacies and inefficiencies of the Bolivian system, and that we would get home as scheduled. The following is an excerpt from that e-mail message:

Last night we got an e-mail message from one of our missionary friends here in La Paz. In it he included the outline of a sermon he had recently preached in the campo. The text of the message was taken from 1 Samuel 17, dealing with David's battle with Goliath. I won't reprint the whole thing here, but we went over it last night as a family, and we found great encouragement in the message. We realized that we, too, are, in a sense, facing Goliath, and the fact that some who seem to be in our own camp tell us that it can't be done, and the fact that the Enemy himself laughs at us, doesn't matter a bit. The battle is God's battle, and we will win it because He will fight for us. After I got all riled up this morning, I remembered that sermon and I realized that I have been acting more like the Israelite army than David. I have been sort of sitting around and waiting for Goliath to fall, or just go away. Now I am going to try to find those five smooth stones and a good leather sling, and I am praying that I will face the Enemy in the knowledge that this is God's fight, and that the Enemy has not defied us, but God Himself. I am asking all of you to join me (us) in this fight by praying for the victory.

Church in the sky

The next day, Sunday, we awoke still feeling heavy and apprehensive about getting out of Bolivia in time. But we forced ourselves to get out of bed, knowing that our family had been given the immense privilege of traveling up to El Alto that morning with Dean and Linda to attend a worship service at an Aymaran church they had helped to establish. The experience was both uplifting and humbling for all of us, and it helped us regain perspective and get our focus back on the Author of Colin's adoption story, and off our own fears. Once we were all in and seated, Dean introduced us to the congregation, including the fact that we were in La Paz to adopt Colin. We then went through a little ritual in which our entire family stood at the front of the church while the congregation came up front and greeted us, one at a time. The whole group couldn't have been more than about thirty worshippers, and the processional-type greeting ceremony was quite emotional. Many of the women cried openly as they hugged us and thanked us for adopting a little blind Bolivian boy, gently and lovingly stroking his cheeks as they passed by.

The whole experience of worshipping with these Bolivian peasants was, as I said, both uplifting and humbling. For us to see the joy in these weather-worn faces, despite lives that were hard and harsh beyond our imagining, to see the zeal with which they approached the reality of their faith and the outworking of their Christianity, to be so embraced by them and to enjoy the brief time of sweet fellowship with them, despite barriers of culture and language, all left an indelible impression on us. And we think we are not the same people—not the people we otherwise would have been—because of the experience.

That was Sunday. Being up on the *altiplano* at nearly 14,000 feet, worshipping with Believers who serve the same God who brought us to Bolivia, Believers whose lives were dramatically different than our own, was what is often referred to as a "mountaintop" experience. After mountaintop times, though, usually come valleys, and Bolivian adoptions are no exception. As we moved into the final stages of our adoption process, we prepared ourselves for the next valley, and we prayed that God would take us safely through whatever ups and downs still lay between us and our goal.

153

Chapter 8

Out of the Valley

The marvelous richness of human experience would lose
something of rewarding joy if there were no limitations to
overcome. The hilltop hour would not be half so wonderful
if there were no dark valleys to traverse.

Helen Keller

The final stages in La Paz

After Sunday and our delightful experience on the *altiplano*,
we got back to the business of getting out of Bolivia. On
Monday morning, December 4, Kathy and I went with Carola to
meet with the director of ex-ONAMFA to plead Colin's case with
her. We had learned, in the meeting between our attorney and the
judge, that a key step in the process, the one that was holding up
everything and preventing the assignment of the final *audiencia*
appointment, was the obtaining of a signature from the director of
ex-ONAMFA. So we had arranged for a meeting with her on Monday
morning. She was kind to us, though we could not understand a

word she said, and she agreed to sign the papers that very day. We left her office feeling optimistic and happy, encouraged that we just might be able to finish the process and leave according to schedule. (More on what finishing "the process" meant a bit later on.)

We then contacted the airline, Lloyd Aero Boliviano (LAB), to make sure everything was OK for our return flights home, and to ask, once again, when the next available flights would be, if we missed our deadline. They gave us two pieces of bad news: first, the next available flights out of La Paz would definitely not be until January 20, owing to the size of our group and the holiday season; second, they told us that Kristen, Erin, and Allan had all been bumped from the return flight on December 14. No reason was given for the cancelation of these three tickets—which had been bought and paid for—and we learned quickly that we had absolutely no power to fight this decision that had been made without our knowledge or consent. We now had no way to get three of our children home with us, even if we did manage somehow to get Colin's process finished in time to make our scheduled flights on December 14. This was almost more than we could take, and we had no idea what we were going to do about it as we headed back to the hotel.

There was a bright spot to the day, though, and it came to us in an unexpected way. When Kathy and I returned from town after our meeting at ex-ONAMFA, we received a message inviting our family to Colin's orphanage to meet with what we thought was a group of volunteers who helped care for the children. One of our constant prayers was that our family would be a light and a testimony to anyone we met in Bolivia, so even though we didn't feel

155

much like socializing at that moment, we felt like it was right for us to accept this invitation. We piled everyone into taxis and headed off, still reeling from the events of the morning.

When we got to *Carlos de Villegas*, we discovered that the group we were meeting were not volunteer orphanage workers, but were instead the board of directors of the *hogar*. This group of women did, in fact, volunteer their time serving on the board, but they were all well-to-do, prominent citizens of La Paz. They wanted to meet the family that was adopting Colin, and they were all very gracious and grateful to us for giving this child a home. They told us, through an interpreter, that they just hadn't known what they were going to do with Colin, and several of them had tears in their eyes as this was being translated to us. It seemed inconceivable to them that anyone would actually choose to adopt a blind child.

All in all, it was a very warm and encouraging meeting, and we were blessed to see these ladies and their hearts for the orphans of Bolivia, and we were honored to realize that God was using our adoption story to open their eyes to the true value He placed on the life of one little blind boy.

Frustration and peace

Later that evening, we found out from Carola that the director of ex-ONAMFA had not, as she had promised, signed our papers that day. This complication made it a virtual certainty that we would not be able to have Colin's final *audiencia* in time to finish the rest of the process. When we went to bed that night, after our day of high "ups" and very low "downs," we were once again at an extremely low point emotionally, and we almost dreaded the next day's coming.[19]

Our dear friend Dean spent the next couple of days, both on the phone and at the office of LAB, pleading our case, begging and cajoling a supervisor there to find a way to get all of us confirmed on a flight out of La Paz together. In the end, they managed to change all of our tickets and get all of us confirmed. However, seven of us were to leave at 7:00 on the morning of December 14, and the other three were not to leave until noon. Even though we were all to meet up in Santa Cruz and make the remainder of the journey together, Kathy's heart was struggling mightily with the fact that she would have to fly out of La Paz and leave three of her children behind. Dean assured us that he would stay with them, watch over them, and make sure they all got on the plane safely, and knowing that Dean would be with them did help immensely.

Carola spent most of the day on Tuesday with the director of ex-ONAMFA, begging her to sign the papers. Carola found out that something had happened during the meeting on Monday that had offended the director, so much so that she had deliberately decided not to sign the papers that day. We missed whatever it was that had happened during the meeting, because the whole discourse had been conducted in rapid and formal Spanish, and we were not able to understand any of it, but it had apparently been significant. In the end—thankfully—Carola was able to appease the director and get the papers signed. After that, we received an appointment for the final *audiencia* with the judge: Friday morning, December 8.

While this appointment was great news, we were again facing the end-of-the-line time crunch that we went through with Nathan. The estimated timeline for all the remaining steps, placed end-to-end, and if everything flowed smoothly, was about a week and a half. We needed to make it all happen in less than four days!

One of the lessons God began to teach us in the course of our adoptions, and especially through the Bolivian ones, is that there are times when you simply have to leave matters in His hands and trust Him to take care of things. This is, of course, something we all hear taught from our childhood, when we have been reared in the church. But God was now teaching it to us through the school of experience rather than lecture.

On that Friday morning in early December—after our final *audiencia* in which Colin's adoption was completed and he officially became our son—as we contemplated the impossibility of the remaining steps, we came to the realization that it was now time to let go. We knew that we had done all we could do and that nothing more could happen before Monday morning. We also really wanted to take some time to celebrate and savor the reality that Colin was now truly and indisputably a Rosenow. There is something about having to fight so hard for a thing that makes it that much sweeter when it is finally gained. We chose to forget about the fact that we still had a huge battle ahead of us, and instead we decided to go, now officially as a family of ten, with Dean and Linda to visit the La Paz zoo—since we still had not yet seen the world's highest zoo. During the afternoon's adventure, we saw Andean Condors and Gray Eagles, peccaries and monkeys, toucans and exotic parrots, pumas and jaguars and lions and bears. It was a delightful diversion, and everyone had a great time.

The final dash

We took a bus back to our hotel, and we were shocked to find that our attorney's assistant, Gloria, who had committed to helping us get the final steps done as quickly as possible, had been trying to reach us for nearly three hours—to tell us that Colin's birth certificate was ready! We needed to get Colin immediately to the ID office to apply for his *carnet*. Even Gloria was amazed. She said that it usually takes forty-eight to seventy-two hours to get the birth certificate, but that it could sometimes be done in as little as twenty-four hours, as we had seen in Nathan's case. *Colin's had been completed in four hours!* No one knew how it had happened, but Gloria told us that she had lain awake during the previous night, Thursday, praying that God would help her figure out a way to help us finish the post-adoption process and get us on the plane on December 14, as scheduled.

Gloria was a jewel, one of the bright spots during our final days in La Paz. She took an instant liking to our family, and an immediate and intense interest in making sure that Colin got out in time to see his specialist on December 20. She was an attorney who worked for our primary attorney in La Paz; however, she was full-blooded Native South American, and as such she belonged to a lower social class than both our attorney and our in-country representative. We are sad to say that Gloria was at most points treated badly by her superior, due to her social standing. But as I said, she was a jewel and a delight to us, and we loved the time we were able to spend with her. She would sit in our apartment for hours, even on her days off, helping us make sure our documents were completed perfectly, all in her attempt to avoid unnecessary delays as we sprinted toward finishing Colin's process. We will always cherish the special bond we formed with her during our time there and the love she felt for our new son.

At this point, on Friday afternoon, it suddenly looked like we could, barring any major catastrophic events, finish the process and get out of the country on time. What a time of rejoicing we had that evening. To make this long story a bit shorter, I will say that we did finish all of the steps in the process, though not without drama. Our day at the immigration office, where we had to apply for Colin's passport, was very tense and "down to the wire." The office closes promptly at 4:30 in the afternoon, and it was 4:29 on Monday, December 11, when we finally got all of the pieces in place and finished the passport application process. We picked up the passport Tuesday afternoon and spent most of the day on Wednesday at the Consulate, getting Colin's US visa.

The wrap-up

We had arrived in La Paz on November 9. We didn't see Colin until November 12, and we didn't have our first (or more accurately, our second) *audiencia* until November 21. During our five weeks in country, our agency liaison, in her concern for us and her attempts to keep us from getting our hopes up, repeatedly told us that it would be impossible for us to make our scheduled departure date of December 14. But God did not listen to her. Late on the afternoon of December 13, 2000, we checked out of *Hotel Calacoto* and piled into three taxis with all of our baggage and carry-ons, and headed up to the rim of the *altiplano*, toward El Alto and the airport. We were going to spend the evening and night with Dean and Linda at their apartment, and Dean was going to take us to the airport for our flight the next morning.

As we were enjoying that final evening together, laughing and reminiscing with this godly couple who had done so much to make our trip to La Paz the success that it was, we got word that Al Gore had, that very day, conceded the presidential election to George W. Bush. The grueling saga that had begun the day before we left the country had finally wrapped up the day before we were to return. We found that fact a bit humorous, and we agreed that we didn't mind having missed America's election ordeal, perhaps because we had been struggling through an ordeal of our own the whole time.

Very, very early on the morning of Thursday, December 14, we said our tearful good-byes to Linda, and Dean drove all of us to the airport. Dean had promised to sit with Kristen, Erin, and Allan until their noon flight, and we planned to meet up with them in Santa Cruz for the flight to Miami. Our relief was immense, however, when a short while after we sat down on the plane, while we were waiting for final passengers to board so we could leave, we saw our three oldest children walk down the aisle. Dean had somehow managed to finagle stand-by tickets for all three of them, and so we were all heading home together. We absolutely loved the time we spent in Bolivia, and the memories still stir our hearts in several ways. But the joy we felt in leaving, and knowing we'd be home in time for Colin's appointment—and for Christmas—was intoxicating. We had an uneventful layover in Santa Cruz, and within a few hours we were airborne en route to Miami, Florida, USA, where we had hotel reservations for a much-desired night of sleep before heading on to Dayton the next morning.

We landed in Miami late in the evening and began the long process of entering the United States officially. The first step was to check in with immigration to get Colin his final authorization for permanent resident status. As I mentioned earlier, this is the necessary last step for all parents bringing their adopted children into the country, and it can be quick and relatively easy, or it can be long and drawn out and exhausting. That Thursday evening in mid-December, it was long and drawn out and exhausting. After what seemed like an eternity, we were finally cleared through immigration and on our way. We gathered up our bags, piled them high onto several baggage carts and, about to drop from fatigue, headed toward Customs. This is normally little more than a formality, but in this instance that was not to be the case. We had, before we left Bolivia, agreed to deliver a package from some friends there to their family in the States. One of the items in that package was something called *chuño*, a sort of freeze-dried potato product peculiar to parts of Bolivia and Peru. A specific variety of potato is allowed to freeze in the cold night conditions of the *altiplano*, and is subsequently trampled (by foot) and then sun-dried in the harsh sunlight of the highlands. The preparation, according to the traditional method, takes five days to complete, with repeated nighttime freezings as part of the process.

And so, as we were waiting in the customs line, when the customs officer asked if we had any foodstuffs in our bags, we said yes, as a matter of fact we did, but that it was "only some *chuño*, dried-out potatoes from Bolivia." She then directed us from our relatively short, "nothing to declare" line over to the very long, "something to declare" line. Our hearts dropped into our shoes at this, since it was by then around midnight, and we knew that we would have to get up at 4:00 in the morning to be able to catch our final flight to Dayton the next day. But, being the law-abiding citizens we are, we began the relocation from the first line to the second — no small feat because of our numerous bags and the cumbersome baggage carts.

Right at that moment, however, Colin began to sing. It was utterly spontaneous, since he had no idea what was going on around him and what still lay ahead for us. He was just feeling a particular joy in his heart at that moment, and so he began to belt out "Jingle Bells" in his sweet little voice. The customs officer, who had already witnessed our state of exhaustion and dejectedness at having to move to the other line, heard Colin singing, and it seemed that her heart just melted. She said to us something like, "Just how dried-out are those potatoes?" We said, "Oh, they're EXTREMELY dried-out!" So she told us to just move on through the "nothing to declare" line. We were so happy, and so grateful, we could've begun singing ourselves, if we hadn't been so tired and so focused on getting out of there.

Home

We did finally get to our hotel room, but we knew we had to bathe all of the little ones before we could put them into bed. So by the time we got checked into our rooms and got everyone settled, and got all four little ones bathed, and crashed into our beds, it was about 2:00 in the morning. We set our alarms for 4:00, two short hours later, and reminded ourselves that we would soon be home. Home! Able to sleep in our own beds, able to celebrate Christmas in our own house. We were weary to our very souls, but we were also very happy.

We made it to the airport again the next morning, and we caught our final flight to Dayton. When we touched down that afternoon, there was snow on the ground. We had come home on Friday, December 15, ten days before Christmas, and there was snow on the ground. It was wonderful!

In wrapping up this portion of the story, I will say that Colin did get to his appointment with the eye specialist on December 20, but the visit turned out to be a bit of a disappointment for us. The specialist told us some things about Colin's eyes that we hadn't known before, including that his right eye was essentially useless to him because of a botched surgery he had apparently been subjected to in Bolivia, and that his right pupil was completely gone. Both of his retinas were fully detached, but he did retain a measure of light perception in his left eye. The specialist, however, did not seem sufficiently concerned about holding on to the level of vision that Colin had, reasoning that it was almost inevitable that his eyes would continue to atrophy and would someday, in all probability, have to be removed and replaced with prosthetic eyes. This fatalistic resignation, which the specialist presented as healthy realism, struck us as inappropriate, and at the very least as premature. We decided to seek other, more committed, specialists before giving up all hope of retaining the light perception that Colin had.

Our Christmas that year was one of the most meaningful we had ever experienced. I believe that the time we spent in Bolivia, witnessing the poverty of her people and the hopelessness in so many faces, and sharing in the joy and faithfulness of the Believers we met there, helped us to appreciate in fresh ways the blessings of our own life here in America and the amazing beneficence of our God in sending His Son for us. Our celebration that year was punctuated by profound thankfulness, both for the family God was building around us, and for the blessings of our salvation and fellowship with our Lord. And on top of all of that, Christmas morning with two two-year-olds and a three-year-old and a four-year-old, was magical for all of us.

Welcome 2001

As we moved into a new year, we had many changes to adapt to. Just two months earlier, we had been the parents of six children, and now we had eight. We had to look into corrective surgery for Robyn and find a retina specialist for Colin. We made arrangements to take Colin to a retina specialist in Tennessee. We made plans, too, for Robyn to see a reconstructive micro-surgeon in Kentucky — the same one who had done so much for Ryan over the years.

We had already made adjustments to our home-schooling regimen while in Bolivia, and so Kathy and the kids were able to slip rather easily back into the daily routine in that area. I returned to work, and we made plans for the various road trips that would be required for all of the out-of-state doctor visits for Colin and Robyn. But in and through it all, we savored this new family dynamic, thinking that we would now have a break from everything associated with adoptions for a while.

As is so often the case, however, God's ways are not our ways, His thoughts are not our thoughts, and the plans He has for us are often very different than we envisage for ourselves. But at least we did make it through the month of January, safe in our thoughts and plans.

Chapter 9

The Glory of the Climb

❋

The feeling remains that God is on the journey, too.

St. Teresa of Avila

Romania

The fall of Communism swept across Eastern Europe during the late eighties and early nineties. One of the consequences of this change in the country of Romania was the discovery by the rest of the world of the atrocities that had been committed against the Romanian people under the tyrant Nicolae Ceauşescu. The utterly deplorable conditions found within the many state-run orphanages caused an international outcry. Hundreds of concerned people from all over the world flocked to Romania to help rescue some of the many thousands of children suffering in Ceauşescu's orphanages. Unfortunately, there will always be tares among the wheat:[20] many of those who got involved in the adoption business in post-Ceauşescu Romania were not concerned for the welfare of the children, but for the padding of their own pockets. And so began—or rather, so continued—the notorious trafficking of children from Romania. There were, of course, many truly benevolent workers trying to improve the lives of these disadvantaged children, and thousands of legitimate and happy adoptions resulted. But there were also documented cases of kidnapping and extortion, and of children being purchased from desperate parents. The decade of the nineties was a dark time for the orphans of Romania, and especially for those who had the misfortune to be born with any sort of special need.

Though we saw the reports on TV and heard of these atrocities, Kathy and I were largely uninformed on the subject of Romania and Romanian orphans while all of this was unfolding. We had our own life we were living, our own children we were raising, and toward the end of the decade, our own adoption stories and rescues we were effecting. Truthfully, the goings-on in a small formerly-Communist country five thousand miles away just didn't make it onto our radar screen.

Developments at home

In January, after taking Colin to see a number of ophthalmic specialists, we decided that the one we trusted most was Dr. Michael Trese (pronounced "Tracy"), in Detroit. Testing done by Dr. Trese indicated that, while Colin's right eye was permanently sightless, his left eye retained a measure of viable retinal tissue. This finding provided the green light for surgery. Dr. Trese operated on Colin's eyes on Friday, February 9. By all accounts, the surgery was successful. Colin recovered well. The retina in the left eye was found to be largely intact, and following the procedure, it lay down nicely against the posterior interior of Colin's eye.[21] After staying one night in the hospital in Detroit, we brought Colin home for him to recover—sleeping in a car seat every night for the next twelve weeks because it was necessary to keep him in an upright position throughout the healing process. We were thankful that the surgery had gone so well, and we were optimistic that Colin would retain his light perception, and perhaps even enjoy some slight improvement in his vision.

Mariana

Through one of the families associated with our fledgling ministry, our daughter Kristen had been given the opportunity to travel to Romania for a couple of weeks late in February 2001. She was accompanying an adoptive mom who was traveling to visit her still-waiting child residing in an institution in the city of Ploieşti (ploy-ESHT), about an hour north of Bucharest. Kristen was very excited to be taking this trip, especially because she had also arranged to spend some time working with an established American missions organization while there. This non-governmental organization (NGO) was primarily concerned with caring for orphans in and around the city of Bucharest. As we put Kristen on the plane the day she left for Romania, we jokingly said to her, "Find us a cute one while you are over there."

An American neurosurgeon from UCLA Medical Center, Dr. Jorge Lazareff, happened to be in Ploieşti during this same time, having traveled to Romania to perform surgical operations on a number of children, and to train Romanian surgeons in modern neurosurgery procedures. On the fourth day of Kristen's trip over there, she wrote to us via e-mail to let us know that she had, she thought, actually found the next Rosenow child. She knew that we had just brought home two new children, and that the timing was, at least by the world's standards, about as bad as it could be for us even to think about another adoption. But there was a little girl called Mariana, only three months old, who had at the last minute been added to Dr. Lazareff's surgery docket. She was born with a form of spina bifida that Dr. Lazareff had been able to correct quite successfully. Dr. Lazareff believed that Mariana, as a result of the corrective surgery, would be able to walk and even run, although it was probable that she would still be at risk for some of the other long-term effects of spina bifida, including the potential for hydrocephalus and problems with both her urinary tract and her gastrointestinal tract. On top of these potential risks, Mariana was an orphan, having been abandoned by her birth mother at the maternity hospital shortly after birth. Her chances for a normal, healthy life would be virtually non-existent if she were left to grow up in the Romanian orphanage system.

Kathy and I agreed with Kristen: though this child's need was great, the timing did seem less than opportune. We decided, however, to pray about it and to discuss it with the rest of the family. After just a few days, we all came to the conclusion that God was leading us to begin another adoption process. The inconvenience to us, in having to go through all of the adoption red tape and headaches again so soon, paled to insignificance compared to this little girl's need. We wrote back to Kristen and told her that we indeed felt led to bring Mariana home, even though we didn't have a clue how to begin a Romanian adoption. But we were willing to begin a new adventure, and we committed our course, once again, to the Author and Perfector of our faith.

The details of this adoption are many and intricate. We contacted an agency we knew of that handled Romanian adoptions, and this agency said that they would help us. They graciously agreed to reduce all fees to the bare minimum, in the interests of helping this little girl get home to her family as quickly as possible. There was, however, considerable unrest in Romania at the time, due in large part to recent presidential elections, widespread political instability, and growing concern over the conditions associated with orphans and intercountry adoptions in Romania. Thankfully, God provided a loving contact there in Romania so that we could get regular updates on Mariana's situation while we tried to unravel the mystery of how to adopt a child from Romania. This contact, Alison Gutterud, was a neonatal nurse working with the American NGO as a missionary to the children in Romania, and we had no idea what an integral part of our lives she would eventually become.

Early in the process to adopt Mariana, we began to hear rumors that intercountry adoptions from Romania were being suspended, perhaps for as long as two years. This news was devastating to us, since we were convinced that Mariana needed to get out of Romania and get to the medical care available here in the States—and to the love and nurturing waiting for her in our family. But once again we were forced to leave this in God's hands and trust His timing.

The appearances of hopelessness did not change the fact that we had been called to pursue the rescue of this little child, and so we continued doing what we could and praying for God's provision in every way.

We decided to name this newest Rosenow Carlin Jessica, which means "little champion beheld by God." We were utterly convinced both that she was a little champion—one who had striven and fought for life against huge odds—and that she was "beheld by God" and protected by His loving Providence for the purposes He alone had planned for her.

Life goes on

As March rolled into April, and then April into May, our lives were punctuated by the events associated with our growing and somewhat unusual family. In April, we traveled to Louisville for reconstructive procedures for both Ryan, who was eleven, and Robyn, who had just turned three. (Robyn was having the extra toes removed from both feet.) Some friends of ours held a massive rummage sale to raise funds toward our adoption of Carlin. Most significantly, we began to see some changes in Colin and his development. The following is excerpted from an e-mail sent by Kathy in May 2001, which expresses our joy over one of his accomplishments:

About two weeks ago, we began to be more concerned about Colin's lack of communication. He continues to 'parrot' but does almost no real communicating. We decided to start praying about it, and yesterday something happened that I've read about, but have never actually witnessed. I told Colin to go upstairs to get ready for his bath, then realized that someone was saying, "Mommy? Mommy? Mommy?" over and over again. It was Colin, and as if this little bit wasn't remarkable enough, I answered him and he said, "I need go upstairs now?" I told him yes the best I could with my mouth hanging open, and he smiled and said, "Okay," and went up the stairs. It continued throughout the evening and on into today with conversations like,

"Mommy?"

"Yes, Colin."

"Wha's that music?"

"That is on the TV."

"The TV?"

"Yes, the TV."

"I like that music." Then, when the music stopped, "Uh-oh. Music stopped."

Or, "Momma, is that the refrigadator?" as he is patting the refrigerator door.

We are all just blown away and holding our breaths to see what he comes out with next. It's like he has just been storing all of this up for the last six months and has decided to hit the play button. We are so grateful for another answer to prayer concerning him and can't wait to see where he goes now. Stay tuned.

Not all of the events in our family were happy, though. Behavioral difficulties with eleven-year-old Raiza began to escalate during the months after we returned from Bolivia. We continued praying for wisdom and for softening in her heart as we kept doing our best to love and parent this little girl who had touched our lives so dramatically.

Also throughout these months, we received spurts of news from Romania about Carlin's health. She was hospitalized several times for respiratory illnesses and for chicken pox. During the time she was in the hospital with chicken pox, Alison did her best to make frequent trips to the hospital to care for her, while also juggling all of her regular missionary duties there in Romania. On one trip, Alison arrived at the hospital and saw that Carlin had been moved from her crib. She began to search the hospital and finally located our tiny daughter in a back corner of a dark room, all alone, soaked in urine, staring into space. She appeared to have cried for so long with no response from anyone at the hospital, that she finally gave up and stopped crying. This is a common problem for orphans whose needs go unmet: eventually they give up and are never able to respond normally to others. Alison cleaned Carlin up, changed her clothes, and held her close to feed her a bottle. She made it a priority to spend as much time as possible with Carlin during the rest of her time in the hospital, praying that she had not slipped away completely during her time alone in that room. Our hearts were absolutely broken over this report about our little Carlin, and we thanked God continually for placing Alison in Carlin's life to care for her while we kept fighting the adoption battles across the ocean.

There were also ongoing developments in our fledgling ministry. We participated in a couple of meetings in which people who were interested in the topic of intercountry adoption listened to our story and then asked questions on the topic. We were exceptionally pleased when, largely as a result of these meetings, four families committed to the adoptions of children associated with our ministry. We were beginning to believe that The Shepherd's Crook Orphan Ministry might turn into a real ministry, in spite of our own shortcomings and limitations.

In June, we were met with three more developments, each significant in its own way. First, we learned that Romania had, in fact, declared a moratorium on intercountry adoptions, and that our adoption agency had ended their Romania program, leaving us without an agency. Second, we received word that Back 2 Back, the ministry serving as our parent organization, was beginning the process to nudge us, as it were, out of the nest. They were asking us to begin the steps necessary for us to become an independent entity, because the load imposed upon their bookkeeper by all of our donations and disbursements was becoming too much for her to keep up with. This had been the plan all along, and their prompting at this time simply represented the natural outworking of that original plan. Third, we found ourselves beginning another international adoption.

Lin Hou

Dick Graham, the director of IAAP, had traveled to China in March to visit some orphanages and make arrangements for some future projects they were involved in. While he was there, he visited an orphanage in Siping, Jilin Province. One of the children he met there was a newborn baby boy with a severe cleft lip and palate. The orphanage workers were calling this child Lin Hou,[22] and Dick immediately felt drawn to him—and almost immediately shared his picture and story with us so we could help find a family for him. After praying about this child and his situation for several weeks, we came to the inescapable conclusion that God was leading us to adopt Lin Hou ourselves.

An e-mail I wrote to our friends and followers, when Kathy and I announced our decision to pursue Lin Hou's adoption, sheds a little light on our mindset at the time. An excerpt from that e-mail, dated June 19, 2001, follows:

We are just "normal" people like the rest of you. We have our days when we wonder what on earth God is up to, and even if He's really listening to our prayers. I am continually reminded of one of my favorite passages in Scripture, 2 Cor. 4:7–9. "But we have this treasure in jars of clay to show that this all-surpassing power is from God and not from us. We are hard pressed on every side, but not crushed; perplexed, but not in despair; persecuted, but not abandoned; struck down, but not destroyed." Paul amazes me in this overall passage. He states, as a reminder to us all, that God has placed the treasure of "the light of the gospel of the glory of Christ" within the frail and inadequate human flesh that is us. We may be, indeed we are, inadequate and frail, and we often fall down, but the very Spirit of Jesus Christ resides within us! What an amazing and inspiring truth!! Anyway, what's the point of all of this? I want you to know that I am at times fearful that I might not be able to take care of all of these children God is sending me. Now, don't laugh. I know what it looks like from this side, but you have to picture yourself down in the trenches with me. It's easy to lose sight of the overall battlefield when all you can see is the wall of mud in front of your face. If I can only lift myself up above the edge of the trench a little bit, I can see the angels of the Living God out there fighting on our behalf. And then I am encouraged. Then I can recognize the imbecility of a statement like, "Will I be able to take care of the children God is sending me?" I know that if God is sending them to me, He will give me what I need to take care of them! So, when I first heard about this baby, I was at that time down in the trenches over a couple of other issues, and I couldn't see the beauty of God's plan. I could only see my own weakness and inadequacy, and I was afraid.

After spending several weeks praying over this, and having long conversations with my wonderful "help-meet" (Kathy), I realized that God was leading us to go after this little guy. And so, let the forces of Hell get out of the way. We're on a mission again. . . . And please pray for us, since we know that these "jars of clay" will again, and repeatedly, be buffeted by the forces of an Enemy who can't seem to get over the fact that he's already defeated.

We decided to rename our newest little guy Aidan Matthew, which means "fiery little gift from God." We had been told that he exhibited a lot of spunk, and it was obvious to us that he was a gift from God. Our hearts were full of joy and anticipation as we dove into the preparation of another international adoption dossier, and as we looked forward to welcoming another gift from God into our family.

We also found much encouragement in the knowledge that, while we were fighting what appeared to be an impossible battle to complete Carlin's adoption in Romania, Chinese adoptions flowed smoothly and relatively predictably. We felt confident that we would have our little Aidan home with us in about six months, and that dream helped us as we kept up the fight for Carlin.

A sunny day and a dark, dark cloud

Birthdays are very special in our family. We devote the entire day to making it special for the birthday person, who gets to choose what birthday cake Kathy will bake and what we will eat for the evening meal. That person, too, doesn't have to do any work all day, and we don't do any school that day, either. At the dinner table, everyone gets a turn telling at least one thing about the birthday person that he or she particularly likes. It is a real treat, and everyone in the family looks forward to his or her birthday.

We all woke up on the morning of Nathan's fourth birthday that September in 2001, pretty much as usual. Before I went off to work, we gathered in the family room while Nathan opened his birthday presents. I don't remember what he got that year. I left for work, and Kathy fed the kids their breakfast and began working on Nathan's birthday cake. Just a normal day in the life of a normal American family.

At exactly 8:46 AM, Eastern Time, on September 11, 2001, our normal world changed.

I was sitting in the conference room at work, along with four or five others, when one of the secretaries stuck her head into the room and told us to turn on the TV. She said that a plane had crashed into one of the Twin Towers of the World Trade Center in New York City. At that moment and in the hours that followed it, our country was plunged into a darkness that changed forever the way we live and the things we take for granted.

Nathan's birthday celebration was very nearly ruined. We did our best to make it as normal as possible for him, but we were all very much preoccupied with what was unfolding around us, and even Nathan, though he was only four, recognized the significance of what had happened. For a long time after that day, Nathan would say that "Bim-Labbim Bim-Labbim" had messed up his birthday celebration, and he actually cried about the pain he knew so many people had suffered that day. In fact, for several years after this, he would cry on his birthday for those who had lost loved ones in these attacks.

The events of 9/11 did not directly impact the world of inter-country adoption, but the secondary consequences did. Many adoptions that were in process at the time were interrupted, some temporarily and some permanently. Travel to and from foreign countries became much more difficult. And people began to look at other people a little differently than before. Fortunately, however, the number of adoptions to the US from other countries did not decline as a result of that infamous September morning.

As America began to recover from the events of 9/11, over the days and weeks that followed, and as we all began to tear ourselves away from the TV screens and the daily updates on the tragedy played out in New York, Washington, D.C., and Pennsylvania, Kathy and I realized that we were still in the midst of two international adoptions and we still had eight kids at home who needed our time and attention. It was time to get back to living.

Turmoil

All through the year, as I mentioned earlier, we had been struggling with behavioral issues from Raiza. Shortly after we returned from Bolivia with Colin, Raiza came back to us after staying with our friends in Mississippi. Her behavior continued to be a challenge to us, partly because of its tendency to disrupt our family life, and partly because of its negative influence on Meghan, in particular. Meghan seemed to be especially drawn toward Raiza, and we were constantly finding ourselves working to undo damage wrought by Raiza's unwholesome influence. Raiza's demeanor was usually morose, and her propensity to manipulate and lie seemed to grow stronger with each passing week.

In August, the doctors at Shriner's Hospital told us that Raiza, because of the severity of her burns and the fact that she was moving into puberty, would require another two years of treatment, at least. This was difficult news because she had already been away from home for nearly two years. We discussed the situation with Healing the Children and RockSalt, and they concluded that the best thing for Raiza would be, at some point in the near future, to send her home for an extended visit with her family before resuming her treatments.

From bad to worse

Unfortunately, the situation with Raiza continued to deteriorate, even while plans were being made for her visit to Bolivia. During the month of October, after Raiza turned twelve, things degenerated to the point that everyone associated with the Bolivia burn program came to the difficult conclusion that ours was no longer the best host family for Raiza. We questioned this decision for quite a while, praying for clear leading, and examining our hearts and all of the ways in which we had tried to help Raiza. We were weary beyond words from the strain of trying to help her, to bring her back into our family circle, and at the same time protect our children from her negative influence over the past two years. Yet we loved her and had made a commitment to parent her for as long as she was in the States for medical treatment. Eventually, we did reach a place where we could accept the difficult truth that our home, in fact, was no longer the best place for Raiza during her temporary stays in the US. We felt like a piece of our hearts was being taken away from us. We truly did love this child as one of our own children. But the decision was made and our path was now clear—difficult, painful, but clear. Plans were made for her to return home to Bolivia for a few weeks while everyone continued searching for a new host family. The day Raiza left our home, Kathy sat and held her as they both wept. We will always believe that Raiza loved us, but she could never seem to break free of the attitudes or inner turmoil that controlled her actions.

Another host family was found, and Raiza did return to the States for only a few months. Sadly, her anger and rebellion increased rather than diminished, and she had to be removed from the burn program and returned to Bolivia, permanently. The day she flew back to Bolivia, Kristen met her at the airport and gave her a letter from Kathy. In this letter, Kathy expressed our deep love for her and a promise that we would never stop praying that she would submit her life completely to God. Our prayer was that she would allow Him to change her from the inside, so that she could reach her full potential and realize His great love for her.

We were heartbroken over what appeared to be the ending of this story, and we felt a bit like we had failed her. In the end, though, we knew that we had to commend her to God's provision and trust her future with Him, as we ultimately have to do with all of our children. For years we tried to find out what happened to Raiza after she returned to Bolivia. We never forgot her or stopped loving her, and many nights Kathy would awaken during the night, crying about this lost child and wondering where she was. We kept our promise to pray for her well-being and for her heart. We continued to hope that we might someday see her again, changed and whole and ready to commit her life fully to the One who created her and brought her to us for a season—and that just maybe her story wasn't over yet.

The end of 2001

November brought us the unexpected news that Aidan would definitely not be coming out of China before the end of the year. This was bad news because our INS approval would be expiring in December. To this day, we still don't know all of the reasons for the delay in processing Aidan's adoption, but we received word that was considered reliable that the adoption couldn't be completed until early 2002, at the soonest. So, we began applying for INS approval all over again. This was discouraging, both because of the costs involved and because of the headaches associated with this type of red tape. This also meant that we would miss his first birthday in January, and we had been dreaming of celebrating this special day as a family. The disappointment was compounded by the fact that we were already missing the first birthday of our little Carlin in November.

Our spirits were lifted a few days later, though, when the ladies at our home church hosted what they termed a "shower" for our family. They showered us with gifts — mostly staples such as paper products and household necessities — and expressions of their support for what we were doing in adopting these children. Our hearts were lifted at this outpouring of encouragement, and we were deeply blessed by the material gifts, too.

Near the end of this momentous year, The Shepherd's Crook took the final steps necessary toward establishing itself as an independent ministry. An attorney from our church helped us with the procedures necessary for incorporation, and he advised our newly formed Board of Trustees as to the nature and functioning of a non-profit corporation. He also helped us apply for tax-exempt status as a charitable organization under Internal Revenue Service regulations. A wonderful woman here in town heard about what was going on and volunteered to serve as our bookkeeper, which was one of the final steps needed. It was an exciting time for all of us, and our excitement was punctuated by the addition of three more children to our website — two babies with cleft palates and an eleven-year-old boy who had tragically lost both hands in a fire.

As if this were not enough for us, Kathy and I also committed in November to a third adoption, this time of a little girl in Haiti. Her name was Macula Jean Luis, and she was three years old. We learned of her through an agency that wanted to list children on our website. This little girl's need immediately captured our hearts. She had been preliminarily diagnosed as exhibiting signs of Reactive Attachment Disorder, and the chances that she would be adopted were extremely slim. This seemed like precisely the type of child the Rosenows felt called to adopt, and our wrestling over this decision did not last very long. We knew that we could be getting in over our heads, but we also knew that God had called us into some areas we considered very scary, and that our job was always to trust Him to provide whatever was needed to fulfill His calling. We chose the name Madlin Arielle for her, which means "precious lioness of God."

Our Christmas celebration that year was memorable. We had a rich and full year behind us and the promise of another exciting year ahead of us. And the events of 9/11 had made all of us, all Americans, more aware of two thoughts that are key to embracing and savoring life: first, that we are blessed beyond measure, and not just in material ways. The friends and families we have are blessings in themselves, and they enrich our lives and often bring us clearer images of the ways in which God loves His children. Second, we knew more clearly than before just how tenuous all of this is, how easily it can all be taken away, and how important it is to live in the present and to be aware of what we have.

So, we closed out the year 2001 with full hearts. We were perhaps a little older and wiser than we had been at the beginning of the year, but we were also a bit more connected with the things that give life meaning and purpose. And how we looked forward to what God would bring us in 2002! We had every expectation that, whatever it was, it would include at least three new little Rosenows. It's amusing sometimes to see how many of the things we expect to come to us are not the things that actually come.

Chapter 10

Dark Clouds and Sunbeams

A Christian may for many days together see neither sun
nor star, neither light in God's countenance, nor light in his
own heart, though even at that time God darts some beams
through those clouds upon the soul; the soul again by a spirit
of faith sees some light through those thickest clouds, enough
to keep it from utter despair.

Richard Sibbes

And the beat goes on

The year 2002 was eventful and even dizzying for us as a family, but in ways that were different from previous years. In addition to all of the chaos and activity that come from pursuing three international adoptions simultaneously—from Romania, China, and Haiti—and at the same time, raising eight children, we now had an independent and rapidly growing ministry to watch over. I was still working full-time as an engineer with a local firm, and Kathy continued to home-school the kids every day, including three preschoolers, a first grader, a middle-schooler, and a high-schooler. With a tremendous amount of hard work, Erin had successfully met Ohio's minimum requirements for high school graduation the previous year and had graduated in a special ceremony with a group of local home-schoolers. She had since taken up her post as Kathy's right hand in the running of the household, and her servant's heart was thriving as she lovingly helped us care for the children each day. Our full and busy days meant that the running of The Shepherd's Crook, which involved maintaining a website, learning the ins and outs of managing a non-profit corporation, communicating with various adoption agencies, and corresponding—via both telephone and e-mail—with a growing number of families pursuing the adoptions of children listed on our website, had to happen in our "spare time." It truly was an exciting time for all of us, but the downside of our busy lifestyle was lack of sleep: Kathy and I often found ourselves working on ministry concerns from around 10:00 each evening—after we had finished our family reading time, put all of the kids to bed, and finished our household chores—until as late as 2:00 or 3:00 in the morning. Then we would wake up at 5:30 or 6:00 the next morning and start it all over again.

In January, we made contact with an adoption agency that felt they would be able to help us with Carlin's adoption from Romania. Kathy had been researching grant possibilities for one of our adoptive families, and her winding search unexpectedly led to a phone conversation with this new contact, Nicole Baila—a native Romanian now living in Oregon, working with an adoption agency in their Romania program. This development was enormously encouraging to us. We had already experienced so many disappointments that we were afraid to get very excited about this new possibility, but from the beginning, the information that Nicole shared with us seemed more hopeful than anything we had yet stumbled upon. We had by then been trying for roughly a year to bring Carlin home, and we had nothing tangible to show for it. The agency Nicole worked for had a person in Romania who talked with Alison Gutterud—the missionary nurse we introduced in the last chapter—to get all of the background information on Carlin. This in-country contact then went to the Romanian Adoption Committee to find out exactly where things stood with Carlin's process. To us, this represented the first real bit of movement we had seen in quite a long time.

Soon after starting Madlin's adoption, we got the idea of wearing ribbons as reminders of our three little ones waiting to come home. We chose the color red for Aidan, white for Carlin, and yellow for Madlin. Kathy bought thin satin ribbon in these colors, and we all tied them on our wrists. The idea was that we would wear these ribbons as reminders to pray for our little ones and as a way to keep them close to our hearts. As each child came home to us, our plan was to cut that child's ribbons from our arms and tape them in his or her baby book, as tangible evidence of the love and anticipation that had accompanied his or her adoption process.

While we waited for any movement, on any of the three adoptions, life marched on. We began to experience the struggles that might be expected when a family's income doesn't match the demands of its size. We climbed to new levels of learning to trust God for daily provision, and the lessons He taught us through these struggles, and His amazing answers to our prayers, deepened our relationship with Him—and would fill another book. We were forced to face our own weak faith and sinful fears over and over again, as we began to live this new life of complete dependency. Often we had nowhere to turn when we needed money for an emergency dental surgery, or glasses for the children, or groceries to feed the family, with many days remaining before the next payday. This new way of life also brought a sweetness and richness that we had never even imagined could be found in our earthly walk as children of God.

Car troubles and faith-building

There is a long list of things you don't want to experience while driving a car on the interstate. The list includes such things as hearing gunfire or explosions; suddenly feeling the wind in your face, even when all the windows are rolled up; seeing smoke billowing out from under your hood; and recognizing certain unmistakable odors, such as gasoline, or burning rubber . . . or antifreeze. Antifreeze is one of those fluids that are essential to the health and proper running of an engine, but which have their proper place and context. It is not good when they are seen outside of that context or that proper place.

Early in March, Kathy drove our fifteen-passenger van to western Pennsylvania to pick up Kristen and a friend from school. As they were leaving campus that evening, Kathy began to smell antifreeze. The further they drove toward home, the more unmistakable the smell became. They rolled the windows down to minimize the offensiveness of the acrid odor, their teeth chattering because of the cold. They finally arrived home at around 1:00 in the morning with their hair and clothes reeking of antifreeze. The carpet in the van, in the area of the front passenger seat, was saturated with the slimy green liquid. I determined that the heater core had developed a leak and would need to be replaced. To make matters worse, we had no money for the repairs, and our other primary vehicle was also out of commission and in need of repairs.

Now, we have an interesting stress-coping mechanism in our family. The gist of it is, when you can't beat the dragon, throw a party. When Kathy and the girls got home that night and we were able to absorb the problem facing us, we decided that the only thing for us to do at that moment was to have some ice cream and laugh for a little while. So we did. We knew that the car repairs would be waiting for us in the morning, but that was tomorrow. Jesus said, "Therefore do not worry about tomorrow, for tomorrow will worry about itself. Each day has enough trouble of its own."[23] We have found that to be true. So, at the end of that trying day, rather than worrying about tomorrow, we had some ice cream. Then we all went to bed, praying that God would send the necessary help to take care of this need.

The next day, a friend stopped by the house to drop off their family dog for us to keep while they went out of town for a few days. As this friend was leaving, she handed me a check, telling me that God had blessed them and that they wanted to share that blessing with us. After she left, I looked at the check and was amazed to see that it was just the amount I would need to buy replacement parts for repairing both vehicles. Kathy and I couldn't believe it: couldn't believe God's amazing timing and provision. And to make it even more interesting, this friend later told us that she and her husband had intended to give us their gift quite some time earlier, but that they had repeatedly forgotten to do so. We were able to relate to them not only how perfectly God had matched the size of their gift with the size of our need, but how He also had perfectly arranged the timing of the gift to meet the timing of our need.

How precious and poignant it is when God so tangibly and unmistakably reminds us that He is in control, and that He will meet our needs and provide for us in every way. Our responsibility, as Jesus so clearly stated in Matthew's gospel,[23] is to seek Him before all other concerns, to be passionate about His causes and His righteousness. The material and physical needs we have are known to the Father, and He will provide for them. Our job is to be His stewards and servants, and to depend on Him for everything.

Near the end of April, we received word from the agency facilitating Madlin's adoption that she was legally ours. On April 24, 2002, Macula Jean Luis officially became Madlin Arielle Rosenow. This was a strange thing for us. We had previously completed four intercountry adoptions, and were at that time in the midst of three more. And yet we had never had an adoption completed without our even having traveled to the country or having met our child. As I said, this was a first, but was not to be the last of such strange adoption stories. We hoped to travel within a month or so, but we were also advised that it could be as late as August before we could pick up our newest child, and our fifth daughter, from Haiti. August. Remember that I said that.

The first annual TSC Celebration Banquet

On May 31, 2002, we held the first annual banquet of The Shepherd's Crook Orphan Ministry. This became an annual event for the next several years, and we used it to share with people the ways God was moving in the world of adoption through this tiny ministry. The day began ominously, with bad news from Haiti and China. The US representative of INS at the Consulate in Haiti had become very difficult to work with. He seemed to think it his duty to prevent all adoptions of Haitian children by Americans, and the roadblocks he threw up for countless hopeful families are the stuff of legend. In fact, there was at the time a large groundswell of opposition to his continuing in the post he held. Agencies and their clients were writing to this man's supervisor to request – or demand – his removal from office. Our case was to be no exception. This field officer was refusing to complete the processing of the adoption investigation, which was a necessary step in granting an immigrant visa for adopted children. So we were being forced to wait, without any idea as to how long the wait might be. Even though Madlin was our daughter, legally, we could not bring her home.

The news from China was that things were hopelessly stuck concerning Aidan's adoption. We had, days earlier, been hopeful that we would soon be receiving our travel authorization. But on this day we learned that the delay would be many more weeks, if not months. All in all, the day was very disheartening for us.

And so we went to our first annual celebration banquet feeling sad, discouraged, weary, and unworthy. Who were we to stand up in front of a hundred and fifty people and talk about adoption and trusting God to do the impossible? We were convinced the whole night would turn into a disaster. But we serve a marvelous God. He took our unworthiness and turned the evening into a true celebration, a tangible witness to the things He had done and was doing in the lives of orphans all over the world. There was laughter, there were praises, there was celebration, there were tears. After the evening was over, we had several people come up to us and say that they had sensed God's presence throughout the evening, and that they could perceive His hand in the work of The Shepherd's Crook Orphan Ministry. This was music to our ears, and the very thing we had been praying for.

Heartbreak brings blessing

The last day of June finally brought us one of the phone calls we had been praying would come. The day is still vividly preserved in both our memories. We had dreamed of this day for so long. Kathy and I were actually out on a date together, browsing through a local bookstore. My cell phone rang, and we saw that it was IAAP's number. We stepped outside to talk to Cheryl. The summer heat was intense as we sat on a wooden bench in front of the bookstore, listening to Cheryl's words: "Well, China finally sent your referral letter, and it's for a little boy — but it's not your little boy."

She went on to tell us that officials in China had unofficially stated that Aidan would not be leaving China, ever, and that this letter matched us with a little boy named Wu Hai He (woo high huh), living with a foster family in Wuhan, China. She said that he had just turned two, had also been born with a cleft lip and cleft palate—although not as severe as Aidan's—and that he had the cutest little "bow mouth" in his accompanying picture. We tried hard to sound positive, in spite of the fact that we were too shocked to feel much of anything. Cheryl told us that she would send us the referral letter immediately and that we would have to mark the box beside either, "We Accept the Adoptee Mentioned Above" or, "We Cannot Accept the Adoptee Mentioned Above," and return the letter to them. Even in our shock, we knew that we couldn't imagine refusing to accept a child that had been assigned to us, but we needed a few minutes to let our brains and hearts absorb all of this information.

We left the bookstore immediately and went to sit in our van. We just needed to talk about everything. As we talked about how this could possibly have happened, we realized that our battle for Aidan was truly over. This beautiful small child was left stranded in China, in desperate need of surgery and a family. The reality of it all—the indescribable grief and pain—suddenly washed over us like a tidal wave. Kathy sank to the floor of the van and began sobbing from the deep places inside her, places we're not even aware of until something inflicts enough pain to expose them. She sobbed herself to the point of exhaustion while I pulled her from the floor and cradled her in my arms. When she finally stopped crying and recovered a bit, we drove home, where a sleepless night awaited us. The next morning, a FedEx truck arrived at our house. The driver left a packet that contained our Referral Letter and a picture of this beautiful little boy, this other child, whom we had never even heard of until the day before—our new son.

We called the family together and told everyone the devastating news about Aidan, and also the news about the referral of the other little boy who was to be their brother. There were many shared tears for the loss of Aidan. It's not that we were unaware of the fact that we had been given another referral. We just had to deal with the loss of the son whose homecoming we had anticipated for so long, before we could turn and face the new reality that had been thrust upon us.

Over the next few days, we moved through a multitude of emotions. The following excerpt from an e-mail update, dated July 2, 2002, gives a snapshot of those days:

The first couple of days after we heard this news, we fluctuated between feelings of anger, numbness, intense sadness, and peace. On Sunday, we were granted much peace, although the deep sadness has remained. It occurred to us that we need to deal with what we do know for sure. And we know now that we have a son in China that needs to come home, and we must pick ourselves up, dust ourselves off, and get busy getting our baby out of China and into our home. We cannot understand God's ways, and so we have to trust Him to handle the things we don't understand. We made a commitment that this would be God's ministry, and that we would allow Him to choose for us which children are ours. Now we have to examine whether we truly believe these words.

This is not the first time that we started an adoption of one child, only to end up with another. Sunday after church while we were eating dinner, Nathan laid his little head on the table and just sobbed his heart out saying, "Aidan can't come home, Aidan can't come home. . . ."

Scott tenderly told him the story of how he came to us — how we started out to bring home little Lourdes, how God changed that so that we were adopting him instead, and then asked Nathan how he thought we would feel if we had never gotten him.

He said, "You would be so sad."

We tried to help him understand that we have to let God lead in this and bring us the child He wants to be with us. It also helps us in our grief right now to look at little Nathan and remember that we wouldn't have him if we had brought home the child we started out to get. Even though we never had enough time to attach to Lourdes like we have with Aidan, we can't imagine our lives without Nathan, and we have to trust God in this, too.

Finally, we met again in the family room for a solemn ceremony to say good-bye to our dearly loved Aidan Matthew. Those who wished to do so wrote letters to a baby brother who would never receive them. We cut the red ribbons from our arms, we took turns hugging Aidan's teddy bear, which had been waiting in his crib for months, and then we packed all of these things lovingly into a box to keep. We talked about our heartbreak, we prayed together, and we cried some more.

After a while, we brushed away our tears and began preparing to receive this new gift God had surprised us with. Kathy and I would be traveling for him in about four weeks, and we all needed to begin immediately to embrace him with our aching hearts. He, like Aidan, was an orphan, with no family and a huge need to be loved and accepted for the precious child of God that he was. We chose the name Stephen Isaiah for him, because the name means, "Crowned one saved by God." We chose Isaiah, too, because of Isaiah 15:24: "Surely, as I have planned, so it will be, and as I have purposed, so it will stand." We knew that God had not made any mistakes. This child was intended to be our son even though we hadn't known anything about him before Cheryl's phone call. We would trust God to bring us through the emotions involved in releasing Aidan to His care and clutching this new son to our hearts with the passionate love of parents. We chose purple for Stephen's color and cut new ribbons to wear for the next few weeks, as we waited for him to join our family. We ended this private family ceremony by tying Stephen's purple ribbons onto our wrists, alongside of Carlin's white ribbon and Madlin's yellow, both now dingy and worn.

China, again

In early August, Kathy and I traveled to China. The majority of the trip was not significantly different from our previous trips to China. We arrived late in the day and were escorted to our hotel. We spent some time settling into our hotel room and getting used to our new setting before it was time to travel to the civil affairs building, which was where we were to be given custody of our new son.

When Stephen was handed over to us by his orphanage representative, she said something to us that didn't really make a lot of sense. She said, "He likes to cry." We just smiled and said, "OK," wondering if she had meant to say something different that got lost in the translation. He was crying, and judging by the speckled color of the skin all over his face, he had been crying for awhile. This was no surprise to us after Robyn's traumatic hand-off two years earlier, so we calmly took him in our arms. We then headed back to our hotel room to try to start the bonding process, for which there are no shortcuts. He cried all the way back to the hotel. He cried all the way up to our room. He cried all through that first day, for hours at a time. In addition to crying, he stood at the hotel room door and banged on it with his little fists, yelling, "Ma-ma! Ma-ma! Ma-ma!"[24] over and over and over. Now we understood what was meant by, "He likes to cry." No translation problems; he liked to cry. He was grieving deeply, though, for the foster mother who had been caring for him for the past year, and it was heartbreaking not to be able to get close enough to him to offer any comfort or to calm his fears.

Finally, after many hours of relentless crying and fist-pounding, he suddenly quieted a bit. He, in fact, became slightly intrigued by my attempts to involve him in a game of peek-a-boo from behind the bed. Before the night was over, he was at least allowing me to play with him and touch him, and had even shared a few shy smiles. He continued to refuse any contact with Kathy, though. Several days of this became almost more painful than Kathy's still-grieving heart could bear. She understood all of the reasons behind his rejection of her after his time of attachment with a foster mother, and she knew from experience that it would eventually pass. But the pain of losing Aidan was still so raw that Stephen's ongoing rejection of her, while she watched him draw closer and closer to me with each passing day, made it hard to rise above her emotions—emotions that hadn't really had time to work all the way to the surface. In spite of her pain, she continued to look for ways to quietly express her love for this new son, while still giving him the space he needed to work through his own fears and loss. And she waited.

On the fifth day of our time with Stephen, we awoke, showered, dressed, and headed down to the hotel lobby for breakfast. We locked our hotel room door and began to walk down the long hall to the elevator, just as we had done every morning since Stephen had come to be with us. Stephen and I started out together, with Kathy following just behind. He had become more animated and joyous each day, and he delighted in doing what we quickly dubbed his "kicky-dance" whenever we walked anywhere. He would try to skip but always kicked his legs behind him wildly as he propelled himself forward, grinning for all he was worth.

Suddenly, about halfway to the elevator, he stopped, stood still, and turned back to look at Kathy. He seemed at that point to make a definite decision. He walked calmly to her and fell in step beside her. While looking up into her face as we all continued walking to the elevator, he reached up and slipped his tiny hand into hers.

199

Kathy held her breath. Her heart soared and tears filled her eyes. Stephen never looked back after that morning. His grieving ended abruptly and completely at that moment, and he embraced his new life and his new parents with all the might his little heart possessed.

After this dramatic final step into his life as Stephen Isaiah, he spent most of his days giving expression to the joy that he obviously felt inside. He would kicky-dance all through the hotel lobby or restaurant or streets of Wuhan, pushing his stroller and singing. He would wave his little hand and greet everyone we met with a very high-pitched and nasal "Hewwo! Hewwo!" The hotel employees all began to call him "the hello boy," and fell in love with his good-natured disposition and winsome grin. Once again, we had been handed a precious gem, and we praised God for this unexpected gift.

Say what?!

On Sunday, August 18, we headed to the Guangzhou International Airport to begin our trip home. When we arrived at the airport, we were met with an interesting problem. We checked in at the gate and found that Kathy and I had been assigned seats in Economy Class, but Stephen had been assigned a seat in Business Class. Our two-year-old was going to be sitting by himself—in a roomy and comfortable seat—for the thirteen-hour flight across the Pacific. While we found the situation merely comical and ridiculous, it seemed to present an insurmountable dilemma to the airport staff.

More than forty-five minutes were required for them to work out an acceptable solution. In the end, Kathy and I were pleased to have our tickets upgraded to Business Class at no extra cost. Our assumption was that the flight attendants had decided that they didn't want to handle this toddler who "liked to cry," without his parents, for the long flight. Whatever the reason, we enjoyed a more-pleasant-than-usual trip from Guangzhou to Los Angeles, where we spent the night at a hotel before heading home the next morning.

Stephen was instantly a hit with his new brothers and sisters. They would race each other to his room each morning to be the one to get him out of bed and play with him for a while. He settled in quickly, too, to the new routine in this large family.

Days continued to pass as our hearts longed to get our other two waiting little ones home. Things had actually continued to progress with Carlin's adoption once Nicole entered the picture, but we still didn't know if our adoption would ever finally be granted. Our hopes would soar with reports from Romania that court dates had been set for finalization of the adoption, and then we would be left with more disappointment when word came that, once again, the adoption had been denied for some reason. The following entries from Kathy's "Carlin" journal, written to Carlin as we went through her adoption process, detail some of the pain our hearts were experiencing during that time.

Sept. 12, 2002, 12:10 a.m.: *If all goes well, you will finally become our daughter sometime today. I can barely believe it, and*

I feel almost like I still dare not. So many, many months have passed since we first learned about you — since Kristen held you and e-mailed us about you — nineteen long, painful, dreamlike months. Are they truly about to come to an end? Will you really be home in a few weeks now? It is just after 7:00 a.m. in Romania. Nicole has said she will call me when your adoption has been completed. How can I sleep as I dream of you eating your breakfast and dressing to go to court? I ache to hold you, feel your fuzzy hair against my face, know you.

Sept. 12, 2002 – evening: *So much discouragement. The judge refused to grant your adoption today. He didn't like the adoption agency's choice for our representative in court. We have to sign and notarize a new Power of Attorney and send it to Romania. They will hold another hearing in three weeks, on Oct. 3. How long!!?*

Another phone call, another wild ride

The journey to adopt from another country is never dull, and we were learning this lesson only too well. On September 28, we got a phone call from Dick Graham, telling us that he and Cheryl, through pure happenstance, had discovered that Aidan was listed now on another agency's website. In spite of what Dick had been told, unofficially, by the Chinese officials, Aidan had been placed on another agency's list of children and was now suddenly available for adoption.

Our heads immediately began spinning. We contacted the agency now holding Aidan's information and asked permission to pursue his adoption. This was not a straightforward conversation, since we had to fill them in on the whole history of our attempts to make this child our son. The obstacles we had to overcome were many and large: (1) We had too many children in our home, since China's new policy was not to allow families with more than five children already in the home to adopt; (2) We had just brought Stephen home a couple of months earlier, and as we mentioned previously, China's policy was not to allow adoptions of any Chinese child within twelve months of a previous Chinese adoption; (3) Our income was insufficient according to the CCAA's new requirements; and (4) We would have to raise the money for another adoption—on the order of $25,000—while still in the process of raising funds for two other ongoing adoptions.

But we felt strongly that God was leading us to try again to adopt this child, regardless of the outcome, and we made the decision to rest in God's wisdom in spite of the obstacles we could see ahead of us. We asked this new agency if they would help us, and they agreed, although they stipulated that they could offer no guarantees. They had seen some surprising things from China in the context of special-needs adoptions, and they felt that there was a pretty good chance we would be approved. And so, once again, we were plunged into the ice-cold water of a risky adoption. The risk in this case was intensified by the fact that we had been down that very road before. We were still bruised from our previous heartbreak at losing this child, and we worried about what another failure would do to all of us.

On the other hand, we knew we had no choice but to try, to pursue this adoption with all of our energy and resources. We had been called by God to live this life, and sometimes—often—following God's calling entails accepting the risk of pain and heartbreak. We do not go into battle so as to remain safe and comfortable, but to offer our very lives in service to our King. It is His cause that is important, not our comfort and safety. So we did our best to don our armor and prepare for the battle ahead, and we dove in.

And then there were ten . . . or was it eleven?

Meanwhile, back to Carlin's story. The last thing we had been told, in mid-September, was that another adoption hearing was to be held on October 3. The adoption, however, was once again denied at that hearing. This time the judge decided that she wanted a letter from the American Embassy stating that they, the Embassy, knew we were planning to adopt this little girl with spina bifida. We began to think that it was just possible that Romania would never approve Carlin's adoption—that we would just continue to be given senseless reasons for denials and that she would never come home to us.

Then came the afternoon of October 24: we received a phone call from Nicole, telling us that Carlin's adoption had suddenly been completed. It was done! Nicole told us that as of October 24, Carlin Jessica Rosenow was officially our daughter. After having fought so hard for twenty months, she was finally, incontrovertibly ours. We were stunned by this news. It almost didn't seem real. There were still a few steps in the process to be completed, but we were told that we could probably plan to travel in about three weeks to bring her home.

We decided that Kathy and Kristen would make the trip to Romania, while I would stay home with the kids. We thought that it would not be good for Stephen to have both of us gone so soon after his own homecoming, and it would be much better for the whole family if Kathy and Kristen made the quick trip. We also knew that it would be very special for Kristen to travel back to Romania with Kathy to bring home this baby sister that God had brought to us through her time in Romania almost two years earlier. Kathy and I really hated that we wouldn't be traveling together, and I hated the fact that I wasn't going to get to see Carlin's homeland. But we knew that the plan was best for everyone concerned, even if not the one that would make all of us the happiest, at least in the short-term.

Unfortunately, the plans for traveling three weeks after Carlin's adoption was finalized did not come to pass. We hit delay after delay as we waited for US Immigration on the Romania end to wrap up their part of the process toward granting Carlin's immigrant visa. Like Madlin, Carlin was legally and officially our daughter, but we still couldn't travel to bring her home.

On November 17, 2002, Carlin turned two years old. We cried as we pondered the truth that we had now missed two of her birthdays since starting her adoption process so long ago. And we wondered if we would also miss Thanksgiving and Christmas with our baby. Then suddenly, on November 27, we got the word we had been waiting for. Kathy's entry in Carlin's journal for that day proclaims this news:

> *You are coming home!!!! We have booked flights, leaving Dayton at 1:30 December 12 — only two weeks from tomorrow — and we return home on December 18. Tomorrow is Thanksgiving, and you are coming home! Is it really true?*

We bring Carlin home

On December 13, Kathy and Kristen touched down at the Bucharest International Airport, just outside of the sprawling capital city of nearly two million people. Kathy and Kristen were taken almost immediately to meet Carlin at her foster home. Carlin was animated, happy, and friendly. Her foster parents, Renee and Valentin, quite obviously cared deeply for her, and there was a special relationship between Carlin and Valentin. Both Renee and Valentin knew that Carlin's adoption was best for her, but they were having a difficult time letting her go.

After a couple of days of visiting Carlin at her foster home, Kathy was permitted to take her to the apartment where she and Kristen were staying. The whole period was almost like walking in a dream for Kathy. She had for so long looked forward to holding this beautiful child in her arms, and now it was really happening. The three of them arrived home on December 18. In an e-mail sent out on December 27, Kathy reported the following:

Praying that all of you had a blessed Christmas Day. It was just magical at our house. Quite a few of you have written to ask for an update and for pictures . . . [Carlin] and Stephen are a funny pair – and deadly at times. They share a room; their cribs sit opposite each other against the walls. One of their favorite antics at bedtime is to stand in their cribs and chatter and throw their stuffed puppies across the room to each other. We have managed to catch them at this a couple of times and hope to break it soon – but they are pretty darn cute, even when being naughty. Carlin, just like a girl, is pretty adept at dropping to her stomach and looking innocent as soon as she realizes we're coming. Stephen, just like a boy, is almost always caught still standing with his arm in mid-swing, with a look on his face that says, "What?? Is there something wrong with this?" Carlin has proved to be a much more normal child than she first appeared – she is not always angelic. She has a strong will and has decided to challenge us on a few points. Just like all of the others, though, each time she finally accepts that we won't back down and that she won't win, her love toward us grows. She has filled our home with giggles and activity – and we thought we were already overflowing in these areas. We still marvel multiple times each day at the miracle her presence here represents.

It seems the term "magical" was becoming our standard descriptor for Christmas celebrations at our house. So much of that was due to the realization of what these children brought to all of us, just as much as the realization of how their lives had changed.

Our joy was tempered, though, by the knowledge that we still had two little ones who weren't home yet. We closed out the year wondering, "When will Madlin and Aidan come home?"

Chapter 11

Finding God in Surprising Places

✳

Did you never run for shelter in a storm, and find fruit which
you expected not? Did you never go to God for safeguard,
driven by outward storms, and there find unexpected fruit?

John Owen

Aidan, the final chapter

On January 21, 2003, right after Aidan turned two, we got
word from the agency handling his adoption — the second
time around — that China had finally denied our request to adopt
him. This was a blow to be sure, and one we found even heavier
than when we had originally been told we couldn't adopt him.
When we asked if there might be any basis for an appeal, we were
told that we had to wait until the official letter arrived and see what
reason was given for the denial.

*E-mail excerpt, January 21, 2003: We have cried buckets of
tears and, if possible, are grieving even more deeply than we did*

the first time we got similar news from China about Aidan. We have been whining to God that to lose Aidan once was unbearable, how can He expect us to face the grief of losing him again. We have been constantly reminded of the story in Daniel 3 when Shadrach, Meshach, and Abednego are about to be thrown into the furnace. In verses 17 and 18 they say, "If we are thrown into the blazing furnace, the God we serve is able to save us from it, and He will rescue us from your hand, O king. But even if He does not, we want you to know, O king, that we will not serve your gods or worship the image of gold you have set up." It appears that our long battle for Aidan is over. Right now, the thought that Aidan is finally free to leave China but that we will not be allowed to have him, after fighting for him for nineteen months, is causing us almost overwhelming and paralyzing sadness. But our prayer is that if God's answer to our request to make Aidan our son is no, He will give us the strength to state emphatically that we will continue to serve Him with all our hearts — even if we can't understand His reasons for leading us through the same dark valley twice.

The agency handling Aidan's adoption eventually told us that no official letter from China would be coming, but that they had been told that we would not ever be permitted to adopt Aidan. Thus, our attempts to adopt this beautiful child came fully, finally to a close.

We immediately petitioned this same agency for the chance to try to find another family for Aidan, whom we once again began to call Lin Hou. We couldn't bear the thought of his remaining forever in a Chinese orphanage, and we knew that the next best thing we could do for him, since we couldn't bring him into our family, would be to find another Christian family for him to grow up in. The agency agreed to give us some time before sending Lin Hou's papers back to the CCAA, and so we began our search.

Melodrama in the Caribbean

Near the end of January, we got word that Frank, the INS officer in Haiti who had been blocking our efforts to obtain a visa for Madlin, would be willing to approve the visa request if our attorney in Haiti could provide one final legal document, called a *négatif*. About a week later, the attorney obtained the *négatif* and took it to Frank. Frank thereupon insisted that the document, which was in French, be translated into English before he would accept it. We were told that this was a first, that Frank had never asked for this before. The attorney was told to return to the INS office by the end of the week to present the translated document. We learned late in the day on Friday that our attorney had not, in fact, gone to Frank's office as he had been told to do, but we weren't given a satisfactory reason for his failure to do so.

The following Monday, our representative in Port au Prince did finally present the translated *négatif* to Frank. Then, just to continue the sensation that we were somehow watching a badly written soap opera, Frank told our representative that they would have to submit DNA evidence that the birth mother was who she claimed to be. This meant once again tracking down the birth mother, convincing her to travel to Port au Prince to have a blood sample drawn, paying several hundred more dollars, and waiting for the lab results—which, we were told, would take at least three weeks, and perhaps much longer. When we heard this, I actually called Frank to discuss the situation with him and find out if there were anything we could do either to avoid this step or to make it happen more quickly. The phone call was neither pleasant nor productive.

E-mail excerpt, February 10, 2003: *This whole episode brings to mind a number of questions and concerns. We, together with many of our friends and many of you out there in cyberspace, have been praying fervently that God would overrule the hearts and minds of those trying to block Madlin's homecoming, and that she would receive her INS clearance today. This didn't happen. Does that mean that God didn't answer our prayers? Does it mean he doesn't care about Madlin, or us? . . .*

What am I to do with my feelings of frustration and anger over the fact that my desires – to bring Madlin home right now – have been thwarted, and my prayers have gone unanswered? . . . I guess this is an area where I am forced to interpret the unknown by the light of what I do know. I do know that God is good. I do know, from His very Word, that He will never leave us nor forsake us. I do know that He causes all things to work together for the good of those who love Him and are called according to His purpose. I do know that He loves me and my family, and that He would never, never do anything to harm us. I do know that He is all-powerful, and that nothing in all of creation can impede or alter

His infinite plans. Nothing. Not you, not me, not the Haitian INS agent, and not Satan himself. So, as I meditate on these truths, I begin to sense that what is happening must be ultimately for my good, and for my family's good, and even for Madlin's good. And most of all, it is to glorify His holy name. So, I will give thanks to God even in these circumstances. Thanks for His goodness and faithfulness, even when I don't understand – and sometimes don't want to understand – what is going on in the big picture. Thanks that He is working all things out according to the counsel of His own will. Thanks that, even in this circumstance, His name is being glorified in all the earth. Praise God!

Just in time

We took Carlin to several specialists after the first of the year, and learned more about life with spina bifida. Because of her lack of bladder control, we began catheterizing Carlin every four hours. This was to prevent damage to her kidneys arising from the fact that she couldn't empty her bladder when necessary.

We learned early in March that Carlin was suffering from a condition called tethered spinal cord syndrome. Without launching into a lengthy and scholastic explanation—for which I am utterly unqualified—suffice it to say that the lower end of the spinal cord is supposed to hang freely within the protective structures of the spine. In tethered spinal cord syndrome, the free end becomes stuck, or tethered, usually within some sort of fatty mass or scar tissue. As the child grows, this attachment begins to stretch the cord itself, resulting in damage to the spinal nerves. Carlin's neurosurgeon recommended surgical correction, which is delicate and somewhat dangerous, as the attempt to remove the tethering mass can result in further damage to the nerves of the spinal cord.

Kathy and I spent some time praying and giving careful consideration to everything involved. We ultimately came to the conclusion that we really didn't have any choice, and that we trusted her neurosurgeon to do the procedure. The operation was scheduled for April, just before Easter. Once again we were struck by the fact that we got her out of Romania, and apparently just in time. If the tethered spinal cord syndrome had been allowed to progress, Carlin would most likely have begun to lose function in her feet and legs, and in all probability she would have suffered further loss of bladder and bowel function. This was all the more striking in light of the fact that no other children were coming out of Romania. We had hoped that Carlin's adoption would signal the resumption of adoptions, but that did not happen. We thanked God for bringing our little girl out, and we prayed that He would, in His perfect timing, open up the doors again to all of the thousands of children waiting, and waiting, and waiting in Romania.

Return to the bizarre

In mid-March, we learned that Madlin, who was now four and a half, was coming home to us. Out of the blue, we got word from our contacts in Haiti that Frank had approved Madlin's visa request and that he had scheduled her consular appointment. The visa was granted on March 18, and she was to come home to us on Wednesday, the nineteenth. The really bizarre aspect of this is that

Frank didn't wait for the DNA results, as he had formerly insisted—even though he had made us pay for the procedure and go through all of the steps. He just finalized the investigation and approved the request. Just like that. While we were stunned and flabbergasted, we were also elated. After sixteen months of struggles and trials, suddenly our little girl was coming home to us.

We had arranged for an escort to accompany Madlin from Port au Prince to Miami, where we would meet them and pick up our new daughter. Kristen just happened to be home from college for spring break, and thus was able to stay with the children for us. So, in spite of the incredibly short notice, we were able to drop everything and make the quick trip to Miami. On Wednesday evening, March 19, 2003, Allan drove Kathy and me to the Dayton International Airport to catch a quick flight to Miami. Fairly routine for us, who had become world travelers over the past five years or so. Then again, this was an international adoption, and nothing is really routine in an international adoption. We arrived at the airport and checked in with plenty of time to spare, and then we made our way to the security checkpoint.

The bizarre becomes surreal

As we passed through the TSA checkpoint, we noticed that the agents seemed to be giving a lot of attention to one of our carry-on bags as it went through the x-ray machine. One of the agents took the bag aside and asked Kathy if it was her bag. Kathy said yes, it was her bag. The agent then reached into the outside pocket of the bag, which was unzipped, and pulled out a small box. We had no idea that the box was even in there, and we were pretty surprised by the discovery. The agent then opened the small box and pulled out what looked like a decorative fan or something. But it wasn't a fan. It was a knife.

At that point, according to airport protocol, the affair was turned over to the Dayton Police, who provide law-enforcement presence and have legal jurisdiction at the airport. The police officer told us that traveling with a "concealed weapon" was illegal and the knife would be confiscated. Well, this was all confusing because we hadn't even known that the knife was in Kathy's bag, and all of the attention and accusing looks were disconcerting and embarrassing. But we were fine with their keeping the knife and anxious to have the whole scary event behind us so we could be on our way. As we stood waiting to be told we could leave, more discussion took place among the officers. They then told us that we would have to be taken to the police department offices at the airport for questioning. We were still pretty shaken by all of this, but we felt confident that everything would be ironed out in time for us to catch our plane. Once we reached the police offices, however, the duty sergeant explained that Kathy was going to be put under arrest. While our heads began to spin, he quickly told us that it probably wasn't a big deal, and that she would most likely be released on her own recognizance so that we could go get our daughter. We could wrap up the details when we returned from Miami. We would have to issue signed statements and so forth, but the sergeant didn't see any reason why we wouldn't make our flight and be on our way. He then told us he had to leave to make a few phone calls.

While we were waiting for everything to come together, we were permitted to call home and talk to the kids. Kristen, when she heard what had happened, remembered that she had bought that knife at a flea market in Florida several months earlier, when she and some friends had gone down there for a vacation. Kristen had been wondering what had happened to that knife. She must've dropped it into the pocket of the suitcase and thereafter forgotten about it. It was just our luck that we decided to borrow Kristen's suitcase for the quick trip to Miami, wasn't it?

Things then went from bad to worse, when the duty sergeant came back and explained that the Dayton Police Chief would have to be notified about the incident. He also said that the FBI would have to be notified, since the attempted concealment and discovery had occurred at an airport security checkpoint. Kathy and I sat down and wrote out our formal statements, explaining in detail what had happened. We learned later that our statements had been backed up by the official report of the TSA officer who had searched the bag and found the knife. Her report included the fact that the pocket in which the knife had been found wasn't even zipped, indicating to her that we weren't trying to conceal anything.

The surreal becomes a nightmare

While we waited in the conference room, we watched television coverage of an event taking place on the other side of the world. The combined armed forces of the United States and her allies were beginning an intense and prolonged bombing attack on Baghdad, the capital of Iraq. Operation Iraqi Freedom had begun.

We wondered if there were some increase in security awareness at US airports in response to the attack on Baghdad, and if that might explain, in part, the insanity behind the arrest of Kathy on such ridiculous charges. We didn't know, but we wondered.

About a half hour after we submitted our written statements, the sergeant came back to tell us that the City of Dayton had decided to charge Kathy with Carrying a Concealed Weapon (CCW), a third-degree felony, and that she was to be taken downtown to the police station for booking. There would be no releasing her on her own recognizance, after all. No flight to Miami to pick up our daughter. He also said that the US attorney's office was considering whether or not to charge Kathy with additional offenses, on the federal level. He read her Miranda rights to her as the two of us listened in shocked horror. How could this be happening! The sergeant told me to tell Kathy goodbye, that she would be held overnight and arraigned in the morning, and that there wasn't anything I could do about it—bail prior to arraignment isn't even an option in felony cases.

One of the police officers escorted me back to the front of the airport and turned me over to our airline's ticket agent. My last view of Kathy had been when they put her hands behind her back and placed handcuffs on her wrists. She looked scared to death, and we were both too surprised and frightened to know what to think. The ticket agent helped me cancel our flight for that evening. In a show of determined optimism, I booked the same flight again for the next evening. I called our contact at the adoption agency and explained what had happened, and they made arrangements to cancel Madlin's and her escort's trip from Haiti to Miami. I told her that we would try to make it the next evening, but that I had no idea what was going to happen. I then called home and told Kristen to have Allan come back and get me as soon as he got home.

I sat in the airport waiting for Allan to come back, and I wondered, "What on earth is God doing in this? What are we going to do? What is going to happen to Kathy?" And I prayed. Once Allan picked me up, I began calling people in our church, beginning with our pastor, Walter Wood. Walter told me that there were a few attorneys in our congregation, and he put me in touch with one of them for help and advice. I thus began learning about legal procedure — arraignments and so forth — and I began preparing for what I would need to do in the morning. So much for me and what I was doing. While I was trying to remain calm and track down anyone who could help, Kathy was experiencing her own nightmare-like experience in a world completely foreign to us.

Kathy's night

After I was led away from her, Kathy was taken to a holding cell to await transport downtown. As she sat in that cell, trying to gain control of the mounting panic she felt in her heart, she managed to gather her thoughts enough to pray about the whole bizarre episode. From the moment she was placed under arrest, she was filled with an assurance that this would not have happened outside of God's will, and her prayers mainly focused on asking three things of God. First, she prayed for Him to stay close beside her through whatever was ahead. Second, she prayed that He would keep her eyes open so that she didn't miss anything He wanted to teach her through all of it. Third, she asked God to help her remain willing to be used by Him through the night, in any way He deemed best. It took constant focus on these things to keep her emotions under control.

Kathy was next transported from the airport to the Montgomery County Jail. Humiliation continued to be one of her most keenly felt emotions that night, second only to fear. One of the most humiliating experiences of all was when they had her face a wall, place her forehead against a padded section, and submit to a body search. While she was undergoing this demeaning procedure, it occurred to her that Easter was just a month away. While she was frisked, she pondered the humiliation that Christ suffered on her behalf during those hours leading up to his crucifixion. She felt Him close by her side and was even able, somehow, to thank Him for this opportunity to identify with His suffering in a new way.

Once she had been frisked, her handcuffs were removed and she was taken to a desk, where she was ordered to hand over all of her personal belongings. The only things she had were her wedding rings, and these were promptly removed and placed in a bag. Then, to her surprise, Madlin's tattered and stained yellow ribbon—the only one remaining on her wrist, since Carlin's had been tenderly taped into her baby book when she came home—was hastily cut, removed, and placed in the bag with the wedding rings. This act almost caused Kathy to lose all control of her emotions, as her heart screamed inside her, "But she isn't home yet! That ribbon can't be removed!"

Next, she was processed in, posed for a mug shot, and exchanged her street clothes for Montgomery County prison attire. The rest of the night seemed interminable. She spent many hours sitting on the women's side of a very large processing room. As she watched the TV hanging on the wall and tried to absorb the surreal scene of bombs falling on Iraq, she found herself wondering what was going to happen to our family. Could our children be taken from us because of this? Would TSC be shut down? Would the FBI choose to press federal charges along with the local charges? Would she go to prison? If so, how would she ever survive? What was going on outside the very small world she now found herself confined in? What was her husband doing? Was he OK? What would happen to Madlin now? Would she, Madlin, spend the rest of her childhood in that Haitian orphanage because of this?

As these thoughts whirled through Kathy's head, she kept returning to her focused belief that God had her there for a reason and that He would not leave her alone. She had to force herself continually to commit Madlin and the rest of her fears to God's keeping. This was the only way to subdue the panic when it began to rise inside her.

Sanity makes a come-back

The first thing the next morning, I drove back up to Dayton to be ready for Kathy's arraignment, which was supposed to happen around 8:00. I got to the courthouse and did my best to figure out where I was supposed to be and what I was supposed to be doing, but mostly I was pretty overwhelmed and bewildered.

After wandering around for a little over an hour, my cell phone rang and it was a number I didn't recognize. I was surprised when the call turned out to be from a Dayton Police Detective, asking if I was Kathy's husband, and asking where I was. I told him that I was outside of the courthouse, trying to find out where and when Kathy's arraignment was supposed to occur. He said, "There isn't going to be any arraignment." He then told me that Kathy was with him and how to get to his office.

When I got there, I was tremendously relieved to see Kathy, although she looked exhausted. The detective said that Kathy should never have been arrested, that she wasn't going to be charged with anything, and that he was going to see to it that she got out of there as quickly as possible so that the two of us could get down to Miami to pick up our daughter. I don't mind telling you that I had never before heard such wonderful words. It took about two more hours for Kathy to be processed out. We then drove back home, where Kathy planned to grab a quick shower and spend a few minutes with our kids before the two of us headed back to the airport, for round two. We had reservations for that evening, again, to fly down to Miami to pick up Madlin, and we were determined, in spite of our fears, to give it a go.

Reflection

That afternoon, Kathy put together an e-mail update to let everyone know what she had experienced during that long night.

E-mail update, March 20, 2003: We are trying to finish re-packing and attempt passing through the security checkpoint at the Dayton airport again, but I feel the need to type this update while details are still so fresh in my mind. I will never be able to thank you all for the overwhelming outpouring of love I witnessed on our e-mail and voice mail when I returned home this afternoon. I was, frankly, shocked by the sheer volume of messages and the depth of love and concern they conveyed for our family.

I will also probably never be able to adequately express just how terrifying parts of last night were for me. I think that, just possibly, it was when I was finally taken to my cell at about 4:00 a.m. The door closed and locked behind me, and as my eyes adjusted to the darkness of the small cell, a huge lump rose in my throat as I saw the Goliath of a woman occupying the bottom bunk. I can assure you that I took great pains not to awaken this woman whose snores more than matched her bulk, as I climbed the ladder to the steel platform that served as my bed, and tried my best to spread the very thin sheet over the thin pad to make something that resembled a place to rest.

But I wasn't always scared, and never for one minute throughout the whole ordeal did I ever doubt that I was there because God wanted me there. I was also able to keep sight of the fact that God continues to hold Madlin securely in His very capable hands. I am not always able to feel the truth of God's perfect will and love with such certainty, and I know that all of your prayers are responsible for my being able to know it deep in my heart this time. As strange as it sounds, and as surprised as I am to be able to say this so soon after this adventure, the experience is also something that I will in some ways always be thankful for. All through the night, I forced myself to focus on the fact that God was truly in control, and to ask Him not to let me miss any opportunities to learn a lesson from Him or to be a witness for Him.

There were times when I was scared beyond words, and the panic at what I might be facing almost overwhelmed me. When I felt this happen, I would pull my knees to my chest, lay my head on them, and quote scripture or sing praise songs in my head. When I couldn't remember any scripture or songs because the panic was too great, I would repeat The Lord's Prayer. In some ways, it was a precious time alone with God. When I was finally taken to the detectives for interrogation this morning, I was greeted by several detectives who looked at me and said kindly, "We are so sorry you had to go through this. You have no business in a jail cell, and this never should've happened. We are going to see that you get out of here as soon as possible, and we will try to get you on a plane today so you can go get your daughter." I almost collapsed in tears just out of sheer gratitude for their acknowledgement of my innocence and their concern for my state of mind. Thankfully, I was able to stay the flow until I was alone in the car with Scott later.

One of the surprises for me was the women I was surrounded by much of the night. Many times, especially during the morning and afternoon today, I was only surrounded by very angry and really scary women, and at those times, I would resort to my knees-to-chest-scripture-recitation method of controlling the fear. But for much of the night I was surrounded by women with sad,

sad stories. Their faces haunted me through the night and have continued to haunt me today. When I was allowed to walk out of jail this afternoon, free and wearing my own clothes again, the first thing I saw when I opened the door of the lobby, was Scott waiting for me. The physical and emotional exhaustion of the long night combined with the sight of my beloved husband's teary eyes made it impossible for me to walk to the car without his help. And being able to come in the front door of my happy, happy home to cheers of "Hi Mommy!! We missed you so much!!" was beautiful. But later as I showered (a wonderful experience), I thought of all of those women who didn't have this kind of love to go home to. I remembered the girl who spent a large part of the night sharing her story with me. She is addicted to heroin and is in a treatment program so she can someday hope to get her three small children back from foster care. But her boyfriend continues urging her to use the heroin he gets for her, and she "loves" him too much to say no. So she feels like there is no hope. I longed to share openly that God could heal her, but they all made it clear early on that they weren't interested in "religious talk." One taught me how to use the phones to make collect calls. They would all look for opportunities to explain to me what to expect with the next step in case we were separated. This went a long way in easing my fears each time my name was called to be moved to another holding place. They begged to hear the details of our story about how I had ended up in jail and wanted to know all about the kids and their adoptions and their disabilities.

*The most touching part of the night, I think, is when the girl with the heroin problem looked at me with tears in her eyes and said, "I wish I could've been adopted by you. I wonder how different my life would be now?" It reminded me for the millionth time that we can **never** underestimate the difference we are making in these children's lives when we take them into our arms and give them our names and make them our own and introduce them to Christ. I have prayed so much for all of these women who touched my life, and I am thankful that I had the opportunity to witness the sad, even disturbing snapshots of their lives. (Although I have no desire whatsoever to repeat it anytime soon.) I will try to continue to pray for them and I will be ever more grateful for all that God has given me.*

And now, we must get on with the business of facing that scary security checkpoint again. I really am scared about going back through there with all of the memories of my arrest still fresh in my mind. But our daughter waits on the other side of that checkpoint, and we will never stop trying to get her home unless God makes it clear in some way that it is not His will for her to be with us.

Our quick trip to Miami

On Thursday evening, March 20, Kathy and I returned to Dayton International Airport and once again faced the security checkpoint. This time, though, we breezed through without incident, though not without considerable butterflies in our stomachs. The TSA officer who had found the knife the previous evening was once again on duty, and she actually gave Kathy a hug once we got through the screening. She said that they had all been so worried about Kathy, after hearing that she had been arrested, and they were greatly relieved to see her there again. We later ran into the duty sergeant from the previous evening, as we were heading to our gate, and he said that he, too, was glad that Kathy was all right and that everything had been cleared up. He explained that he hadn't really wanted to arrest her but that federal regulations required it.

We then flew down to Miami and spent the night in a hotel near the airport. The next morning we went back to the airport and met Madlin and her escort. We spent a few minutes introducing ourselves to Madlin, and then the escort left us to catch her flight back to Haiti — and we were on our own with our new, almost-five-year-old daughter, who didn't speak a word of English. We spent an hour or so with her while we waited for our return flight, and then we headed home. When we landed in Dayton, we were met by a couple of police officers, who were waiting for us with a gift basket for Madlin and more hugs for Kathy. We actually remained in touch with these officers for several years after this incident, introducing them to more new Rosenows as we brought them home through the Dayton International Airport.

Over the course of the next several months, we began to get to know our new daughter as she began to get to know her new family. Madlin seemed to settle in pretty smoothly from the beginning, but there was a "flatness" about her, an emptiness and numbness that we couldn't seem to break through. There were no struggles with rebellion like we faced when Colin came home to us, but neglect, mistreatment, and multiple abandonments by her birth family had left deep marks. Although her insecurities and inability to trust us did lead to acts of deception and very poor social skills, Madlin was, most of the time, too-quietly compliant and at times seemed vacant. We were plagued by the feeling that we could not reach deeply enough inside her to get to the "real" Madlin. She seemed unable to break out of the robot-like behavior that defined her.

We didn't know then that it would be more than six years before we finally realized our desire to capture Madlin's heart and had the blessed honor of fully knowing her as our daughter. This wouldn't happen until that incredible day when she sat at our feet in our family room and prayed to receive Christ as her Savior, fully surrendering her heart to Him. In the meantime, though, we thanked God for bringing her to us, prayed constantly that He would help us find ways to reach her, and loved her in spite of the fact that she didn't seem to be really able to feel this love or believe that it was genuine and unconditional.

Interestingly, we encountered with Carlin something similar to what we found with Madlin, and it began around this same time. Carlin, like Madlin, seemed on the surface to bond well and become a natural part of the family, but closer examination—and more time—revealed that this was merely illusion. In Carlin's case, the resistance to bonding manifested itself differently. At some times she was openly rebellious, but most of the time it was more like she was protecting herself, not allowing herself to attach to us, not allowing us to see what was really going on in her heart. She had been through so many hurts in her short lifetime, and we think that she unconsciously developed mechanisms for ensuring that she didn't have to suffer again in the same way. In her case, too, it took nearly six years before we felt like we had won her heart, and her trust. As with Madlin, the real turning point came later, when she surrendered her heart to Christ and His love. The battle to win these little souls is protracted and often intense. It makes us understand how jealously Satan holds onto every life he claims as his own, and how there is rejoicing in heaven whenever Satan's grip is broken.

Synopsis of the other major events of 2003

The rest of the year was a whirlwind of activity, and even now, many years later, it remains a blur to us. Shortly after we returned from Miami with Madlin, we got word that a family had come forward to pursue the adoption of Lin Hou. We were still grieving through our own loss, but we could now rejoice, both on behalf of Lin Hou and for the sake of the new family adopting him. This was a case of God turning our "mourning into joy," as we knew that this baby would not have to spend his life in an orphanage in China.

We had three more surgeries that year: Carlin's tethered cord release in April; one for Stephen in July, to form a pharyngeal flap — which helps kids with repaired cleft palates avoid the nasal sound caused by air from the larynx flowing up into the nasal passages rather than through the mouth; and one for Meghan in November, to do some additional corrective work on her hands and feet.

Real life

All of these events — the loss of Aidan, the struggle to get Madlin home, with all of its complications, and our emotional battles to gain the hearts of our new children — left us somewhat frazzled and exhausted as the year drew to a close. In fact, the weariness and doubts we were feeling at this time were what led to Kathy's writing of the e-mail excerpted in the Preface to this book. These emotional and spiritual struggles were compounded, near the end of the year, by some comments we received having to do with trials — suggesting that we did not go through the same difficulties others face, or that somehow God blesses us above and beyond His treatment of others. This caused us both pain and concern. We were concerned that our e-mail updates might have been conveying, without our realizing it, the misconception that life was easy for us and that God answered all of our prayers just exactly as we asked. This concern prompted us to address this topic with our e-mail update list in an effort to clear up any misconceptions.

E-mail excerpt, November 24, 2003: We mentioned in a recent update that we have been passing through a fairly intense season of testing. During this period we have regularly received letters from other TSC families, asking us to help them understand what it means when they pass through times of silence, when it seems that God isn't hearing them, asking us why He seems to meet all of our needs but doesn't seem to be listening to them. Several people have said to us that they are afraid to follow God into adoption because they "are not the Rosenows. People won't just

230

give [them] everything like they do to the Rosenow family." It has concerned us that maybe we have been giving the false impression that we, the Rosenows, just submit our "order" to a Santa-Claus-type-God for whatever we want and then see that "order" filled immediately, making it possible for us to live a life of ease. We don't care so much, for ourselves, what others are thinking about the life we live, but we have felt great concern for those families who long to obey God when they can't see past the next step in front of them. We believe that it is important that they know that there will be many times when the need will be great, and even overwhelming, and when God will remain silent – that they know we also pass through trying times like this. But because we also believe that sometimes God calls us to reveal our needs only to Him until the time that He chooses to meet those needs, we have been struggling with how to make it clear to people that this is a fact of life when trying to learn how to live a life of total dependence on God. We walk a fine line always between trying to share our struggles honestly and at the right time, or giving the impression that we view ourselves either as struggling martyrs or wealthy, comfortable recipients of a constant stream of "goodies." Because we feel a responsibility to share with the world that God truly can be trusted, but that there will be times when we all – even the Rosenows – will wonder if this is true, we feel that the time to share some personal and specific things has now come. . . .

As we have been praying and praying for help in many areas – some of these are areas that require huge, miraculous, even impossible, answers to prayer – we have been greeted most often, lately, with a frightening silence from God. Or even worse, an increasing need in some of the areas that most need answers has been met with still greater need. . . . We have prayed for help with repairs that we knew were needed on the van, and in answer to this plea for help, the water pump has gone out, or the fuel pump or . . . the list goes on and on. . . .

God continued to care for us in small ways, but our fearful and clouded human vision caused us to view these instances of help more like Band-Aids when we felt like we needed major surgery. A gift card to Meijer from an anonymous giver made it possible for Scott to get a couple of new pairs of pants for work, since the ones he was wearing literally had holes forming in the seats. Another gift replaced his shoes which had holes in the soles. Hand-me-downs provided, once again, clothes the children needed for the changing weather, and birthday money from grandparents provided new pajamas for all of them. Our dentist wrote off everything insurance wouldn't cover when I broke a tooth and had to have it repaired. You would think that all of these things would be enough to keep our trembling hearts fixed solidly on His face, but we are not as strong as people seem to think we are, and the growing list of needs seemed always much bigger than these reminders that God was still there.

Then suddenly, about two weeks ago, after many months of our wondering if God was even hearing our cries for help, He began showering us with blessings over a period of a few days. An example of this came when we opened our mailbox one day and found an unbelievably generous gift for our family from a dear *family we know. We praised God and began calculating how far we could stretch this amazing blessing, and exactly what should be paid with it. We thought that we could, first and foremost, get our checking account back in balance and pay off all of the overdraft charges for the medical and car repair bills. . . . We decided to keep just enough to put new tires on the van, since two of them were already into the wear markers and snow will be coming soon. These tires had been a huge burden on Scott's mind for months, and he was so excited to finally be able to replace them. We paid the money out to all of these areas, but just before we bought the tires, we realized that, somehow, we had forgotten to take out the tithe portion of this gift. We readily did that, knowing that there was now no longer enough money to buy tires. However, God had restored our confidence in trusting Him, and we were able to boldly ask Him to provide money for the tires. Tears literally flowed when about four hours later, a DHL truck drove into our driveway and delivered a gift check from someone else! That was on a Friday. The next morning, Scott went out to investigate buying tires, even though we weren't sure there was quite enough to cover the expense once we also took out our tithe portion of this most recent gift. He found a dealer who was having a sale — buy three, get one free — on the exact tires we needed for the van. It cost us $1.37 over the amount we had to spend. . . . We cannot ever possibly know all the reasons God handles our prayer requests in the ways He chooses to do so. We cannot understand all the ways He may use our situations to further His Kingdom — even, maybe especially, when He tarries in answer to our cries. We must only* *trust Him. "'For my thoughts are not your thoughts, neither are your ways my ways,' declares the* LORD.*" (Isaiah 55:8)*

We closed out the year 2003 with renewed conviction that we were on the road God had laid out for us, with reinvigorated determination to trust in Him alone, and with refreshed dedication to follow Him wherever He led. After our painful experience with Aidan, though, our eyes were opened to the fact—in a new and poignant way—that beginning an adoption does not guarantee its completion. Sometimes God may lead us into the fight for a child without intending for us to bring that child home. In our service to God, it is usually the battle that matters, as the outcome is His. This truth caused us to wrestle, a bit, with our resolution, knowing the heartache that can come in such struggles. We also wondered how many more children were out there, waiting for us to come and fight for them, and what their stories might look like.

Over and above everything, though, we knew that we could trust the One who held the answers to all such questions safely in the palm of His hand.

Chapter 12

Awed by Answered Prayers

There are more tears shed over answered
prayers than over unanswered prayers.

St. Teresa of Avila

Welcome, 2004

Any parent who has experienced the birth of a child knows that there is almost nothing in the world to compare with it. The emotional impact is life-changing, as is everything that follows. And any parent who has experienced the *rebirth* of a child—the new birth into the kingdom of God—knows that there is almost nothing in the world to compare with that, too. But I think that, if possible, the rebirth of an adopted child is even more impactful, even more emotional. Not only is your child's name written in the Lamb's book of life,[25] but your child has been snatched from the very hand of Satan, from a destiny of hopelessness and utter lostness. It is undeniable that *all* children are lost and face a destiny of hopelessness, were it not for God's saving grace, but somehow

235

this outcome seems even more certain for a child growing up in an orphanage, far removed from the regular proclamation of the gospel, than for a child growing up in a Christian home.

Meghan came to us one day in January 2004, when she was almost eight, and said that she wanted to become a Christian. Whenever one of our children tells us that he or she wants to become a Christian, we sit down with them and discuss it, examining both their motivation and their understanding. One of our children, some years earlier, after having said that he wanted to become a Christian, admitted in our discussion that the reason was because he wanted to be able to drink the grape juice when the church observed Communion. (We decided that he was not yet ready, by the way.)

Kathy and I sat down with Meghan and talked about everything involved in becoming a Christian and what it means to be a Christian. After about half an hour of discussion, we came to the conclusion that she really did understand what she was undertaking, and that her heart was genuinely desirous of being a child of God. She knew for a certainty that she was a sinner, that as such she deserved God's wrath and eternal punishment, and that the only way she could be saved was through the finished work of Christ on the cross, appropriated through faith in Him. We sat with her as she prayed to God for His salvation, to become a member of His family through adoption.

It was a powerful moment for Kathy and me, to see this child who had come to us from an orphanage in Communist China, who had challenged us in so many areas, who had once or twice made us wonder if we had heard God correctly when He called us to adopt her — to see her on our couch, surrendering her life and her heart to the saving grace and lordship of Jesus Christ. Every Christian parent prays for the salvation of his or her children, and it is quite simply an awesome thing to see those prayers answered.

Once again we were struck with the heartfelt conviction that we would continue doing this, continue adopting children as God led us, for however long He chose to use us in this ministry.

Che Lan Lan

During the first three months of 2004, on top of our busy and demanding life, an amazing story unfolded involving our family and China. To tell the story, though, I have to back up just a bit.

The Xi'an Railway Station in Shaanxi Province, China, is huge, covering more than six million square feet and serving more than eighty thousand passengers daily. One day in February of 2003, someone placed a small bundle on one of the seats in the second waiting hall of this busy railway station, and walked away. The bundle was a little girl only two years old. She was beautiful, with big dark eyes, a tiny button nose, and lots of curly black hair. But she was also a little bit broken: she had been born with a form of spina bifida that had left her unable to walk, paralyzed from about the knees down in both legs. She also was completely unable to control her bladder and bowel functions.

Later in the day, this baby girl was taken to the Xi'an Social Welfare Institute[26] (SWI) and committed to the care of the special-needs unit on the fourth floor. They decided to call her Che Lan

Lan (chuh lahn lahn). Lan Lan was described as being withdrawn and not connecting well with either her caregivers or the other children at the SWI. She appeared to be a very sad little girl. The trauma Lan Lan must have felt when she was abandoned at the train station left her, like our Robyn, with deep and long-lasting emotional scars.

When IAAP sent the information and picture of Lan Lan to TSC for posting on our website, back in the fall of '03, Kathy was immediately struck by Lan Lan's beauty and how unusual it was for a Chinese child to have naturally curly hair. She printed out a picture and left it on the kitchen table, just to show me when I came home from work. Allan, who by this time was a commuting student at the University of Cincinnati, came in from classes that afternoon and spotted Lan Lan's picture on the table. He picked it up and said something like, "Who's the little girl?"

Kathy explained that she had been among IAAP's new children to be listed on our website and told him that she had printed it out because of all that curly hair. Allan then asked, "Are we going to adopt her?"

We knew the realities, however: China at the time was not even considering large families for adoption, and their definition of large was "more than five children in the home." We had ten children still in the home, and we felt certain, after the outcome of our battle for Aidan, that the Chinese officials wouldn't give us a second glance. Allan felt that we should at least try and urged us to do so, but we felt it would be ridiculous even to consider it, and we dismissed the suggestion.

Lan Lan was on IAAP's list of waiting children and on TSC's website for several months. Her information and picture were viewed nearly two thousand times on IAAP's website, and not once did a serious inquiry result. It seemed that everyone, like Kathy, was struck by her beauty and drawn to her listing. But as soon as they read the extent of her disabilities, their interest would end. Not one of these families expressed any desire to adopt this beautiful but needy child. Kathy mentioned to Dick in a phone conversation that Allan had been urging us to try to adopt Lan Lan, and that we would love to have her but knew it would not ever be possible.

In January of 2004, Dick and Cheryl told us that China had recently approved a family with nine children, and if we were still interested, they would be willing to advocate for our adoption of Lan Lan—who at the time still had never had anyone consider adopting her. We submitted the necessary pre-approval paperwork, not even allowing ourselves to hope at all. Then, we waited.

In early February, the Chinese officials contacted Dick and Cheryl to express concern over our ability to care for so many children adequately. They were requesting information on how we were able to meet the needs of the children, love them all, feed them all, and so forth. This was amazing to us because it meant that they were actually *considering* us. The fact that they hadn't immediately said no, but were instead asking for more information, seemed like a very good sign to us, and it did to Dick and Cheryl, too. We began to feel just a flicker of hope in our hearts.

Dick suggested that we contact all of our friends and ask them to write letters of endorsement on our behalf, to help convince the officials at the CCAA (China Center of Adoption Affairs) that our family could be exactly what Lan Lan needed. We wrote to all of our friends and supporters and explained the situation. We invited any who felt they knew us and had seen us interact with our children, to write letters on our behalf. We wanted to send a large number of such letters to China, to strengthen our case and show the CCAA that we really could take care of one more child.

Our friends responded enthusiastically. So many letters were sent in on our behalf that Dick's contact in China asked us to stop. She couldn't handle any more letters. She diligently translated them all and sent them to the CCAA. And again, we waited.

Finally, on April 2, we got word that China had approved us to adopt Che Lan Lan! We almost couldn't believe it. God had answered the prayers of hundreds of people and granted our petition to make this child a Rosenow. The incongruity of it all served to reinforce in our minds the conviction that God had brought this child into our lives, that she was truly a Rosenow, and that our exciting overseas adventures had not yet come to an end.

We threw ourselves, heart and soul, into the adoption dossier preparations and fund-raising, and we made the decision to change Lan Lan's name to Caelyn Karina, which means "Loved forever, dear little one." We all fell deeply in love with her soon after committing to pursuing her adoption, and those feelings had only grown as we had worked and prayed to obtain approval from the CCAA. And we knew that God loved her before we knew she existed, and even before she was born.

TSC's Celebration Banquet

Our annual Celebration Banquet was more impactful than usual in 2004. We were pleased to welcome some very special guests for our evening of celebration, reflection, praise, and fellowship. Dick Graham, the founder and director of International Assistance and Adoption Project (IAAP), made the trip up from Tennessee to be with us, and Hannah, IAAP's in-country liaison, flew over from China, to be with us, too. Many of TSC's China families were thrilled to be able to join us that evening and to see Hannah again. Hannah was, in turn, more than a little excited to see many of the children whose adoptions she had been so instrumental in facilitating. There were very few dry eyes in the banquet hall that evening, as the real-life impact of the work we were doing was felt by so many.

While Hannah was visiting in the States, Kathy and I were privileged to welcome her into our home for a couple of days. It was amusing for us to see her, again and again, exclaim with disbelief as she saw how beautifully the children were doing. She was especially taken with Meghan, whose transformation was, for Hannah, nothing short of miraculous. She repeatedly said to Kathy, "It's a miracle! I can't believe it's the same girl! She was *so* bad, and look at her now."

Hannah went from room to room throughout the time she spent with us, making notes in a little notebook she had brought with her. She explained that she wanted to be able to tell the officials back in China, and to back it up with documentation, that it is possible for a large family to meet the needs of the children, and that each child was loved and nurtured without exception.

China, here we come — again

Shortly after our Celebration Banquet, we received our travel authorization (TA) for Che Lan Lan, soon to be known officially as Caelyn Karina Rosenow, now three and a half. We realized, based on the shock we felt when we received the TA, that we had been subconsciously expecting that somehow the Chinese government would, in the end, find a reason not to let us finish Caelyn's adoption. But that was not to be the case. We were set to travel to China from July 6 through July 23.

As thrilled as we were that we were about to travel, we were also faced with a situation God had never brought to us before. We didn't have all of the money needed to complete Caelyn's adoption. We hadn't received as many donations as we'd hoped, and a small government reimbursement grant that had been awarded to us with our previous adoptions was no longer available for international adoptions. We continued praying and asking God to send the needed funds as we watched the days tick away. Finally, it became clear that the money was not going to come this time.

For the first time ever, we had to take on debt to complete an adoption. But we were so convinced that God had brought this little girl to us and had orchestrated every step in Caelyn's adoption journey, that we decided to trust Him in every area — even in taking on debt to bring her home. We could not imagine God's being pleased with us if we had said, "No, we're not going to get her, because it is more important for us to remain debt-free than it is to save the life of another human being." So we borrowed the needed funds, and we headed to China.

We arrived at our hotel in Xi'an at around 10:00 p.m. on July 11. Imagine our surprise when we found several orphanage officials waiting for us in the lobby, along with a sleeping Caelyn Karina— who was, incidentally, running a fever of 104 degrees Fahrenheit. She didn't really wake up as we were going through all of the greetings and formalities, and she didn't really wake up when we took her to our room, along with one of the workers from the orphanage. We got her settled into her bed for the night, said good-bye to the orphanage worker, and prepared to get ready for bed. Then Caelyn woke up. Needless to say, she was not happy.

We had a very long night with our little curly-headed wonder. We gave her some medicine for her fever and settled her back into bed. Even attempting to hold her sent her into hysterics of fear, and as pitiful as it was to hear her lie in bed and cry, and as much as it broke our hearts not to be able to offer her comfort, we had no choice, as she clearly preferred not to have any physical contact with us. She eventually fell asleep. Kathy and I woke frequently during the night to check on her, to see that her fever hadn't gone up and to make sure she was all right. We were concerned that her fever might be due to a urinary tract infection, which is not at all uncommon in kids with spina bifida. We were greatly relieved in the wee hours of the morning when we heard Caelyn begin coughing, as it looked like her fever might be due to a cold or flu rather than a urinary tract infection.

The next morning, Caelyn was very sullen and withdrawn, much as Stephen had been initially—though without the wailing and crying. We spent the morning going through all of the usual steps to complete the adoption, and by about 11:00 a.m., we were done. We went back to our hotel and felt that we could actually, finally begin the process of trying to get to know this newest little Rosenow, who wasn't at all interested in getting to know us. By this time, we were well enough acquainted with this early stage of rejection not to feel any concern over it, and Kathy and I tried to give Caelyn as much space as possible, to let her begin to get to know us in her own way and in her own time. We very patiently, very slowly made it possible for Caelyn to move toward us.

For example, we had brought a cookie matching game with us. I would sit near Caelyn on the floor and play with plastic cookies, placing them one at a time into the cookie jar, and then dumping them out and starting over again. Every once in a while, I would offer one of the cookies to Caelyn, to see if she would like to place it in the jar. For a long time she would simply ignore the cookie, in which case I would, after a minute or so, pick the cookie up myself and place it into the cookie jar.

Finally, though, she picked up one of the cookies and placed it into the jar herself. Kathy sat close by, watching this game, occasionally sneaking pictures with the camera, and she marveled over the miracle that God had actually gifted us with this newest daughter. It still seemed almost impossible, even though she was right there in front of us. Gradually, Caelyn began playing the game with me, and then with Kathy and me together. Initially, if we tried to talk to her or make eye contact with her during the game, she would slowly drop her cookie and turn her face away, staring blankly into space. It was agonizing for us to see the pain manifested in this precious child's innocent face and actions. She clearly desired to play with toys and just be a little girl, but the inculcated mistrust of adults, the ones who should've protected her and cared for her but hadn't, left her unable to do so. We knew that it would take time for her to know that we were in her life to stay forever, and that we would love and defend her to the point of even giving our lives for her, if necessary.

Kathy and I are continually amazed at the transformation that occurs in the lives of these little ones. Within a couple of days, Caelyn was allowing us to hold her and talk to her, to dress her, and to hold her hand when we walked beside her stroller. In fact, she quickly became so attached to us and so dependent upon us that she would seem to grow frightened when we all left the hotel room, and she would stay very close to us in such situations. I think we can only imagine the metamorphosis that takes place in their minds, these children who are adopted into a new family. They must process an overpowering fear, which quickly becomes familiarity that then becomes dependence, and eventually it blooms into love. The first few steps happen very quickly, while the ultimate transformation from fear and mistrust into a child's love for her parents can take months, or even years. Caelyn, as the other little Rosenows before her, progressed to a certain point in attaching and trusting us, but her ability to surrender her heart completely to us did, indeed, take years. And as with the others, it was a beautiful process.

The remainder of our trip to China was fairly uneventful, and we returned home near the end of July. We immediately began the long list of medical appointments, tests, and evaluations for Caelyn.

We first had her evaluated by the neurosurgeon. His conclusion was that Caelyn was suffering from tethered spinal cord syndrome, as Carlin had, and he told us that surgery to release the tethered cord was needed as soon as possible. We also had her evaluated by Carlin's urology specialist, who determined that she, like Carlin, would need to be catheterized regularly because of her neurological damage. We put the two girls on the same schedule, and team catheterizations every four hours became a way of life for us.

An unexpected turn

Just four days after we returned from China with Caelyn, we received an e-mail from TSC's Guatemala contact, Melissa. She was writing to tell us about a baby girl in Guatemala City who was about three months old, and who was exhibiting some pretty significant issues, including microcephaly[27] and brain damage. Melissa had been given only a very short time to find a family for this baby before she was to be officially declared "unadoptable" and moved to a horrible institution for the mentally disabled. Melissa was very familiar with this facility and she knew that, if this baby were institutionalized there, she would spend the remainder of her life in emotional darkness, left alone in an enclosed crib with virtually no human touch.

Six other families had briefly considered adopting this precious little girl, but all had changed their minds, one by one. As Melissa sat that afternoon and rocked this baby, praying that God would bring a family to her before it was too late, our names came to mind. She knew we had just arrived home four days earlier with a child who had significant special needs; she knew that we had accumulated debt during that adoption; and she knew that it was probably crazy for her to approach us. But she also felt unmistakably that this was exactly what God was prompting her to do. So she contacted us and boldly asked if we would pray about adopting this baby no one else seemed to want.

Many years earlier, when we began looking into the question of adoption, we gave consideration to the various special needs we thought we could "handle." Our experience with Erin and Ryan and their various medical issues had made us feel comfortable with a variety of possible disabilities, such as missing limbs, spina bifida, cleft palate/lip, and so forth. We did not formulate an exhaustive list but, as we related in an earlier chapter, we did feel that any significant cognitive impairment would be more than we could handle. Thus, we left that "special need" off of our list of children we would consider adopting.

Interestingly, it was our experience with Erin and her cognitive difficulties that led us, in part, to conclude that we were not equipped to take on a child with mental disabilities. We felt that we had been stretched to the very limit, and beyond. These feelings of inadequacy, and our multiplication of that inadequacy should the demands be even greater, convinced us that God had not equipped us or called us to adopt a child with this type of special need.

It is important, by the way, for adopting families to give thoughtful consideration to their own strengths and weaknesses—the ways in which God has equipped them—before saying yes or no to any referral. There are two important sides to this question.

The first has to do with adoptions that don't "work out"; the second has to do with being used by God in spite of our own inadequacies.

As to the first side, we see over and over again cases in which families end up dissolving a legally completed adoption because the child turns out to be more than the family can handle. There are more and more of these dissolutions occurring every year. We urge prospective adoptive families to pray diligently before committing to the adoption of a child. It is critically important to seek God's face in such a life-changing decision, and it would be utterly foolish for a Christian to approach it with less than such an attitude of dependence.

As to the second side, however, I will add that Kathy and I are suggesting that the family pray for the equipping and commitment and perseverance from the Lord to be able to handle whatever comes. We are not recommending a window-shopping approach to adoption, in which the prospective adopter says, "Let me see what you've got and I'll choose my child." Rather, we are advocating a more responsible, more committed approach that says, "Lord, lead me to the child You have for me and then, please Lord, give me whatever I'll need to be that child's parent, forever." We simply cannot do this, this adopting of children, on our strength alone. We must depend on and utilize the strength that only God can—and will—supply. More on that will come out later in this book.

So when Melissa shared the information with us on this little girl in Guatemala, whose name was Zoila, we were utterly taken aback. The information indicated that she would most likely exhibit severe cognitive impairment, probably would have cerebral palsy, and would almost certainly suffer from seizures. There were even opinions suggesting that she might be blind and deaf, on top of the other issues. Based on these descriptions, and based on what we knew of ourselves, we felt ill-equipped to parent this child. We experienced fear.

Our whole family took this situation to God in prayer. We had committed to pursuing the adoptions of as many children as God led us to, but we hadn't reckoned on this turn of events—that God might lead us to pursue the adoption of a child with severe brain damage. In fact, we had been certain that God would not lead us into such an adoption. We had eight little children at home now, in addition to the four older ones. How could we meet the needs of all those children *and* a severely brain-damaged baby? These thoughts—in addition to the fact that we had just arrived home from China, we were experiencing the worst jetlag we had ever known, and we were struggling with our confusion about the debt we had been left with from Caelyn's adoption—led us to think it almost impossible that God would really take us there.

I'm going to include an excerpt from a story Kathy wrote, some years later, about this whole experience. This excerpt deals, in particular, with how she, Kathy, wrestled with God over this huge decision for our family.

Our whole family was scared to death to move forward with even considering the adoption of this little girl. In spite of his fear, though, Scott was ready to obey God. I, on the other hand, was just so terrified that I obstinately refused to even open my heart to

249

any leading from God in this area. One night, I'm ashamed to say, I even stated aloud to Scott and our older kids that I absolutely would not agree to adopt this child under any circumstances. After a shocked silence from all of them, I went to bed and spent the night crying and wrestling with God in my sin and misery. Finally about 4:00 a.m. I got up to pray. Pouring my fears out to God, I confessed the sinfulness of my heart, surrendered my will to His, and told Him that I would obey Him if it was His plan to bring this child to us, but that I would need so much more from Him than I had ever needed up to that point. By the next evening, Scott and I both knew that God was indeed asking us to move forward with adopting this little girl.

Once we all became convinced of this, we threw ourselves into the paperwork and fund-raising aspects. By early September, we were once again in the midst of an international adoption process, with full vigor and conviction. We still had concerns and fears about the future, but we were certain that God was leading us to do this, and we committed ourselves to trusting Him for the outcome, every step along the way.

We submitted Zoila's CT scan images to some physicians here in the States for interpretation. Their findings confirmed what we had been told earlier and reinforced our fears. The images revealed significant brain damage, and that she was missing portions of her brain, including a large part of her right frontal lobe. We were told that she could be essentially unable to interact with us or her surroundings, even unable to know us or recognize us as her family.

This represented new ground for us, in pursuing the adoption of a child who might be so isolated from us and so cut off from our love.

Zoila's prognosis continued to intimidate us, and the questions about her future loomed large on the horizon of our imagination, but we were now convinced that we were where God wanted us to be. This conviction gave us the courage to ask the tough questions and face the uncertain future. We began to get excited about bringing this baby home. She was our daughter, and she was way too far away from us—especially in light of her great need. We decided, in faith, to name her Kathryn Felicity, meaning "pure joy." It was our prayer and our desire that this child would be able to experience joy and be able to give joy to others, in spite of the dire predictions we had been given about her.

In the context of Kathryn's adoption, we came to know an adoption facilitator in Guatemala, named Mary, without whose help we would never have been able to bring Kathryn home. She worked diligently with the listing attorney in Guatemala City to move the case along as quickly as possible, and she helped tremendously with the fund-raising on our behalf. In fact, she and a co-worker donated their Christmas bonuses to Kathryn's adoption, generously caring more about this little girl than about how they might've been able to use their bonuses on themselves. We are truly grateful to Mary and the ways in which she helped us in Guatemala.

End of '04

The fall of 2004 was lost in the mists of busyness, both on the ministry front and on the home front. We were scrambling to put together a dossier for Guatemala, a country we had never adopted from before, and we were working hard to get all of Caelyn's medical visits and procedures taken care of. During the month of August, we racked up a total of forty-six appointments, a new one-month record for us. Kathy was now home-schooling nine kids, ranging from high school to preschool, some of whom could barely speak and understand English. We were trying to learn as much as we could about what we might be facing with Kathryn when she came home from Guatemala.

Late in September, Caelyn underwent surgery to release her tethered spinal cord. The surgery went beautifully, and her recovery was actually faster than we anticipated. It took several months before all of her strength returned, but both we and her neurosurgeon were pleased with the outcome.

In November, the Rosenow family assembled in the Butler County Probate courtroom for the re-adoption of our eight adopted children. The probate judge, Randy Rogers—who is locally famous for his massive and loving heart toward adoption—made sure the entire experience was a beautiful and memorable one for all of us.

A few weeks before this re-adoption ceremony, Nathan became our second adopted child to embrace the gift of salvation by accepting Christ as his Savior. He was only seven at this time, but he had from a very young age exhibited a deeper grasp of spiritual matters than one would expect in such a young child. We felt certain that he fully understood the decision he had made that day in our family room. Our hearts once again soared as a result of this victory, and that day in court our eyes filled with tears when Nathan proudly proclaimed to Judge Rogers that he had now been adopted three times: "Once in Bolivia when Mommy and Daddy came for me, once into God's family when I became a Christian, and again today." We couldn't have expressed this better ourselves, and we praised God one more time, as we continued praying that all of our children would, in time, come to Christ themselves.

Late in December, right after Christmas, we received word that our adoption of Kathryn had been completed in Guatemala. We had never had an adoption go so smoothly or so quickly, and as always, we rejoiced at the way God had answered our prayers. Kathryn was just eight months old, her adoption had taken only four months to complete, and in contrast with Caelyn's case, God had provided all of the money needed for the adoption—even for all of the travel expenses. We were told that we could plan to fly to Guatemala to pick up our newest daughter sometime late in January, in plenty of time to be able to celebrate her first birthday together.

We ended 2004 awed by the fact that we had completed two adoptions, neither of which had even been started at the beginning of the year. One of these children was home with us, and we were eager to travel shortly after the new year to bring the other one home.

Chapter 13

Fearfully Heeding His Voice

To know that our faith is weak is

the first step toward its strengthening.

George MacDonald

Scott goes to work, differently

The previous September, we had written to all of TSC's supporters to let them know that The Shepherd's Crook had reached the point at which we could no longer function as we were. As I described a few chapters back, we were often staying up until very late at night, taking care of the running of the ministry, and we would have to get up early the next morning for the start of the new day. We were exhausted, and we were approaching burnout. Plus, we were regularly forced to turn away agencies who appealed to us for help in placing their waiting children. We simply could not handle any increase in our workload.

Our Board of Trustees came to the conclusion that we needed to hire a full-time director and that it logically needed to be me.

This was partly because I was already acting as the director, albeit in my "spare time," partly because Kathy and I had founded The Shepherd's Crook and established its vision for ministry, and partly because my heart had pretty much left the world of engineering and was longing to be doing the work of the ministry full time. So, we wrote to our supporters to let them know the situation and what our Board had decided. We invited people to pray with us on behalf of the ministry, and we asked any who might be interested in doing so to support TSC financially on an ongoing, monthly basis, to make this move possible.

By January 2005, we had received enough commitments of ongoing support to make it possible for me to transition to part-time work with The Shepherd's Crook while remaining with my engineering employer, also on a part-time basis. I have to say that my employer, PEDCO E&A Services, was absolutely wonderful throughout the whole of this period. They were very accommo-dating of my demanding schedule and my frequent absences for the adoptions and the many medical appointments, and they were very supportive of my decision to transition to part-time work, on the way toward a complete transition from engineering to directing the ministry.

So beginning on January 17, 2005, my new work schedule featured three days each week at PEDCO and two days each week, plus weekends, at home as Director of The Shepherd's Crook Orphan Ministry. This made it possible for me to accomplish what Kathy and I had been doing late at night, but it wasn't enough yet for us to move the ministry forward. It was survival mode, but we welcomed it enthusiastically and gratefully.

Guatemala

During this same time, we were making plans to travel to Guatemala to pick up our little girl who was, without even knowing it, waiting there for us. There was considerable anxiety for us as we looked forward to meeting Kathryn and beginning to get to know her, partly because of what we knew of her condition, and partly because of the unknowns surrounding her prognosis. In an e-mail Kathy wrote to her mother just before we traveled, she related the following thoughts:

When I was having to change [Kathryn's] appointments the other day over the phone, the nurse was reading some things from Kathryn's chart that had already been started there. She said, "Girl, born May 9, 2004, adopted from Guatemala, severe microcephaly . . ." I never heard anything after that until I realized that she was asking me to OK a date she had chosen for the appointment. It wasn't anything new to hear, but for some reason it was like someone had punched me in the stomach. . . . I felt so heavy, so sad, so scared. I think that since we can't know for sure what we are dealing with, we have been able to kind of not "go there" for now. We have "been there" several times since making the decision to adopt her, but for now, we had left it all in God's hands. And once I started buying and packing all of her little baby things, I was able to mostly just focus on bringing home my little baby girl. There was always some anxiety and a bit of a cloud over it all, but mostly she was just my new baby girl. . . . Hearing the nurse's words suddenly robbed me of all of that, and I was plunged into the fear of it all again."

On Sunday morning, January 23, 2005, Kathy and I boarded a plane bound for Guatemala City, Guatemala. The fact was not lost on us that this date was Sanctity of Human Life Sunday, the date on which many Americans pause to reflect on the true value of every human life. President Ronald Reagan established National Sanctity of Human Life Day in 1984,[28] to be observed on Sunday, January 23 of that year. In his proclamation, President Reagan called upon "the citizens of this blessed land to gather on that day in homes and places of worship to give thanks for the gift of life, and to reaffirm our commitment to the dignity of every human being and the sanctity of each human life." The Sunday closest to January 22 has been observed each year in the same way by millions of concerned Americans.[29] Kathy and I were keenly aware, as we boarded that plane and headed toward our daughter, that many people would consider this beautiful and cherished child not fit to live. In spite of our very human fears about our own ability to meet Kathryn's needs, it exhilarated our hearts to know that God had called us to play a part in demonstrating to the watching world just how precious her life, and every human life, is to Him.

We landed at the airport in Guatemala City, caught the shuttle bus to our hotel, and quickly got settled in. Later, our adoption facilitator, Mary, picked us up at the hotel and took us to the *hogar,* or orphanage, where Kathryn was living. Our hearts were broken when we first laid eyes on this sweet baby, who appeared to be locked in a world that had very little contact with our own. Her big, dark eyes seemed to look at the objects around her, including the people, without really seeing any of them. Though she was eight months old, she did not respond when addressed by name, and she seemed in almost every way like a newborn baby After spending about an hour at the orphanage, we took Kathryn back to our hotel and Mary left us alone to begin to get acquainted with Kathryn. To paint an accurate picture of what that afternoon looked like, I'm going to include another excerpt from the talk Kathy delivered about our first experiences with Kathryn.

> **Excerpt from "Kathryn's Story"**: *When we brought [Kathryn] to our hotel room, she was like a little body with no one inside at all — she was like an empty shell. She stared into space and wouldn't respond to any sound, no matter how sudden or how loud. She did indeed appear to be deaf and possibly blind, just as we had been told. I started to cry, placed her in Scott's arms, and went into the bathroom where I sat on the floor and cried while I begged God to help me know how to love a child who would never be able to love me back. I just kept saying, "God, I'm so scared. This is too big. I can't do this."*
>
> *I had to make a choice on that hotel bathroom floor to listen to what I knew God was calling me to do, regardless of what the future held, because I knew that this was for His glory. It wasn't about me or my comfort or pleasure. I found tremendous peace*

and courage in remembering that it was God who had brought us to that hotel in Guatemala, and that He was the One who had placed that brain-damaged baby in our arms as our child. That knowledge gave me enough courage and strength to start that first day with little Kathryn Felicity.

When we bring a new child into our family, we always choose a song to be that child's special song, and when I came back out into the hotel room, Scott was singing Kathryn's special song to her. Whether she could hear him or even know that he was there with her, Kathryn's daddy was singing to her. By the end of that first afternoon, Kathryn had made very brief eye contact with us. We kept singing to her, and by the next day, she had smiled at us. Music and love continued to unlock the world where Kathryn had locked herself safely away, and she rapidly became the brightest little light that God had ever brought into the life of the Rosenows. . . .

Rarely does a day pass when I don't think to myself, "I almost missed this because I was too afraid to go where God told me to go." And even when I was so obstinate and sinful in my fear, He chose to bless me with this beautiful gift anyway. He didn't need me to fulfill His plans for Kathryn's life. He could've accomplished these plans without me — in any way He liked. But He brought her to me. What a merciful Father we serve.

We can't always know how things will turn out when God calls us to step out in faith, but we can know that we will never have peace or be content if we refuse to obey Him. And He will *bring joy and peace into our lives when we do obey, and this joy can sometimes come from very surprising circumstances.*

The trip was a quick one. Because the adoption itself had been completed back in December, we were there primarily to pick up our new daughter, get her US immigrant visa, and take her home. We did manage to spend some time with Melissa, the TSC volunteer who had brought Kathryn to our attention the previous August. Melissa took us on a quick sightseeing and souvenir-buying trip one afternoon, and to an authentic Guatemalan steak house for dinner that evening. After a mere four days, we were done and headed home.

Home from Guatemala

We brought Kathryn home on Wednesday, January 26, and truly our world has not been the same since. We got home very late that night and woke up all of Kathryn's new brothers and sisters so they could meet her. They greeted their new baby sister, literally, with open arms and beaming smiles, completely unperturbed by her considerable disabilities. Kathryn, it turned out, was neither blind nor hearing impaired, though she did have some mild visual impairment. But she was and is profoundly brain-damaged, and she has significant cerebral palsy (CP). As Kathy said in her talk, above, Kathryn has turned out to be one of the brightest blessings God has brought us since we started adopting. Her future remains a bit of a mystery, but God answered our prayers concerning the name we chose for her: her smiles and giggles fill our home with joy, just as we asked of Him when we chose it. Every day with her brings increased happiness to the whole family, and we thank God for overcoming our fears and doubts by bringing this most precious child to us.

Once we got Kathryn home and began her battery of tests and evaluations, it was determined that she had a condition called schizencephaly. This is a rare developmental disorder in which abnormal clefts form in the brain. We further learned that Kathryn's type of schizencephaly was the more severe type, with what are called open- and closed-lip clefts on both sides of her brain. Schizencephaly is often accompanied by microcephaly, as in Kathryn's case.

The MRI which revealed the schizencephaly also showed that significant portions of Kathryn's brain were missing, especially in the area of her right frontal lobe. These findings reinforced some of the dire predictions that had been made about Kathryn's future, and they brought to light some issues we hadn't known about before. For example, we learned that kids with schizencephaly, and especially the bilateral type (i.e., on both sides of the brain), almost always have seizures, and the seizure activity often intensifies as the child grows older. An EEG of Kathryn's brain, recorded around this same time, indicated abnormal activity in certain areas of her brain, which strongly suggested either past seizures or the likelihood of future seizures — or both. But God has a significant role for her to play in this world, limited though her abilities may be, and we are honored that He chose us to be a part of her life and the discovery of that role for her.

Sunshine from the Midwest

In March, Kathy and I got an interesting e-mail from an adoption attorney we had worked with a number of times. The message told about a family in a nearby state who was looking to dissolve their adoption of a little boy from Guatemala. The family had adopted this child about seven months earlier, and they felt they had reached the point where his continued presence in their home was damaging the entire family. This little boy, who was just twenty-one months old, had already been labeled with reactive attachment disorder (RAD), attention deficit/hyperactivity disorder (ADHD), hyposensitivity (high pain threshold), and a host of other negative conditions.

Kathy called the adoptive mom to get more information about this little boy so we could begin to try to find a new family for him. That phone call was chilling. This woman made it clear that the child was not a welcome member of the family, was considered to be in the way, and could not leave too soon for the family's liking. She said that she couldn't stand the sight of him, and that they were more or less just feeding and bathing him until they could find another home for him.

We were heartbroken for this child and the conditions he was enduring. These people who were supposed to have been the answer to his prayers, whether actually spoken or not, had turned out to be another chapter in the nightmare of his young life. We immediately began to love this little lost boy and decided that our family might be the best place for him to heal from the hurts he had endured. We exchanged a few e-mails with the parents, and they concluded that we would be the right family for him.

We sensed an urgency in the situation, as the mother confessed to Kathy that neither she nor her husband would have any physical contact with this child. Though the adoptive mom stayed home every day and cared for their other children, she was sending this little boy to day care because she couldn't stand to have him in the house any more than was absolutely necessary. We called our adoption attorney to ask what could be done to get the child out of there as soon as possible, and he made arrangements for us to fly to a metropolitan city in the nearby state to meet this mom at the airport and bring this little one to our home on a respite basis. These arrangements called for us to meet her forty-eight hours later, and although we knew we had to do whatever it took to go get him, we also knew that we didn't have the money to buy the plane tickets. But a family in Florida—a friend of TSC and the Rosenows—sent us a monetary gift, which arrived the same day we decided we had to book our flights. This family, in sending the gift to us, stated that they didn't know how God intended to use it for us, but that they just knew He was leading them to send it. They had no idea we were involved in trying to help this little boy, let alone that we were planning to fly to another state to get him. They simply felt led by God to send it to us. The gift was enough to cover the cost of the plane tickets.

Our meeting with this adoptive mom at the airport was just as disturbing as the phone calls with her had been. She spent the whole time reciting all of the deficits—and worse—that characterized his life. When it was time for us to go, she looked at him, this little boy she had traveled to Guatemala to adopt and make her son, and she said to him, "Have a nice life." She did not hug him or even touch him. She seemed immensely relieved just to be rid of him.

This little boy was small for his age, quiet, and clearly frightened, but he came to Kathy's arms immediately, without any hesitation. Only once as we were heading to our gate to catch our flight home did he look around the airport and whisper, "Mama?" We told him that she had "gone bye-bye," that we were taking him to our home now, and that we loved him very much. Our hearts ached as we looked into his very confused face.

When we got him home, he was greeted by all of our kids, who couldn't wait to meet him and make him feel welcome in our home. That first evening, he had a very sudden, prolonged, and deep session of grieving. He crawled into Kathy's lap and sobbed for over an hour with all of the energy his small body possessed. He fell asleep after that, and the next morning he began settling into the routine of life in our home — without ever looking back again.

We knew without any question now that we wanted to move from respite to full-blown adoption, so we again contacted our attorney to find out how to begin this process. We also went through our typical name-selection for him and finally settled on Braedan Josiah, which means, "from a dark valley, God has healed." We truly felt that this little one had spent the first part of his life in a dark valley, and we were immensely blessed that God had chosen to place him into our family for his healing. This child, who was saddled with some terrible labels before coming to us, quickly became another bright beam of sunshine in our home. He would begin each day by running down the hall to our room, just to find Kathy and exclaim to her, "Good morning, Mommy!" His face just glowed, as if greeting the new day, and his new mommy, provided all the joy he needed in life. Time and again we say to ourselves, "That family's loss was our gain."

Family life in the Rosenow household now began to settle into a new form of "normal." I was home two days each week, in addition to the weekends, and that was a help on both the ministry and the family fronts. We now had ten little children, in addition to the four older kids. (Kristen had moved back in with us after finishing school and had taken a teaching job, while she sought God's will and direction for her future.)

Part-time becomes full-time

Throughout the winter and spring, the ministry continued to grow. The demands of running this fledgling enterprise were gradually pressing more and more on me, and on the whole family, to the extent that we realized that two days a week were no longer sufficient for me to be home. At the same time, though, our pleas and prayers for more ongoing monthly support had not been realized. There wasn't enough in the budget to pay my salary and overhead on a full-time basis. And so we continued to pray.

In May, we got some stunning news. A church here in town, Vineyard Community Church, was celebrating its twentieth anniversary. As part of that celebration, they were awarding a gift of $20,000 each month of the year to a local charity or ministry that shared some of the beliefs and missional goals of the Vineyard. Some friends of The Shepherd's Crook nominated TSC for one of the awards and in May, TSC was awarded this amazing gift. This blessing made it possible for The Shepherd's Crook to continue its work, by making it possible for me to transition to full-time with the ministry. We knew that if I were to take a deeper cut in pay than we had been originally anticipating, relative to the salary I was earning as an engineer, we could stretch that $20,000 out to cover the balance of my salary for the remainder of the year.

TSC's Board of Trustees initially struggled with taking this step because they had hoped to be able to pay us more than the amount this gift would enable us to receive. Kathy and I, however, were peaceful with the knowledge that God was clearly calling us to step out in faith and move forward with this smaller-than-expected salary, and to trust Him to provide for our family in His own ways. The Board finally agreed and voted to do this.

My last day with PEDCO was June 10. On Monday, June 13, 2005, I began my career as the full-time paid Director of The Shepherd's Crook Orphan Ministry.

A balm for our souls, and a suntan

There is a great deal of talk in our society about annual family vacations, and there are many opinions as to whether or not these vacations are "necessary." One school of thought promotes the idea that a family needs to get away from the daily grind at least once each year, for time to relax, refresh, and reconnect with each other. The family vacation presents a great opportunity for all of these, and its proponents argue that it is not merely beneficial, but necessary. Another school of thought argues that, while vacations are usually fun and refreshing, they are not "necessary" in the sense that other things, such as food, shelter, and medical care, are. The Bible includes no precept concerning vacations, and it is difficult to reason that they really satisfy any requirement of the term "necessary." And if a family is not spending time all through the year connecting with each other, whether through family devotionals, or over dinner, or when discussing books or movies, or in contemplating the weekly worship services attended together, then a once-a-year vacation is not likely, in and of itself, to bring any sort of long-term connectedness.

Notwithstanding all of these considerations, Kathy and I were feeling, as we neared the summer of 2005, that our family would really benefit from some sort of a vacation. We hadn't had any form of a family vacation in ten or so years, and we were certain that a bit of time away from the pressures and demands of everyday life would be beneficial to all of us. We found ourselves praying that God would provide some sort of get-away for us, some way to recharge our batteries and devote a little focused time to our kids, especially the newest ones.

The answer to these prayers came unexpectedly, as God's answers so often do. A friend of a friend of our family was planning to travel to visit relatives out of state during late July, and they wanted to offer us the use of their home while they were gone. Their house was a bit bigger than ours, especially the kitchen, and they had an in-ground swimming pool. They thought it would be a nice break for us and the kids to be able to get away from the normal, and just settle in for a time of relaxation and swimming and other fun stuff. They were to be gone for a little over a week, and they were offering the use of their home for the whole time.

This little excursion turned out to be one of the nicest vacations our family has ever had. We really did just escape. We shut down the ministry for a week—arranging for another staff volunteer to cover any emergencies that might arise—and we left our computers at home and just took it easy for about eight days. We are still thankful for that time of healing and rest—and we got to enjoy the same thing the next three years, as well. God knew exactly what we needed, and He prompted one of His families to provide it for us.

Colin's vision

In September we took Colin, who was now seven, to see his retina specialist in Detroit for a routine exam under anesthesia. The exam revealed that Colin's left retina, the one that had remained viable and was giving him a measure of light perception, had deteriorated—that most of the improvements of the previous surgeries had been reversed. His retina specialist was deeply distressed at what he found. He told us that the retina had once again detached and that it had apparently developed a small hole or tear. But the fact that Colin was still able to perceive light in that left eye gave the surgeon proof that the retina was still viable, still able to be saved. The surgeon gave us about a fifty percent chance that they would be able once again to repair the damage and help the retina settle back into place, but that another surgery would be required. If this surgery were not performed, the retinal tissue would soon begin to die, and even the small amount of light perception that Colin retained would thereafter be lost. We were scheduled to return to Detroit in about a week for that surgery.

We took Colin back to Detroit on October 3. The surgery was fairly involved and required several important steps, but it went well. The surgeon had been able to complete the several steps he had planned, making it possible for the retina to relax and conform more naturally to the interior contour of the eye — which is necessary for the retina to receive images (or just light) and transmit them to the optic nerve. He also told us that they discovered, once they got inside Colin's eye, that the retina was not torn, as they had previously believed. This was very good news.

Following the surgery, the surgeon again felt that the retina would remain viable and that Colin would retain his light perception. Before, during, and after the surgery, we prayed to the Great Physician that He would do just that — i.e., save Colin's retina and his light perception — and we continue to trust Him in this area. Before we left for Detroit, we met with the elders of our church to pray for Colin and this surgery. One of the prayers that was lifted up that day was that the results would be even better than anyone was expecting. And that was exactly how Colin's surgeon described the results: better than any of them expected. Praise God!

More in store for Caelyn

In October, after the dust had settled following Colin's surgery, we met with the team of surgeons in the urology department at

Cincinnati's Children's Hospital Medical Center (CCHMC). The doctors were discussing plans for a major surgery for Caelyn, which would, if we decided to go forward with it, take place in about a year. Caelyn suffers from bladder and bowel incontinence as a result of the nerve damage caused by her spina bifida. She was looking at the prospect of having to wear diapers all her life because of this condition, and at nearly five years of age, this was becoming an area of concern for her. The surgeons at CCHMC were proposing an operation to modify both her urinary tract and her intestinal tract, to help her achieve what is called social continence, the ability to prevent leaks and lead a more normal life. But the surgery and its recovery would be significant, and not to be entered into lightly.

The plan was to reconstruct her bladder, to prevent further leakage, and to create a Mitrofanoff,[30] through which she would catheterize herself for the rest of her life. If the team determined during the surgery that the reconstruction of the bladder resulted in its being thereafter too small, then they would also increase the size of the bladder by borrowing a portion of Caelyn's large intestine. This is called bladder augmentation. The final step in the long surgery would be to create a Malone[31] to permit Caelyn to flush out her large intestine every day, to keep her bowel clean. These procedures, combined, were required for her to achieve overall social continence. The bad news in all of this was found on several levels. First, the surgery would be lengthy and somewhat dangerous. If augmentation of the bladder were required, Caelyn would be under anesthesia for as long as fourteen hours. That, in itself, is difficult and dangerous. But we also learned that augmenting the bladder can increase the child's risk of developing bladder cancer later on, once he or she becomes a young adult. Caelyn would have to have annual exams starting from her early teens, to monitor the condition of her bladder for possible signs of cancer.

The length of the surgery was intimidating, but we were also told that Caelyn would be in the hospital for somewhere between ten days and two weeks, depending on exactly what they had to do during surgery and how quickly her body would recover. She would begin with two full days of pre-operative preparation, and then eight to twelve days of recovery following the surgery. So in addition to everything involved for Caelyn, we would have to make plans for one or both of us to be with her during her entire time in the hospital — which is no small task for a family with thirteen children, nine of whom were nine or younger.

We spent weeks considering and praying about this surgery. If we elected not to pursue it, then it would mean that Caelyn would spend the rest of her life in diapers of some sort. If we elected to do the surgery, then the risks, both now and down the road, were considerable. After much prayer and discussion, we decided to go ahead with plans for the surgery, weighing the certain against the uncertain, and trusting God's provision no matter which way things went. The surgery was to take place the following October.

Christmas of 2005 found us celebrating with a family of thirteen children. It seemed that every year we found ourselves a larger family than we had been the year before. It wouldn't be quite accurate to say that we had more to be thankful for, but there were definitely more of us being thankful. And our celebrations, all of them, were becoming a bit louder, a bit more energetic.

We were large enough now that it had become difficult to go out as a group without attracting a measure of interest, and usually a comment or question. The children were all very well behaved, and sometimes that fact alone was enough to prompt someone to comment. Other times it was the diversity of our crew that drew remarks. But in every case, we were pleased to be able to relate how God had grown our family and blessed the two of us so much beyond our expectations.

Chapter 14

Broken Hearts

The bitter cup which it may please the Lord that you shall drink
this year will not be mixed by human hands. In the hand of the
Lord is that cup!

Octavius Winslow

Maria Fernanda

In mid-January 2006, we learned of a newborn baby girl in
Guatemala who, unknown to us then, would come to hold a
significant place both in the hearts of the Rosenow family and in
the hearts of many throughout the extended TSC family. TSC's
Guatemala Family Coordinator, Melissa, traveled to Guatemala
City early in the month to check up on the TSC kids there and to
help obtain important medical tests for some of them. She had
learned of the birth of a baby girl just before her trip, and when she
arrived in country, she was told of the serious medical condition
this baby faced. The baby's name was Maria Fernanda, and she
had been born with a life-threatening heart condition. Though we

273

were all committed to doing everything possible to find a family for Maria right away, we also knew that Maria would not survive a typical lengthy adoption process because of the severity of her heart condition.

Melissa and Mary — the same adoption coordinator who was so instrumental in helping us adopt Kathryn — took Maria to UNICAR to seek treatment for her soon after she was born. UNICAR (*Unidad de Cirugía Cardiovascular,* or the Cardiovasular Surgery Unit) is located in Guatemala City and is considered the leading cardiac care facility in all of Central America. The physician Melissa and Mary met with told them that there was nothing that could be done for this baby, and that they should do the best they could to make her comfortable during what would be her short life. These two women, however, were not content with this advice. Melissa contacted us to intercede on behalf of Maria, to ask us to commit ourselves and all of TSC's prayer supporters to pray for this baby, and to see if we might be able to come up with some plan to help her survive.

The unfolding of Maria Fernanda's story was intense and involved, but we decided very early on that the best approach would be for us to obtain an emergency medical visa to bring her to the States for heart surgery. Through a series of events and the help of a number of friends of TSC, we contacted a hospital in the Boston area that agreed to donate medical care for Maria, if we could get her there. While we worked on the many pieces required to obtain the medical visa at this end, Melissa made arrangements to take Maria to stay with her in her hotel room, to begin providing immediate and around-the-clock attention and care for her. We arranged for TSC's Medical Ministries Coordinator, Alison,[32] who is a registered nurse specializing in neonatal care, to fly to Guatemala to stay with Melissa and Maria, to provide any nursing-level medical care that might be needed in the short term. Our plan was to help this fragile baby survive the weekend, God willing, and get her back to UNICAR on Monday morning.

The reason for taking Maria back to UNICAR was twofold: first, we thought it would be advisable to get her on a stabilizing medication, to buy time for her struggling heart; second, we knew that, in order to apply for an emergency medical visa to the United States, we would need documentation from a local physician, stating that the care Maria needed was not available in Guatemala. We thought that this documentation would be no problem, since UNICAR had previously refused to treat Maria. The weekend was very touch-and-go for the baby. There were a few times when Alison and Melissa were afraid they were losing her. But she did survive.

On Monday, Melissa and Alison took Maria to UNICAR and asked the on-duty cardiologist for the letter they would need to take to the US Consulate, to request a medical visa. The cardiologist, who was a different doctor than the one who had turned them away the previous week, stunned them when, after examining Maria Fernanda, she said that she would not write the letter because the surgery the baby needed was, in fact, available in Guatemala—at UNICAR. This compassionate doctor told them that Maria's condition seemed very serious, and she scheduled an echocardiogram (echo) for later that morning.

The results of the echo were grim. Maria's heart was failing, and the doctors felt that she needed surgery immediately. In fact, they said that they did not believe Maria would survive the night if Melissa took her back to the hotel. Her blood oxygen saturation levels, which should be in the upper nineties or even one hundred percent, were hovering in the mid-sixties. Consequently, the surgery was scheduled for that very afternoon. By the time she went in for the surgery, her saturation levels were in the forties—a life-threatening condition. This surgery was considered a stop-gap procedure to keep her alive and allow her body to continue to grow, but she would need a much more major surgery when she was a bit older and stronger, at about four months of age, to repair the damage to her heart. Everyone hoped and prayed that she would be adopted before the need for that surgery arrived, safe in the United States and with access to our advanced medical care.

Kathy and I, back in the States, told Alison that TSC would cover the cost of the surgery, and that they should proceed. We immediately abandoned efforts to obtain a medical visa for Maria, since we now knew we could never get approval, and we began fund-raising for this emergency surgery. By US standards, the cost of the procedure was very low, but we still had to come up with several thousand dollars. We sent appeals out to our e-mail list of supporters and trusted God to provide. Maria still needed to be adopted, and by a family that could and would move very quickly and do whatever was needed to make the adoption happen right away.

Another bend in the road

Mary continued searching frantically for a family to adopt Maria. After three or four days, she contacted us directly and, through her tears of concern for Maria, asked if we would consider adopting this very sick little girl. Because we had already worked with Mary to complete Kathryn's adoption, she knew that we could assemble a dossier quickly. We had already been praying about the possibility of our adopting Maria, seeking God's will for us and for her. When Mary asked us, it seemed to be confirmation that God was leading us to do this. So we said yes, we would be honored to adopt this little girl and work as God's agents in caring for her. We decided to name her Lauren Amelia, which means "victorious work of the Lord."

Maria's — or rather, Lauren's — case, however, wasn't the only one Mary wanted to discuss with us. There was a seven-month-old boy that Mary was also quite urgently trying to find a family for. This baby, whose name was Luis, had a lump on his lower back that very much appeared to be lipomyelomeningocele, the same form of spina bifida that Carlin and Caelyn had. He needed to have corrective surgery as soon as possible to prevent the spina bifida from damaging nerves and causing loss of function in his lower limbs and his urinary tract. But Mary told us that this adoption would be very difficult, and she wanted to discuss the possibility of our adopting him because of that factor, coupled with Luis's urgent need for medical care.

The reason Luis's adoption would be so difficult was that the Guatemalan attorney handling his case was notorious within adoption circles in Guatemala. She reputedly would take money from adoptive families and never finish the adoption. She allegedly lied to families, to adoption agencies, and to others involved in adoptions, and she was inept, at times appearing unfamiliar with long-standing adoption practices and regulations in her own country. Her reputation was so tarnished that no one in the adoption community wanted to work with her, if at all possible.[33]

We knew that we could certainly not ask any other family to go into this adoption, knowing that they could invest a large amount of money, as well as emotional capital, in the adoption of a baby who might never leave Guatemala. But we knew that there was a little boy over there who very much needed a family of his own, a family who would fight for him and try to get him to the States for evaluation and treatment. It was clear that we simply could not leave Luis behind just because he had been assigned to a disreputable and incompetent attorney.

We finally came to the conclusion that even though we could not ask any other family to attempt to adopt Luis, we were being led to try to bring this little boy home ourselves. In our line of reasoning, we referred to what Kathy and I have come to call, for us, the Good Samaritan principle. The story of the Good Samaritan was told by Jesus in the Gospel of Luke, Chapter 10. It is a familiar story often cited to urge people to get involved in helping others in times of need. Kathy and I have committed ourselves to this principle, so that whenever God brings a need across our path, we believe we have a responsibility to consider prayerfully if and how we might be able to meet that need.

So when Luis was brought to our attention and his story was told to us fully, we looked to the Good Samaritan principle and asked God whether He might be calling us to pursue Luis's adoption. As I said, we ultimately came to the conclusion that we were being led to do so, and we committed to both Luis's and Lauren's adoptions very early in February.

Kathy and I immediately jumped into dossier preparation for these two adoptions. We were able to complete our portion of the dossiers in one week, which was a record for us. Unbelievably, we were just one month into the new year and we were already in the midst of two new adoptions.

The march of time

Early in March, we received our preapproval from the USCIS (formerly INS) for our two Guatemalan adoptions, and we took a quick trip to Guatemala to meet both of the babies. Many adoption agencies encourage adopting parents to travel to Guatemala at least once during the process, both to familiarize themselves with their child and to ensure that the child will become a US citizen upon entry into the States.

We were excited to meet both of our children waiting for us there. Lauren was so tiny and frail, but she was doing better than we expected and dared to hope. Luis, whom we had decided to call Evan Michael ("God is good; who is like God?"), was doing very well and showing no outward signs of neurological damage from his spina bifida. We remained concerned, though, because the nerve damage, once it manifests visibly, is irreversible. In both babies' cases, we continued to pray that God would enable us to complete their adoptions in record time so we could get them home, and get them the medical care they both so urgently needed. Kathryn accompanied us on this trip so that those who had been involved in her care and adoption there could see what miraculous progress she had made since her adoption. The testimony of her life impacted a number of people in Guatemala when they saw her again, and it was a very special few days for the two of us with our three babies. At times things were pretty intense, especially when they were all tired or crying for bottles at the same time, but this glimpse of what our lives would be like once we got them all home together was thrilling for us and filled us with even more determination to fight for the two of them with all our strength.

Our world was rocked late in May when we received word from Guatemala that the adoption of Lauren had hit a major stumbling block. It's complicated, and still to this day a little difficult to understand, but the problem involved legal processes in Guatemala and something to do with ways in which Lauren's birth mother had falsified some documents. It took a few days to sort out, but in the end we were told that the adoption was being halted while the courts took custody of Lauren. The whole affair could take at least a year to sort out, and in the meantime, Lauren would be stuck in Guatemala — and might even be moved from her private orphanage to a state-run institution. We were devastated at the thought that this little girl, for whom hope had burned so brightly just a few days earlier, was now facing the possibility of dying in an institution.

We sent an e-mail out to our update list to let everyone know about this turn of events. In that message, Kathy related a story from many, many years earlier, in which God had taught us an important lesson about our ability to understand His ways, and about the way in which we should trust Him in spite of our doubts.

E-mail excerpt, May 12, 2006: Many years ago, we battled through an agonizingly long and painful period of questioning God and His ways after the sudden and tragic death of my brother, who also happened to be Scott's best friend at the time. We were hurt and angered by the sometimes thoughtless explanations and platitudes carelessly tossed our way about this being "for the better" and "God's knowing best." I remember that when I finally moved past a year-long time of fist-shaking at God and truly began to seek answers from Him, an incident happened that is simple and kind of silly, but helped bring things into perspective for both of us. We have used this story when our disabled children have asked us why God made them the way they are, or why He didn't bring home some of the children they thought would be their brothers and sisters. I'll try to relate it briefly here: Our oldest child, Kristen was about two years old and had been struggling with diarrhea for over two weeks, even though she didn't act sick in any other way and had a great appetite. We had tried many things to check this with no success. We thought it was finally over when it suddenly started up again, so we called the doctor and left a message for him to call us back. While we waited, I prepared supper – hamburgers, which happened to be Kristen's favorite at that time in her life. I had just put her in her highchair and was starting to put food on her little plate while she happily chanted, "Hangabugga, hangabugga . . ." when the doctor called. His orders were to begin immediately withholding all solid foods for the next forty-eight hours and then to call him back with a report. If this didn't work, they would have to hospitalize her. I remember feeling like such a bully when I took away her beloved "hangabugga" and handed her a cup of liquid Jell-o instead. The look on her face and her tears clearly expressed the betrayal she felt in her heart, even though her vocabulary was too immature to state such things explicitly. I felt helpless, knowing that no matter how many times I might try to explain to her that I had to do this for her good — that I was doing this out of my great love for her — her baby brain wouldn't be able to comprehend it. No matter what I said, this could only appear to be done out of meanness and to hurt her; she couldn't possibly understand that there could be any good in this situation at all. As I reflected on this, I suddenly saw myself sitting in front of God for the past year, pouting and crying — aching with confusion and what I viewed as betrayal by Him when He seemingly inflicted pain for no good reason on those He loves, or stood by allowing havoc to reign in the world. And suddenly His words from Jeremiah 29:11 ("For I know the plans I have for you," declares the Lord, *"plans to prosper you and not to harm you, plans to give you hope and a future.") seemed true to me. I was then better able to understand Isaiah 55:8 and 9, "For my thoughts are not your thoughts, neither are your ways my ways," declares the* LORD. *"As the heavens are higher than the earth so are my ways higher than your ways and my thoughts than your thoughts." At that moment, He gradually and slowly began to teach both of us to trust Him as we had never trusted Him before — regardless of the circumstances or the whispered lies from the Enemy that God couldn't be trusted.*

After weeks of intense work by some very compassionate people in Guatemala, Lauren was moved to a foster home where she could be monitored and cared for while we waited for the legal situation to be resolved. We prayed intensely for God to overrule the wrangling going on in Guatemala, and to keep her safe and healthy until we could get her to the States for her major surgery — but we knew that time was running out for her.

Vacation

In July, we were again presented with the gift of a mini-vacation. The same family who had loaned us their house and pool while they were traveling in the summer of 2005 offered us the use of their home again this year. We were all so excited about the thought of a time of rest and play like God had given us the year before, and we were tremendously blessed and grateful to this family for their generosity.

Unfortunately, conditions in 2006 were not the same as in the previous year, and we found it much more difficult to escape all of the stresses of life in our get-away. The first challenge facing us was health insurance for TSC's paid employees. When I came home to work as TSC's director eighteen months earlier, I had opted to use

COBRA to extend our health insurance coverage while we searched through other options for the future. The allowed eighteen months on COBRA were now coming to an end, and our futile search for acceptable health insurance had become frantic and urgent. We moved ahead with our vacation plans, but the week was overshadowed with the stress and concern of trying to make final decisions regarding this critical need for our family and any future TSC employees.

The weather was also uncooperative, and the pool developed problems affecting our ability to stabilize the chemicals. These two things alone interrupted the swimming time that had been such a critical part of our family fun the year before.

As we fought valiantly to enjoy this special time with our children, in spite of the weather, the pool's lack of cooperation, and the necessary, almost-consuming preoccupation with our health insurance crisis, we received very distressing news from Guatemala about our little Lauren.

The cardiologist at UNICAR let us know, through Alison, that Lauren could not go any longer without the major corrective surgery for her heart condition. Our baby was out of time. Since her adoption was completely held up, and since there would be no way to obtain a medical visa for her to come to the States for surgery, she would have to have the operation in Guatemala. We knew that the surgeons at UNICAR were fully capable of performing the procedure Lauren needed, but we were also aware of the fact that post-operative care—or the lack thereof—is just as critical as a well-performed surgery. We had learned that in the first half of the year, six babies had received open-heart surgery at UNICAR, and that all six of them had come through well — but all six of them had subsequently died due to complications post-operatively. This was a sobering fact for us, and it made us apprehensive about Lauren's having the surgery there.

The news that Lauren needed surgery was not a complete surprise to us, since we had known all along that she would have to have the corrective procedure sometime between four and six months of age. She was now six months old, and we had been praying and wondering for weeks how much longer she would be able to hold on without this next essential step — dreading the day when this call might come. Yet when the news came, it was devastating, nonetheless. We didn't yet know the date of her surgery, but Kathy and I decided pretty quickly that we needed to be there with her for her operation. While we waited to hear back from the doctors, we decided to cut the rest of our vacation short and head home. We needed to begin making preparations for leaving the children while we flew to Guatemala to be with this child who was our daughter in our hearts, even though we didn't have any papers to prove it, and even though she didn't know us as her parents.

It was another couple of weeks before we finally heard that surgery had been scheduled for Wednesday, August 9. We quickly made plans to fly down on August 7, with the hope that we would be able to spend some time with Lauren before the surgery. God mercifully provided, through generous friends, everything we needed to cover the costs for that trip. Friends also once again worked together to plan meals for the children while we were gone, and our older kids willingly arranged their schedules so that at least one of them would be available at all times to care for the younger ones.

Guatemala, again

When we arrived in Guatemala on Monday, we were able to spend about an hour with our sweet baby at the hotel where we were staying. She looked deceptively healthy and happy. We were so blessed by the way we were treated and received by everyone there. All of the doctors involved with her care recognized us as her parents, and this meant more than we can possibly say. We were invited to meet with the pediatric cardiologist, Dr. Carlos Herrera, the next morning — Tuesday — as he discussed the cardiology team's plans and talked about exactly what they hoped to accomplish through the surgery on Wednesday. We were pleasantly surprised that Dr. Herrera and most of the other doctors at UNICAR spoke English very well.

After our meeting with Dr. Herrera on Tuesday morning, we were able to spend the rest of that day with Lauren, accompanying her foster mother as Lauren went through all of the required pre-operative blood draws and evaluations. These special hours with our daughter were such a gift, and we cherished every minute — every smile. Lauren was very content in Kathy's arms all day, and it was with heavy but grateful hearts that we placed her into her hospital bed at the end of the day and headed back to the hotel, leaving her in the care of her foster mother. It was hard to walk away from her lying there, looking a little bit scared and very tiny and helpless in the adult-sized bed. We knew that it was possible that we would never see her alive again. Kathy stated in an e-mail message that evening to the kids back home, "This day was one of the most amazing experiences of my life so far. Regardless of what the future holds with us and with her, I will cherish those hours for the rest of my life."

We were thankful for the bond Lauren seemed to have formed with her foster mother. This made it easier for us to walk away and leave her at the hospital that evening. The role of foster parent is a role that should never be undervalued. In one of our updates from Guatemala about this day with Lauren, we wrote the following:

> It occurred to us today that foster mothers' roles are of the John the Baptist nature – "He must increase, but I must decrease." (John 3:30) All of their work is dedicated to and directed toward handing the fruits of that work off to another. What a difficult calling, and we are thankful that there are people willing to endure the pain of passing on these precious ones to their new parents, after giving each child in their care a piece of their hearts.

When we got back to the hotel that afternoon, thirteen-month-old Evan was there with his foster mother, waiting to spend some time with us. What an incredible day it was to have these hours with each of our babies. Evan had changed so much since our last visit with him. His face had become even more beautiful and was now framed by a head full of soft curls. He had learned to crawl and made us laugh with his ability to crawl quickly across the floor, and then suddenly reverse directions and crawl backwards at the same speed. We had never, and have still never, seen a baby do this before. We spent a joyful couple of hours with him before his foster mother took him home. We then fell into bed so that we could be up early and head to the hospital the next morning. We had no idea what the day would hold, and we wanted to be prepared to face anything that was ahead.

Lauren's surgery

The next morning, we headed back to the hospital very early and settled in to wait for any word from the team in the OR. The surgery, which was expected to last two hours, ended up taking five because of some unexpected findings with Lauren's anatomy. Instead of a single superior vena cava — which is normal — the team found themselves facing two in Lauren's chest. They were, however, able to find a way to work around this and a few other complicating factors, and Lauren came through the surgery beautifully. We were so relieved when the doctor came to find us and reported this great news. And when he then told us that we could come into ICU to see her for just a few minutes, we were ecstatic. She looked very swollen and blue, but the doctors had prepared us for this, and she still just looked like our beautiful little daughter.

The surgeon then explained to us that Lauren's vital signs looked very good, and that one of the primary factors they were monitoring carefully was her interior venous pressure. Their goal was to keep it below twenty, and Lauren's was holding at eleven or twelve. They were very pleased with this but also cautioned us that the next twenty-four to forty-eight hours would be critical, as Lauren's body tried to learn to cope with the new piping arrangement and begin functioning properly on its own.

We knew we would not be able to see her again that day, so we decided to head back to the hotel that evening and try to get some sleep. We were still struggling with pretty significant sleep-deprivation—and we both fell into a deep sleep very early.

We were startled awake at about 9:30 that evening when the phone in our room rang shrilly. It was Mary. She and our attorney, Javier, were on their way to our hotel to pick us up. They needed us in the lobby within five minutes. The hospital had called to say that Lauren was in trouble and would probably be headed back into surgery.

We threw on clothes as quickly as we could and then dashed down to the lobby and jumped into our attorney's car. As he sped away, we found ourselves searching mentally for words, words we could fashion into a prayer that would express the cries for help that were choking out rational thought. We huddled together in the back seat, clutching each other's hands, and our prayers mostly took shape as silent, panicked whimpers—cries from the hearts of parents begging God to protect their little one.

When we arrived at the hospital, Lauren had been taken to the cath. lab, where the team was attempting to do an exploratory heart catheterization on her. One of the doctors took time to explain that Lauren had suddenly begun to swell horribly, and that in spite of all their efforts, they had not been able to make it stop. They were afraid that there was a blood clot blocking the tube they had inserted that morning, and they were hoping that a heart cath. would help them see what was going on and allow them to clear the clot. He told us that they would let us know as soon as they had any more news.

After about two and a half hours, Lauren's cardiologist came out to talk with us. We knew immediately that he did not have good news. He told us bluntly but kindly that Lauren's situation was very bleak now: they had had a terrible time getting the catheter inserted, and they had actually had to resuscitate her three times during the procedure. Additionally, once they finally managed to get the catheter inserted, they did not find the blockage they expected to see. They did determine that her pulmonary pressures were extremely high, and this had everyone puzzled. Because of the specifics with Lauren's particular combination of heart defects, high pulmonary pressures were unheard of. The cardiologists and surgeons couldn't find any reason to explain it and thus could not come up with any way to correct it. The result of this high pulmonary pressure was that her heart was pumping blood to her upper body, but her body systems were unable to return the blood to the lungs. The blood was backing up, essentially pooling in her upper body and head, causing her head, neck, and shoulders to turn purple and swell to twice their normal size. There was also much concern about possible brain damage because of the elevated pressure the excess blood was exerting on her brain. Her breathing had become very labored, and they had been forced to put her on a respirator. They also inserted drains on both sides of her body in the space between the lungs and the ribs, hoping this might allow her lungs to work better. It was made very clear to us that it was an absolute miracle that she was still alive at all, that the doctors had no idea what else they could do for her, and that there was very little hope that she would survive now.

This was all explained very carefully to us, as they tried to prepare us for what we would find when they took us into ICU to see our baby. In spite of their genuine attempt, however, we were completely thrown by what we found when we got to her bedside. This helpless little baby didn't even resemble our dearly loved Lauren, and she appeared to be already dead. We wept quietly as we stood there, finding ourselves reliving all of the hopes and dreams we had been cherishing in our hearts during the seven months that had passed since we started her adoption.

After a brief visit, we were ushered back out to the ICU waiting room. What a strange, almost surreal experience this was for us, in a foreign country, surrounded by anxious, waiting parents from such a different culture, speaking a different language. Kathy and I sat and read Scripture and prayed silently, as these Guatemalan moms and dads, some wearing their traditional clothing, spoke softly to each other, thumbed through their Spanish Bibles, dozed, or stared at the floor, wiping away tears. Grief erased so many of the differences between us, and although we weren't able to converse, we were all able to communicate the compassion we felt for each other. We found that we figuratively linked arms in the knowledge that we shared the same pain, fears, and sadness. And we all, in our own ways, faced the probable loss of dreams we held so dear to our hearts for our children, who were all fighting for their lives on the other side of those double doors.

At about 3:00 a.m., we were told that we would not be allowed to see Lauren again until the next day. We were urged to go back to our hotel and try to get a few hours of sleep. The doctors, whose passionate concern for our daughter's welfare was obvious, promised that they would call us immediately if there were any changes, so we agreed to leave the hospital for a while. They stated that she was a strong little girl and a tremendous fighter, citing as examples that she had survived when they had almost lost her twice after her first surgery in January, and that no one had ever expected her to grow so well, get so fat, and meet the developmental milestones she had managed so far. As our attorney drove us back to our hotel in those dark wee hours of the morning, we were frightened for our baby and grieving to see her in such a condition. But we still believed that God was holding her firmly in His hands, and that He could still heal her. He had stilled the fears in our hearts enough that we were able to ask Him for the strength to trust Him with Lauren's life.

We grabbed about two hours of sleep, then showered and returned to the hospital. The next morning passed without much change, and we alternately paced outside the ICU doors and sat among the other hurting parents in the waiting room. The medical team attempted a number of measures to help Lauren in her struggle to survive, but none really delivered any results. Finally, her doctors called us into a small room and very gently and compassionately told us the grim reality: our little Lauren had suffered two more cardiac arrests, her systemic blood pressure was near zero, and there simply was nothing else they could do for her. They would very soon be taking her off of life support and declaring her dead.

At about 1:20 p.m. (CST) on August 10, 2006, our precious Lauren Amelia was ushered into the courts of the Almighty and, we are confident, found herself in the arms of her loving Heavenly Father. The following e-mail excerpt written by the two of us together gives a pretty clear picture of where our hearts were at that time:

Kathy and I do not feel quite ready to write this e-mail, but we also recognize that we will never be quite ready for it, and we want to let all of you know as much as possible about Lauren's last days and the mighty ways God was working in and through and around her, here in Guatemala. I am sure we will say things in this message that might be easily misunderstood, the limitations of e-mail being what they are, so I ask you to extend a bit of grace to Kathy and me as you read this.

The last four days, from Tuesday through Friday, have been an overwhelming mixture of hope and optimism, fear and worry, confusion and doubt, and sadness and pain.

I won't even try to tell you what it felt like to lose the battle for the life of this beautiful child who was already our daughter — our daughter both in our hearts and in God's mind, even if the Guatemalan authorities didn't officially realize or recognize it yet. We know that the pain of losing a child whose adoption is in process, while devastating and deeply painful, is not the same as the pain a parent feels who loses a child who has been in their arms and in their home. This is a difficult thought to express adequately. To those of you who have never adopted, I can only say that losing Lauren was like losing one of our other children, in terms of the grief and heart-pain we feel. But to those of you who have lost "actual" children – not adoptions in process, but children already part of your family – we acknowledge that the pain we feel is different, is less, than the pain you have felt. We know several families who have lost children whose adoptions were in process, and we don't in any way want to minimize the pain those families have felt. We now know firsthand how much it hurts and how it does truly change your life. (And many of you never even had – as we did – the privilege of holding your child, of looking into his or her eyes and seeing him or her look back at you, or of being there when your child-to-be went home to the Father. Kathy and I recognize the gift we have been given in this past week, and we are truly thankful to God for it.) But we also know families who have lost "actual" children, including Kathy's own mother, and we truly don't want to present ourselves as feeling the same loss, the same pain that those families have felt, as they had to go home and pack away the clothing and toys and belongings of the children whose voices and laughter would never be heard in their homes again. The truth is, each of us experiences the things that come to us, and we can (almost) never truly know what someone else experiences in the things that come to him or her, even in cases in which the same or very similar experiences are shared. We can sympathize, and sometimes we can even empathize, but we can *never really know precisely what that other person is feeling. But the experiences God brings to us truly do help us to sympathize and empathize with others when they go through similar experiences, and we believe God expects us to use our own experiences to make ourselves better able to help others. Kathy and I now know a pain that we had not known before, and it is probable that God will use that experience to permit us to better help others, even as many of you have been able to help us in a special way because of having experienced similar pain yourselves. Kathy and I want to thank all of you who prayed with us during this ordeal, and especially all of you – literally hundreds of you – who've taken the time to send us notes of encouragement and support this week. We will never be able to respond individually to all of you, but we have read each and every message, and they have touched us and blessed our hearts. Thank you!*

Thursday afternoon, after the death of our baby, we went back to our hotel and were blessed to learn that Mary had gathered a number of other American adoptive families who were staying in the same hotel. Mary had already been a tremendous blessing to us throughout Lauren's short life. In addition to fighting alongside us for Lauren's life throughout her entire ordeal, she had made it possible for us to be a part of Lauren's final days in ways we never imagined. This was a special gift, given to us by God through Mary. Now she had gathered those families who were waiting to embrace us in our grief as they held a brief service of support for us and in remembrance of Lauren. One of the fathers read a passage from

1 Corinthians and spoke on the comfort that can come only from God, and then we all held hands as he prayed for us. It was so moving and touched us so much for them to do this for us, and it was very special.

We had spent many times talking to our children at home, trying to gauge from so far away just how they were doing through all of this. The older kids really pulled together to take care of the younger ones. All of the kids were heartbroken to hear that Lauren had died, but they expressed that they were glad she was with Jesus and free from pain. They expressed their concern for us and how we were doing, and they, especially the older ones, assured us that everyone was doing fine and that we shouldn't worry about things there as we wrapped up the final chapter of Lauren's life.

On Friday we attended Lauren's funeral. We had never attended a Latin American funeral before, and it was quite different from our other funeral experiences. It was a mixture of elaborate public grieving and incongruous nonchalance about the whole thing. We moved through Lauren's burial in a fog, watching the entire drama unfold before us as if in a dream. We can honestly say that we buried a piece of our hearts with our daughter that day, as her tiny coffin was placed in what was locally referred to as the "Wall of Babies" at the cemetery. And we wept more tears when we learned that Mary and Javier had chosen to list us as Lauren's parents on her headstone. She was buried under the name she would've been given had she made it home to her family.

As we began to turn our thoughts toward home, we felt torn. We missed our children and longed to get back to them. But there in the secluded world of our hotel room and among the few people who shared our grief, we were able to grapple with the pain and loss we were experiencing — free to cry and take the time needed to absorb all that we were feeling. As we pictured ourselves leaving behind that small world and returning to our bigger world back home, we recognized that we didn't know how we would continue grieving there. We weren't going home to a funeral and all of the support of extended family and friends that typically accompany one's journey through such a tragic event. There would be no memorial service, no condolences, not even any real acknowledgement of Lauren's brief sojourn on earth or the small but indelible marks her life had left behind. The only sign of her life and passing was on a stone that marked her small grave in a cemetery that would be very far away from us. It occurred to us that this must be the way parents feel as they try to return to normal life after a miscarriage. A lonely, private world of sadness. We were shocked by the number of very loving and comforting e-mails sent to us by those who had been following Lauren's story. And later when we returned home, we were deeply touched by memorial gifts from several friends who did understand our pain and who had a desire to recognize, in some way, the fact that a little girl had lived and died and made an impression on the hearts of many people.

For the most part, though, this was a private journey God asked us to make. Thankfully, He didn't ask us to make it alone. His presence was tangible to us every moment of our time in Guatemala. We felt Him all around us with a clarity and an intensity that we have only experienced a few times during our lives. But the grieving hurt. Even now, years later as we write this book, the tears flow easily over the memory of the events that comprised Lauren's short life.

In the midst of this difficult grieving process, we did begin to force our brains to focus on returning to America and moving on with life. However, as it turned out, God wasn't quite finished with Lauren's story and His plans for us during this visit to Guatemala.

Chapter 15

Bittersweet Sovereignty

Cheer up, Christian! Things are not left to chance: no blind fate rules the world. God hath purposes, and those purposes are fulfilled. God hath plans, and those plans are wise, and never can be dislocated.

C.H. Spurgeon

Joy in the morning

One of our favorite Bible verses is Psalm 30:5, which says, "For His anger is but for a moment, His favor is for life; weeping may endure for a night, but joy comes in the morning." (NKJV) It is a constant delight to God's servants to see the ways in which He changes our weeping of the nighttime into the joy that comes in the morning.

Almost from the moment of Lauren's death, Kathy and I were painfully aware that there was now a completed dossier in Guatemala—a dossier that was no longer connected to any child. We knew with certainty that there were literally hundreds and hundreds of children right there in Guatemala City who needed homes, even hundreds with special needs. Our hearts burned with the question, "How could we walk away and ignore those hundreds of children who need homes and families just as much as Lauren did?" We believed that trying to use Lauren's dossier to save another child from a life of hopelessness and aloneness would be the best way possible to honor Lauren and her struggle for life.

Following Lauren's funeral, we went back to the hotel and headed up to Mary's room to talk to her about what to do with Lauren's dossier, and whether or not we should consider transferring it to another needy child. After listening to our thoughts, Mary walked briskly to her computer and pulled up a picture of a beautiful but malnourished five-week-old baby girl who had, just the day before, become available for adoption. This little girl, whose name was Ana Maria, had been born with a relatively minor cleft lip and partially affected palate. However, because of her cleft, she was unable to suck and swallow properly, and everyone was very concerned about her ability to thrive because of this. Kathy and I both immediately felt that this child was the one God had led us to, the one whose adoption we were supposed to pursue with the dossier we had put together for Lauren.

Mary had this baby brought to our hotel room that very evening, and we were allowed to start trying to feed and care for her while we were in Guatemala. One of TSC's outreach ministries at the time was providing special cleft-palate bottles to orphanages around the world. We contacted our TSC volunteer in charge of this project and had her immediately send a shipment of these special bottles to our hotel, praying it would arrive within the next couple of days so we could spend a little time teaching Ana Maria's foster mother how to use the bottles before we headed back to the US

We were awed by the knowledge that God's perfect plan had brought us there for Lauren and her surgery at just the right time, so that we were in Guatemala when Ana Maria became available and could be brought to us. We felt such clarity that this was exactly what God had called us to do, and that saving Ana Maria's life, God permitting, would be our way of commemorating Lauren and the ways in which she had touched so many people. We felt blessed and thankful to God for giving us the privilege of pursuing the adoption of Ana Maria, this tiny, beautiful child. She was truly a gift to us and our children.

In sharing this unexpected turn of events with our supporters back home, we wrote the following on August 13, 2006:

> . . . *The full name we gave to Lauren is "Lauren Amelia," and it means "victorious work of the Lord." It may seem to some, and at times it seemed to us, that her death here following surgery was anything but a victorious work. We were so prepared to see Him bring her supernaturally through this dangerous surgery and then allow us to complete the adoption and bring her home. Wouldn't that have been a demonstrable "victorious work of the Lord"? How does this ending to her story fit the name we gave her? We, of course, don't know all of the answers to that question. Oh how we wish we did. But we do think we can see just a bit of an answer. First and foremost, Lauren's life was a victorious work*

because it made it possible for us to save another life, little Ana Maria's. Secondly, Lauren's surgery and ordeal brought literally hundreds of people together in prayer for days on end. How Satan hates to see God's people united in prayer! And thirdly, His work in the life of Lauren was victorious because she is now safe with Him, removed forever from pain and suffering and heartache. Truly we can celebrate the life of this victorious work of the Lord that we were so privileged to be a part of, even if only for a while.

Kathy and I hope you will all be able to understand why it is so important for us to pursue this adoption so immediately after losing Lauren, and that you will be able to rejoice with us over Ana Maria and her adoption, even in the midst of our grief over losing Lauren. In all of this, we pray that God will be glorified, both in Lauren and her life and our attempts to save her, and in Ana Maria and her life and her adoption. We are His servants, and our lives are to be lived in that vein. We do not believe we would be serving Him well if we walked away from this country and left Lauren's dossier to gather dust on the shelf. This is the life we have been called to, and serving God according to His call is the only source of joy and fulfillment for any of His servants. We will keep you posted as things develop and unfold, but we wanted to let you know about the final chapter in Lauren's story.

Ana Maria's special bottles did arrive a couple of days later, and we spent several hours with her young foster mother, showing her how to feed the baby so that she wouldn't burn all of her calories working futilely to get the nutrition she so desperately needed.

The next day we flew back home to our children and had a blessed reunion in our family room as we all cried together over the loss of Lauren, and as we rejoiced that God had brought us Ana Maria. We discussed names at length and finally decided on Shannen Mariana. The meaning of this name, "God's gracious gift of bitter grace," seemed like a perfect fit to us. God had used the devastating death of Shannen's sister to bring her to us as His very special and gracious gift to our family.

A new melody

Excerpt from e-mail, August 18, 2006: When Kathy's brother was killed in a shipwreck twenty-five years ago, we came to the realization that a death does change the lives of those left behind, in both subtle and obvious ways, and those left behind never really "get over it." It is more like life goes on, but it has a slightly different sound or melody or color than it had before. God still brings richness and beauty in the new melody (or color, or whatever), but it's simply not the same melody that it was and would have been. All of that is to say that, though we continue to feel the pain of the loss of our little Lauren, we are ready to move on and embrace what is ahead.

We did return to everyday life after getting back from Guatemala. Everyday life included all of the work of running the ministry, and once again all of the effort and attention needed to assemble a dossier for an adoption from Guatemala. Much of the dossier we had put together for Lauren could be used for Ana Maria, but there were still many things that had to be done because it was a different child and a different attorney in Guatemala. And we had to raise funds. The adoption of Ana Maria was going to cost approximately fifty percent more than Lauren's, and we didn't have any of those funds.

Soon after we returned from Guatemala, God began answering our prayers for funding. We received a phone call from a representative of Shaohannah's Hope,[34] one of the organizations we had sent a grant application to, telling us that they had chosen to award our family a grant to help fund our sweet Lauren's adoption. Through tears, Kathy expressed our deep gratitude for this gift, and then went on to explain that we had just buried our precious baby in Guatemala. When Kathy told her about the way God had brought Ana Maria into our lives, following Lauren's death, the representative kindly and generously offered to transfer this grant to be used toward the adoption of this new little daughter. We felt as if God had wrapped His arms around our aching hearts and, once again, confirmed our decision to adopt Ana Maria.

In September, we were all blessed with another shot at a family vacation. Some friends of friends offered to let us use their cabin in the woods of central Pennsylvania. This would be a completely different sort of get-away than the failed attempt in July, but it promised to be refreshing and rejuvenating for all of us — and that's exactly what it turned out to be. We were almost completely isolated in this beautiful cabin in Pennsylvania's Kishacoquillas Valley Amish country. We had no telephone, no cell phone service, no Internet, and no TV. The setting was pastoral and the cabin itself was awesome. It had been designed and built as a retreat center, and it was actually big enough for our entire family to fit in comfortably. Our time there was everything we had hoped it would be, and we were so thankful to have been given the break.

Caelyn the Brave

Have you ever noticed that when a doctor describes an upcoming procedure and tries to prepare you for how tough it's going to be, he invariably forgets to mention one or two key things that turn out to be huge? What ends up happening, then, is that you get mentally prepared for the difficult stuff, and the unexpected catches you by surprise and knocks you down.

Caelyn entered the hospital on October 17, 2006, to begin two days of preparation for her urological reconstruction surgery. These preparations are no fun, but both we and Caelyn had been well prepared for them. She was definitely a trooper, and all of the doctors and nurses were impressed by her spunk and her ability to stay cheerful in the midst of misery. On the morning of October 19, she went into surgery at about 8:00 a.m. We were told to expect the procedure to last between eight and fourteen hours, depending on what they found inside and what exactly they had to do. One of the surgical nurses called out to the waiting room periodically to let us know where they were in the procedure and how Caelyn was doing.

After about seven hours, we got word that the operation was done. It turned out that the procedure was easier than they had anticipated it would be, and they decided not to augment the bladder, since its capacity seemed to them to be adequate. Caelyn was taken to the pediatric intensive care unit (PICU) for observation and monitoring, and it was expected that she would be moved to a regular room later in the day.

When we got our first look at Caelyn, we were a bit shocked—primarily because of the number of tubes coming out of her little body. She looked so helpless and frail on that big hospital bed. She did get moved to a regular room later that afternoon, and Kathy and I began the process of settling in for the next week at the hospital.

Sometime in the evening, Caelyn began to have trouble breathing. We could tell that her throat was hurting her, and her breathing was becoming shallower. Eventually she developed what is called post-surgical stridor, a condition in which the throat, having been irritated by the presence of the breathing tube for the long surgery, becomes inflamed and partially obstructed. The result is a harsh, almost croaking sound with every breath. It is uncomfortable for the patient, and it can lead to further difficulties if not addressed. Because of the amount of trauma to Caelyn's systems, coupled with the new ten-inch-long incision all the way up her abdomen, it was necessary that she work hard to continue breathing deeply, to prevent fluid from settling in her lungs. The stridor made it difficult for her to get those deep breaths, and we were all concerned that she might develop further complications.

The floor nurses decided to send Caelyn back to the PICU for her safety, where she could be monitored more closely. They also called in a respiratory therapist for some breathing treatments. The three of us spent the night in the PICU. Caelyn slept quite well, once the breathing treatments calmed her stridor; Kathy and I, on the other hand, barely slept at all. The next morning, they moved Caelyn back to her regular room, and we actually began to think that the worst was behind us. We were new to this level of reconstructive surgery.

Caelyn mostly slept during those first couple of days following the surgery. On the third day post-operatively, we began to notice that Caelyn seemed to be experiencing increased pain in a semi-cyclical pattern. We learned that she was having terrible bladder spasms, just as Erin had experienced some twenty years earlier following her bladder surgery. For some reason, the surgeon had neglected to warn us about this in Caelyn's case, and we had forgotten that Erin had experienced them.

Caelyn suffered through wave after wave of these excruciating spasms, as the nurses and pain management team tried to find some way to manage the pain. We learned that changing positions seemed to cause the spasms to stop, at least in some cases, and Caelyn was both desperate and amazingly brave as she forced herself to do everything we told her to do to try to ease the pain. Kathy and I even spent hours teaching her the Lamaze breathing we had used during Kathy's deliveries, and Caelyn, at the age of five, learned to focus and faithfully breathe through the agonizing pain. The hospital staff was amazed at Caelyn's persistence and stamina, and especially at her sweet disposition throughout the ordeal. The worst of the spasms lasted for three or four days, though it seemed like three or four weeks.

Rosenow Family Circus

Stephen had had a visit with the craniofacial team at Children's about a week before Caelyn's surgery. We learned at that visit that his tonsils had ballooned in size and were obstructing his airway, exacerbating his breathing issues while sleeping. Just a few days before Caelyn's surgery, Stephen's ENT let us know that Stephen could not wait for his surgery. So, just to add to the excitement for our family, we scheduled Stephen's tonsillectomy/adenoidectomy for the Monday following Caelyn's major surgery, which was on a Thursday. We arranged to have a close family friend come and sit with Caelyn in her room while Kathy and I went downstairs to be with Stephen for his surgery. We would then split up that night, with one of us staying with Caelyn and the other with Stephen.

Everything went pretty much according to plan, except that we were surprised and delighted when Stephen's ENT surgeon arranged for him to be assigned a room on Caelyn's floor. In fact, his room was right across the hall from hers; they could see each other from their beds! This made it so much easier for Kathy and me to take care of the two of them during the night. On the other hand, it was a bit confusing for the nursing staff when it sank in that there were two Rosenow children on their floor, and right across the hall from each other.

Once Stephen got settled in his room after surgery, Caelyn looked across the hall and saw him in his bed. She exclaimed, "Oh, I see Stephen's little head!" We bundled her into one of the hospital wagons and she made the trip across the hall to spend some time in her brother's room. They watched a Disney movie together, at least for a brief time, but after a while, Caelyn's bladder spasms began to get the best of her. Also, Stephen's nurse had to suction his nasal passages, and he started crying because of the pain. Caelyn immediately became upset, on top of the spasms, and so we decided that it was time to return her to her own bed.

Stephen was discharged from the hospital on Wednesday, two days after his surgery. By that time, all of the kids at home were beginning to miss Caelyn terribly and to wonder when—and if— she was coming home. At one point the previous day, Braedan had the chance to talk to Caelyn on the phone. As soon as he heard her voice, he began sobbing and he said, "Caelyn, I love you and I miss you and I need you to come home!"

By this time Caelyn's bladder spasms had become very manageable, and it was hard for us not to become overly eager to be going home. The doctors said that she needed to stay in the hospital till Friday, and though we couldn't understand why it had to be so long, we had no real say in the matter — which was probably a good thing. We promised all the kids we would have a big ice cream party and "I Love Lucy"-fest once we got Caelyn home, and we were all really looking forward to it.

On Friday, after a long week and a half, Caelyn was finally discharged from the hospital. We headed home, tired and excited, ready to settle in with our brood and enjoy some quiet, connecting family time. Because Kristen was working full time and Allan was away at school all day, Alison had flown out from California to help take care of our kids for us while we were in the hospital with

Caelyn. She and the older kids had all of the younger ones prepared for our homecoming by the time we got to the house.

We brought Caelyn in around three in the afternoon and spent some time with all of the kids, making plans for how the rest of the day would play out. At around 4:00, Kathy and I, who were both upstairs, were startled to hear Alison cry out, with obvious alarm in her voice, "Kathy, you'd better get down here—quick!" We bolted downstairs as quickly as we could and found Stephen leaning over the sink in the bathroom, bleeding profusely from the mouth and nose. We grabbed towels and tried to stanch the flow, though with little success. We knew we had to get him back to the hospital right away. So, we made sure Caelyn was settled and as comfortable as possible, gave hurried instructions to Alison and Kristen, and bundled Stephen into the minivan, surrounded by towels and with a plastic basin in his lap to catch the blood.

The doctors in the Emergency Department (ED) at Children's Hospital determined that Stephen's post-surgical scabs had come off too early, resulting in the profuse bleeding from his throat. This is not common following a tonsillectomy, but it does happen about three percent of the time. The ED resident had to cauterize Stephen's throat to stop the blood flow and promote proper healing. Right after the doctor finished the procedure, Stephen, whose stomach had apparently filled up with the flowing blood, threw up all over the floor of the treatment room. We were secretly glad that it happened at the hospital, where someone else would clean up the mess for us.

They admitted Stephen for overnight observation, just to make sure the bleeding wouldn't start up again. Kristen drove down to stay with him for the night so that Kathy and I could go home and care for Caelyn during her first night at home. Late the next afternoon, Stephen was discharged, and he and Kristen came home. We were all, finally, together again. We did go ahead with the planned ice cream party and Lucy-fest that evening, and it was a party indeed — though, for obvious reasons, not as loud or energetic as some of our other parties have been.

The remainder of 2006

We thereafter settled into our temporary routine, which included some pretty extensive daily care for Caelyn. She came home from the hospital with five drainage catheters sticking out of her little body, in addition to the significant surgical incision I mentioned earlier. Every day we had to clean and treat all of her stomas and the incision, as well as flushing her various drains. She was scheduled to go back to the hospital on the day before Thanksgiving, when she would again go into the operating room to have her drains removed and to permit the surgeon to examine her internally via cystoscope.

About three weeks after Caelyn's surgery, Kathy was heading downstairs one morning to begin the day. She was carrying Kathryn in one arm and her Macintosh laptop computer in the other. As she was coming down the stairs, she tripped on one of the steps and fell. Somehow, heroically, she managed to hold onto Kathryn and protect her while she fell. Her computer wasn't so lucky, as it tumbled end over end down to the landing at the bottom. Miraculously, though, neither Kathryn nor the computer sustained any damage. Kathy, however, didn't fare so well. She injured her left knee pretty badly, to the extent that we ended up taking her to see an orthopedic surgeon for exam and treatment. It was determined that she had sprained her medial collateral ligament (MCL) and her anterior cruciate ligament (ACL), and she was confined to a cumbersome knee brace and the use of crutches for several weeks. She also had to visit a physical therapist twice a week for about four weeks. All of the kids were great at helping me carry the extra load around the house while Kathy recovered from her injuries.

On the day before Thanksgiving, Kathy and I took Caelyn back to Children's Hospital for the surgical procedure to remove her drains. We had been told that we would have to spend the night, to make sure that we had enough time to be trained on how to catheterize Caelyn through the new Mitrofanoff and how to flush her large intestine via her new cecostomy. Caelyn's surgeon, however, let us know that he would authorize Caelyn's release that same day if Kathy and I felt comfortable with the new care regimen. We worked diligently all day to master the various techniques required, and we all returned home late that evening, very relieved that we would be sleeping in our own beds that night rather than at the hospital.

In light of our having to spend the day before Thanksgiving at the hospital—coupled with Kathy's physical incapacity due to her knee injury—a group of dear friends worked together to provide a complete Thanksgiving feast for our family. (This was on top of the work they all had to do to provide Thanksgiving dinner for their own families.) Our hearts were warmed, beyond our capacity to express, by the generosity of these special women, and our family enjoyed our Thanksgiving meal that year perhaps more than any other since our second trip to Bolivia. This gracious act also touched our hearts on the question of how members of God's community at large can be involved in adoption, even if not adopting themselves. The following e-mail excerpt relates some of our thoughts on this topic:

> **E-mail excerpt, December 4, 2006**: *We are constantly amazed and so grateful that God has blessed us with such a support system here in Cincinnati. If you are a person who feels confident that God hasn't called you to adopt personally, please consider ways that you can support other families who have been called to adopt. Those who bless our family in such ways tell us all the time how blessed they have been through giving. God just works that way, you know? And our children are surrounded by so many tangible expressions of God's love and examples of the way His children should be living and touching others in the world. We are thankful.*

The Rosenow family closed out 2006 with our eyes fixed on the grace of our Savior, still looking forward to where He would lead us in the year to come. And we remained mindful of the fact that Evan and Shannen were still in Guatemala, waiting to come home to us. How long, O Lord? How long?

Chapter 16

Putting One Foot in Front of the Other

It is a glorious thing to know that your Father God makes no
mistakes in directing or permitting that which crosses the path of
your life. It is the glory of God to conceal a matter. It is our glory
to trust Him, no matter what.

Joni Eareckson Tada

Bruising our bruises

I grew up in a small town in southern Wisconsin situated on the
shores of the Rock River. In the winter, much of the river would
freeze. There was a small lagoon off of the river at Riverside Park.
When the lagoon froze solid each year, public ice skating was permitted on it. My brothers and I often had the pleasure of skating on
the lagoon on weekend afternoons. I say skating, but we younger
three were really *learning* to skate more than actually skating. In
fact, I spent a lot of time falling. Even now, the image in my mind
is fairly comical, as I would scoot along, practically running across

314

the ice, and then my toe pick would catch something and down I would go. Unfortunately, my usual mode of landing would be to catch myself . . . with my elbows. After a couple of hours of skating, and particularly after two or three weeks of this, my elbows would become very bruised. Back then I used to describe them as "mushy," they would get so swollen and tender. I couldn't stand to have anything touch them, and it often took months for them to heal fully, once the skating season was over. It seemed that ordinary little bumps became fierce because of the tenderness of my elbows.

The year 2007 turned out to be, quite possibly, the fullest and most difficult year for us, in many ways, since the beginning of our adoption journeys—and this was coming, remember, on the heels of 2006. By the time we came to the beginning of 2007, I think our emotional state resembled the physical state of my elbows during skating season. We had been battered emotionally to the point that every little thing—even good things—struck us with heightened impact. We cried very easily; we went through our days figuratively wincing as we subconsciously waited for the next blow to fall. Into this milieu came two developments early that year. The first was positive, the second decidedly negative, but both caused intense emotional reactions and tears.

The first thing

In January, we began the adoption of another child from Guatemala. Once again, Kathy and I received a phone call from Mary, the adoption facilitator we had worked with in Guatemala, asking us to adopt a child in trouble—a little boy whose adoptive family had changed their mind. The child was an infant named Miguel Angel. He was an apparently healthy child, and a family had committed to his adoption early on. But when he was three and a half months old, still living with a foster family in Guatemala, he suffered a significant seizure. An MRI and CT scan performed after the seizure revealed that he had a couple of problems with the development of his brain, and his future suddenly became very uncertain. When the adopting family learned about all of this, they decided that the risks associated with this child were too great and they withdrew from his adoption. This caused all of us at TSC great concern, because conditions were shaping themselves in adoption relations between the US and Guatemala that threatened to put a halt to all adoptions from Guatemala to the US

The concerns about ongoing adoptions centered around the Hague Convention[35] and its implementation by the United States. One of the provisions of this Convention, which is effectively a treaty according to US constitutional law, requires, among other things, that member states that have implemented the Convention not conduct intercountry adoptions with any other member state that has implemented the Convention but is not in compliance with its requirements. The United States had previously signed the Convention but had not yet implemented it. Guatemala, on the other hand, had implemented the Convention but was not in compliance with its requirements. The reason intercountry adoptions between Guatemala and the US were in jeopardy was that America was preparing to implement the Convention fully. When that happened, because of the provisions of the Convention, all intercountry adoptions between Guatemala and America would immediately cease. No one knew exactly when the US would implement, but rumors were circulating that it could happen soon. Once that took place, thousands of children would be trapped in Guatemala indefinitely.

If a family didn't commit to pursuing the adoption of this little boy quickly, he would be among those left behind.

After prayer and discussion, we decided that God was leading us to begin this additional adoption in Guatemala. Our hearts, still tender after the bruisings of the previous autumn, committed to the task of bringing this child home, but we were admittedly fearful. We were at that time still in process for two other children in Guatemala, and we were concerned that we might once again begin an adoption that would never be permitted to complete. We had been working on Shannen's adoption for a full five months, and on Evan's for eleven months, and there was nothing official to show that either adoption had even begun. In both cases, we had paid thousands of dollars to attorneys who weren't doing their jobs, and our hearts were already completely linked to our babies.

A minor digression

Soon after making the decision to adopt Shannen several months earlier, our kids had been eager to begin the traditional Rosenow name-choosing process, but Kathy had been resistant to doing so. Typically, this is one of the steps in our children's adoptions that she enjoys the most. Kathy's heart, however was at that time still healing after the loss of Lauren in Guatemala. Her fears that Evan's adoption might never become a reality caused her to hesitate. Mostly due to the insistence of our children, she had finally agreed to move forward with choosing a name, but she continued to refer to Shannen by her Guatemalan name. She also reverted to calling Evan by his Guatemalan name and no longer referred to him as "Evan."

One night months later, Kathy was sitting alone on the sofa in our family room after the kids had gone to bed, and she was trying to pray for our babies—begging God to bring them home to us. Suddenly, she was keenly aware of the fact that her refusal to pray for and talk about these babies by the names we believed God had given us for them, was a sin. Her heart was pierced and broken as she forced herself to look truthfully at what she had been holding back from these little ones, and from the God who had brought them into our lives. She confessed this and made a commitment to begin to call them by their new names from that point forward.

In light of all of this struggling, we made the decision to choose a name for this new little one in Guatemala as soon as we began the adoption process. After a lengthy search, we settled on Ethan Alexander, which means "mighty defender of mankind." We didn't know what his story would look like as it unfolded, but it was our prayer that God would work through this child and, in some way, use any aspects of his story, in the years to come, to save other children waiting to be rescued.

The second thing

As January drew to a close, we began to realize that our adoption of Evan probably was not going to happen. On February 6, we received word from our contacts in Guatemala that the adoption was definitely over. We would never be permitted to bring Evan Michael Rosenow, still officially known as Luis Miguel, out of Guatemala and into our home.

Coming as it did, effectively, on the heels of our loss of Lauren the previous August, this news was a terrific blow to us. Our grief was on two levels: the first was our deep sadness at the realization that this beautiful and special child would not be joining our family, that we would be denied the benefits of being his parents. On the second level, we grieved for Evan, whose spina bifida would remain untreated, and who would never experience the love and security that come from belonging, from being a part of a family.

A few days after learning that Evan would never be coming home to us, Kathy was writing to thank a group of friends for the late Christmas gift of a desperately needed new stove. In that e-mail, she shared some of her thoughts about this most recent painful lesson from God. An excerpt of her e-mail follows:

E-mail excerpt, February 21, 2007: *For reasons I still don't really understand fully, the news that Evan's adoption will never be completed was absolutely devastating for me. I was shaken in deep places in my faith. I cried for days, and asked God so many questions during those dark, painful days. Scott and I think that part of the reason we may have had such a hard time with this* is that our hearts are just still a bit raw from Lauren's death in August and some other areas of grief from this past year. It seemed like these things just kept piling on top of each other – not like each one was a new grief, but more like each one just took up where the last one left off until we felt buried under them all and just kind of lost.

I went through a period earlier in his adoption process when I realized that I was resisting any connection with Evan and Shannen because of the doubts about Evan's ever coming out and the pain I had felt when this happened with some of our other adoptions – when the children didn't actually end up coming home. When I became aware of this, God convicted me of this and made it clear that I was sinning. He had not asked us to pursue these children's adoptions as casual onlookers, but as their parents. He had asked me to accept the responsibility of fighting for these children as their mother. He showed me that if I wouldn't love these children with a mother's heart and the love of a mommy, and if I wouldn't pray for them with a mother's cries for her babies, then I wasn't fully obeying Him and I wasn't glorifying Him. I knew that He was asking me to do this regardless of the pain it might bring later in the process. I confessed this and embraced this little boy and this little girl with all my heart then. So when Evan was snatched away from us, the pain was very real and intense.

A couple of nights ago, I was standing in the kitchen cooking supper. Once again the tears started to flow as I pictured Evan's face and remembered how he had started to really connect with us and bond to us on our last trip to Guatemala. I ached as I

320

pictured his future now — the paralysis that will surely take away the function of his legs, and the loss of kidney function that will very possibly take his life while he is still young. Silently, I was saying, "God, where are you in all of this? Do you care? Do you care about him? Do you care about our pain? Are you still there?" Then I looked down at the food I was stirring and saw my stove. I know that this sounds silly, but in that instant, it was as if God said, "Do you see this stove that I sent to you? This stove is a symbol — a reminder — of My promise that I am still here. That I care. That I will always take care of My children." A little bit of peace began to flicker in my heart at that point.

A couple of nights later, during a family discussion about God and His sovereignty and His "no" answers to our prayers, we noticed that Caelyn, one of our six-year-old daughters with spina bifida, had tears running down her cheeks. We asked her what was wrong, and she started to cry like her heart would break. Then she said, "I wanted so bad for Evan to come home to us and have us for his family." She, with her paralysis and spina bifida complications, knows even better than the rest of us what lies ahead for him — and that he is in a country where he will not have the medical care he needs or the support that our family could've given him.

We, of course, don't have all of the answers for them (or ourselves) about the ways in which God works, but we told them what we do know — that we have to trust in His love for us and Evan and in His perfect knowledge. And we have to leave all of the Evans in His hands and just keep loving them as He brings them across our paths and fighting for them whenever He calls us into battle.

We are doing much better overall and feel like God has helped us regain our footing and balance now. We don't know what God's up to next. It's been a hard year, and our hearts are feeling a little wounded, but we are looking to Him – not for explanations now, but for marching orders for whatever comes next. I'm sure there will be more tears – maybe forever – for all of our babies who don't end up coming home, but He is showing us – and sometimes we are able to see it – that it is an honor to be given the opportunity to cry a mother's and a daddy's tears for these special ones of His. We continue to ask Him to make us worthy of this calling and for grace to do it for no other reason than to obey and glorify Him, and to do it in a way that it will be an acceptable gift to Him. And we continue to thank Him for using others to pass on very tangible reminders of His presence in our lives and His love for those who follow Him.

Shortly after this, we lost all contact with Evan in Guatemala. We have not been able since then to get any word as to how he is doing, whether or not his spina bifida has resulted in loss of function or sensation, or whether he is even still living in his foster home. We still cry tears for this lost son of ours.

♫ "Goin' to the chapel . . ." ♫

Back in October of '06, while Caelyn was in the hospital recovering from her major reconstructive surgery, our oldest daughter, Kristen, began dating a young man she had met in college. They had known each other for several years and had become close friends.

But in October, they had come to the sudden realization that they were in love with each other. They were both very serious about their relationship with God, and they both had a very high view of marriage. Their romance continued to develop, and very soon they knew that they wanted to spend the rest of their lives together. In February, they made it official by announcing their engagement. Kristen Marie Rosenow was committing herself to marry Greg Matthew Godwin. We were very excited for both of them and couldn't have been more pleased. And so, in addition to everything else that characterized our frenetic lifestyle, we began talking about and planning a wedding — a first for all of us Rosenows.

Once Kristen and Greg had begun getting serious about each other, but before Greg had actually proposed, they spoke about the future and family. At one point Kristen said to Greg, "You need to know that I am named as guardian of my brothers and sisters, should anything happen to my parents.Greg said, "I figured that."

"And you're OK with that? I did say 'all' of my brothers and sisters."

"Yeah, I'm OK with that. I pretty much figured that was the case."

I can tell you, when we heard that, the deal was cemented in our minds. This was the son-in-law God had picked out for us, the right husband for our daughter. Truthfully, there were many other signs that let us know that Greg was the one, besides his willingness to become a part of this insanely large family. He was committed to Kristen, and he was committed to his relationship with God. All in all, he was just the sort of young man we would've picked out for Kristen if we'd chosen someone ourselves.

Kristen decided early on that she wanted her brothers and sisters to be in the wedding. Now remember, Kristen at the time had seven sisters and six brothers, so the idea of having all of them participate in her wedding was no small thing. We didn't see how she could make it work, but she was determined that this wedding would be a family affair, and we were certain that she would find a way to do it—and we knew it would be beautiful.

Greg came from a small family, having only one sibling, a brother. But he threw himself into the process of getting to know the large family he was marrying into, and he has done an amazing job from the very beginning. We laughed when we realized that a few of the younger kids were under the mistaken impression that we were planning to adopt Greg, but they all embraced him as a new member of the family in spite of the fact that he already had a family of his own.

Carlin

Early in March, Carlin entered our Children's Hospital for her bladder reconstruction surgery. She was scheduled for the bladder neck reconstruction and Mitrofanoff but not for the Malone.[36] As had been the case with Caelyn, there was the question of whether or not she would also require bladder augmentation—a question that would not be answered until the surgeons made the determination during the lengthy operation.

The surgery began at about 9:00 in the morning and was done by 2:30 that afternoon. The doctors determined that there was no reason to augment Carlin's bladder size, and thus they were able to keep the procedure at just five and a half hours. She did extremely well following the operation. She had much less difficulty with the bladder spasms than Caelyn had, and overall her pain was very manageable. She did have a really bad reaction to morphine, but once we got the Pain Management Team to discontinue that, she improved steadily. After ten days in the hospital, we were able to bring her home. As with Caelyn, she came home accompanied by many drains and tubes and the need for regular drain irrigations and intense post-operative care.

The ministry

The number of TSC adoptions continued to increase, as did the number of TSC families. By this time we had been a part of bringing roughly 150 children home, and close to 100 families had partnered with us as TSC families. We continued to thank God for each and every one of these adoption stories and adoptive families. We had also grown to a staff of over thirty volunteers, and we were in near-urgent need of a full-time administrative assistant. We began to pray that God would provide everything we needed to fill this position. We had neither the funds available for an additional salary nor a person in mind who possessed the skills and temperament we knew this job called for. And we were adamant that the highest requirement for this person would be a passion to serve God through caring for the orphans of the world. In spite of what we needed but didn't have, though, we had confidence that God would supply in every way.

We love Cincinnati Children's Hospital

In April, three of our girls had surgical procedures at Children's Hospital. Carlin had to go in to have all of her drains removed, following her major reconstruction surgery in March. Caelyn had to have her two abdominal stomas revised. (The stoma is the opening in the skin; she has one for her Mitrofanoff and one for her Malone.) Both of these stomas had become problematic. In fact, the Malone stoma had closed up and we were no longer able to insert a catheter into it. So Caelyn had a surgery to revise and reopen those stomas.

Kathryn had to have surgery on her eyes. She had exhibited a form of strabismus since we brought her home, and her ophthalmologist had tried a number of therapeutic techniques to correct it, unsuccessfully. The doctor finally concluded that the muscles controlling Kathryn's eyes required a slight repositioning, to try to correct her problematic wandering. The surgery was minor, and her recovery was relatively simple, especially considering the way in which even minor interruptions to her routine affect her so much. The trip to Children's Hospital for Kathryn's surgery was a little more interesting than it might have been, because Caelyn's surgery was on the same day. But both girls did amazingly well, and the day was pretty unexceptional.

Meanwhile, in Central America . . .

We continued struggling to bring Shannen home from Guatemala, and Ethan's adoption process moved into full swing. We became acutely aware of the difference the right attorney can make in a process like this. Whereas Shannen's process was arduous and seemed to require continual input from us even to keep it viable, Ethan's moved along almost effortlessly. We found ourselves thinking thoughts like, "Sure the process is moving along quickly right now, but it'll stop soon, and then it will end up just like Evan's and Shannen's." But in May, we received our preliminary approval from the USCIS office in Guatemala City, and we moved to the next critical step in the courts of Guatemala — entry into PGN.

We were elated at this news. PGN (*Procuraduría General de la Nación*) is Guatemala's Solicitor General's office and is responsible for, among other things, final adjudication of adoption cases prior to their approval. There are several steps in the process in Guatemala to get to the PGN stage, and here we were, just four months into Ethan's adoption and already entering PGN. Shannen's case, by contrast, had not even cleared the very first step in the overall process. We were, as I said, elated about Ethan's case, but this news left us even more concerned about the final outcome of Shannen's case.

A make-over blessing

We were contacted in April by a group of people who knew our family and loved the work God was doing through us. They were members of a local church that had initiated a community service project, called Go Cincinnati, to encourage members to get involved in helping in the name of the Lord, and to provide much-needed assistance to families and ministries throughout the Cincinnati area. This group knew that we had pretty much outgrown our house, and even though they knew that they couldn't increase our physical space, they wanted to do a major project to spruce the place up and make it more livable for us.

The project in the end included the time and talents of nearly one hundred volunteers, and what they did for us and our house! They painted most of the interior; they replaced the flooring in the dining room and one of the bathrooms; they weeded and mulched our flower beds, front and back; they completely cleaned and organized the garage; they added shelving organizer units in our closet and in the laundry room; they replaced the carpet in the family room and in Erin's bedroom; they cleaned up and organized our basement; and more!

We were, all of us, moved to tears by the outpouring of love and self-sacrifice this group showered on our family. One night shortly after the project was finished, one of our older sons was praying in the family room. He said, "God, I thank You so much for all of the home improvements these people brought to our house. And we thank You for teaching us, first, that we can live without these really not-very-necessary things, like freshly painted walls, nice curtains, matching dishes and new, clean carpet. It was a good thing for us to learn that we don't have to have these things to live for and serve You, and we are so grateful to You now for giving them to us as a gift. Thank You for these people who gave up their time, donated their money, and worked so hard to bring us these things from You."

To hear one of our children pray this prayer was a real encouragement to us, because it helped us know that God is speaking to them, too, as He is speaking to us in all of these circumstances — both the easy times and the hard times.

When it rains, it pours

I've always found that an interesting saying. An older version of it seems a little more acceptable to me: "It never rains but it pours." The meaning is that when things start happening, whether good things or bad things, they seem to come in huge numbers or quantities, rather than just a little at a time. Such often seems to be the case in our lives, particularly with adoptions. We were, at this time, struggling mightily to bring Shannen and Ethan home from Guatemala. It's difficult to say whether it was merely raining or actually pouring, but we were figuratively getting very wet.

In early May, the rain picked up a bit: we learned of a little boy in upstate New York who had been adopted from China about a year earlier, and whose adoptive family wanted to dissolve his adoption and find a new family for him. This little guy, who was five, had a severe cleft lip and cleft palate and had also developed a cholesteatoma in his left ear. A cholesteatoma is a benign[37] tumor that, in this case, grows in the middle ear as a consequence of frequent ear infections.

The family that had adopted this child felt that they could handle all of his medical conditions, but that his behavioral issues were more than they could deal with. They described him as having reactive attachment disorder (RAD), and they explained that they simply did not feel qualified to parent a child with this condition.

As we looked into this child's situation and what The Shepherd's Crook might do for him, we talked with a couple of families we thought might provide a good home for him. In both cases, the families decided, after prayer and consideration, that they were not in a position to adopt this little boy. Kathy and I felt instantly drawn to him, however, and after the other two families let us know their decision, we prayed for God's leading as to whether ours might be this little boy's home. We quickly came to the conclusion that we were supposed to adopt him, and we contacted our adoption attorney and set things in motion to bring him home.

The RAD label that had been attached to this child caused us concern. There have been documented cases of RAD-diagnosed kids acting out in violence and aggression, sometimes even attacking their adoptive parents and siblings. We were concerned, but we were also convinced that if God were calling us to pursue this adoption, then He would guide us throughout. We weren't saying that we believed He would protect us from any harm, or that He would cause things to work out perfectly and happily for all of us, including the child. We were saying that His call is the most important consideration in any situation, and if He called us, our duty was to obey.

And so we began the process to adopt this child, whom we decided to name Ian Matthew, which means, "gracious gift of God."

"Aslan is on the move"

One of our favorite books to read as a family is *The Lion, the Witch, and the Wardrobe*, by C. S. Lewis. This book is the first installment in *The Chronicles of Narnia*, a delightful series written for children and containing some of the profoundest expressions of Christian truth available in extra-biblical form. In this book, the four Pevensie children are transported magically to a land called Narnia, in which the animals talk and act much like humans. This land is ruled by the evil White Witch, who makes it always winter but never Christmas. However, when the Pevensies arrive, they are told that Aslan, the real ruler of Narnia who hasn't been seen in the realm in living memory, has been spotted. It is rumored that he may be returning to overthrow the White Witch and restore Narnia to its rightful situation. Aslan, the largest and most powerful of all lions, is a figure of Christ.

As Mr. Beaver is explaining everything to the children, he tells them, excitedly and with awe in his voice, that "Aslan is on the move." This mysterious reference communicates all of the wonder and hope which only children are capable of understanding. And indeed, Aslan does arrive on the scene and, through the agency of the Penvensie children, overthrows the White Witch and restores peace and harmony to the land of Narnia.

Whenever we Rosenows, here in this concrete world, are sensing that God is putting things in place to answer prayer in a big way, we find ourselves saying to each other, "Aslan is on the move."

While all of these things were going on with Ian and his adoption, we were approached by some friends who had a proposal for us. Frank Riley and his wife, Suzanne, met with us for dinner one evening, and Frank told us what had been on his heart for quite some time. He felt that the Lord had been leading him to head up a project to provide a larger home for our family, one that would meet the unique needs of so many children with so many different disabilities and special requirements. Frank was well qualified to head up such a project: his career has been as a construction project manager in various capacities, and he is currently vice president of client services for a major facilities management company based in the Midwest.

Frank laid out his thoughts and convictions before us, telling us that he felt strongly that God had been leading him to head up such a project for quite some time, but that he had only recently come to the unavoidable conclusion that the time was now. This house would be large enough for our very large family, with room for the children at an older age than they then were, and even with some room for additional children we would, in all probability, adopt in the years to come.

Kathy and I were absolutely overwhelmed at this revelation. We had actually been praying for many years for just such a house, though in secret. Here we seemed to be receiving confirmation that God had heard our prayers and was putting things in place to answer those prayers. How we rejoiced and praised God for this! We also thanked Frank for being willing to be used in this capacity. There is a much larger story here, but the telling of it would require a book all on its own. Suffice it to say, Aslan was on the move.

Trying times and many tears

Kathy and I took a quick trip to Guatemala on May 26. We went primarily to meet nine-month-old Ethan, to make sure that his citizenship would be established upon his arrival in the States, but also to have a meeting with the attorney handling Shannen's case. Our intention was to "lay down the law" to this attorney, to try to induce her to do something, anything, to get the case moving. We had started Shannen's adoption when she was a newborn, and now, at ten months old, she was still no closer to coming home to us. This was a whirlwind trip, but we did have the meeting with the attorney, and we did get to spend some wonderful time with our little Ethan. The meeting with the attorney was intense, and discussions became heated before we finished. The meeting ended abruptly when the attorney stood up, turned her back on us, and stormed out of the hotel room without even bothering to close the door. Tears ran down Kathy's face in the stunned silence that followed, as she tried to accept what we believed was the end of Shannen's adoption process. We came back home on May 27.

Our return home was greeted with such unexpected and frenetic activity that we didn't have much time, initially, to grieve over the outcome of our meeting in Guatemala, which we viewed as nothing short of failure. The day after we got back, Caelyn began having trouble with her Malone. She had had intermittent problems since healing from the operation the previous fall. Sometimes it was extremely difficult to get the catheter fully inserted into the Malone, requiring much patience and persistence. But on that Memorial Day Monday in late May, try as we might, we could not get the catheter inserted. We finally called the urologist to let him know what had happened and to find out what we should do. He told us to bring Caelyn to the Emergency Department (ED) at Children's, which we did. The ED doctor and one of the urology residents tried for well over an hour to get the catheter inserted, but still without success. Finally, Caelyn's doctor, contacted by phone, told the resident to stop trying, and that he wanted to take Caelyn into the operating room to explore the Malone under anesthesia, using an endoscope. He came to the hospital to do the operation himself, even though it was a holiday. The procedure was supposed to take fifteen minutes; after forty minutes, Caelyn's doctor came out and told us, with great difficulty and obvious emotion, that she had lost her Malone — it was no longer usable.

The explanation for why this happened was somewhat involved and difficult to understand fully, but the bottom line was that Caelyn had lost the hope of gaining bowel continence. This was an issue with an emotional impact, especially for a six-year-old little girl dreaming of the day when she would get out of diapers like other little girls. We didn't tell Caelyn what her doctor had said before putting her to bed that night, believing that she would be better able to handle the news the next morning.

Excerpt from Kathy's e-mail, May 29, 2007: *Scott brought Caelyn into bed with us this morning when she woke up, and we talked through everything with her. She is just an amazing little girl. The tears started to fall without her face even moving. Then she just quietly cried her heart out for awhile. She was* *very subdued over the next few hours, but talking well about her feelings concerning all of it. She even told us very openly and innocently that she is a little bit mad at God because she knows He could've saved her Malone and made it work. We had a long talk about that. Then she told us that she wanted to be the one to tell the other kids, so we carried her downstairs to talk to the others, and gathered everyone into our family room. Caelyn swallowed really hard a few times to pull herself together and then very, very clearly explained everything that had happened and what it means for her. When she got to the part where she told them she would have to give up her dreams of ever getting out of diapers, she just slowly buried her face against my neck and broke down again. Scott and I pretty much lost it at that point. After she cried a bit, we asked the others if they had anything they wanted to say, and several of them cried for her, too.*

Madlin didn't cry but went to her and just said how sorry she was that this happened. Colin (who is blind, if you have a hard time keeping them straight) wanted to get across the room to her right away so he could touch her, then cried so hard that we had difficulty understanding him. He said, "Caelyn, I'm so sorry you don't get to be like other girls your age and stop wearing diapers." It was so clearly from his heart. Meghan and Robyn teared up, but didn't talk. Nathan stoically told her how sorry he was, but later when I talked to him alone he cried and told us that he is really, really sad for Caelyn. Braedan said, "I don't want to say anything, but I want to hug Caelyn." Carlin cried when she told Caelyn how sorry she was about all of it and how bad she is going to feel, now that her surgery has been so successful and they can't put away their diapers together. They have talked about this and dreamed of it together since before their surgeries. Stephen came to her and started to cry pretty hard and said he felt really sad for Caelyn. They have all totally rallied around her in a way that actually surprised us a little bit, and we already know what great kids they are. When we did her bowel routine this morning, she just lay on the floor through it all, crying silently.

We didn't know it yet, but this marked merely the beginning of a long period of trying times for Caelyn, which culminated in another massive surgery a few months down the road.

Chapter 17

Richer by the Dozen

Hope fills the afflicted soul with such inward joy and
consolation, that it can laugh while tears are in the eye, sigh
and sing all in a breath; it is called "the rejoicing of hope."
(Hebrews 3:6).

William Gurnall

The exciting times go on

Early in the month of June, Kathy and I drove to the nearby
Columbus airport to meet our new son, Ian, whose adoptive
family was flying in with him for the "hand-off." We had been preparing our other children to meet their new brother, but we really
had little idea what to expect. The litany of potential behavioral
problems presented to us was impressive and a bit scary, but we
also felt in our hearts that at least some exaggeration, whether
intentional or not, had to have been in play.

We took a photo book for Ian with us, to help him "meet"
his new family even before the actual encounter that would take

place later in the day. After picking him up at the airport—which included a tearful and confusing good-bye from the adoptive mom—we headed out to a hotel room, where we had decided to spend a few quiet hours letting him begin to get acquainted with us and beginning our acquaintance with him. He looked at the pictures in the book as we went through it with him, but he did not seem really engaged. More than anything he seemed to be confused and frightened, and we did our absolute best to console and reassure him.

We then went shopping to buy a few needed items of clothing for Ian. Based on what we had been told, we halfway expected some sort of tantrum or other wild behavior in the store; nothing of the sort happened. He was compliant and accommodating, though he was very quiet and still appeared to be somewhat afraid. Next, we went to lunch at a Mexican restaurant. There was a small battle of wills over the question of French fries—none were available—but we got through that, and he ate well and thoroughly. Finally, we climbed into the car for the two-hour drive back home.

Once we got Ian home and into the mix of the family, he seemed to fit in immediately—and the mandatory six-month waiting period for the adoption in Ohio began. We very quickly became aware of two truths about this newest little Rosenow. First, he was very sensitive, and he very much wanted to please us. Second, he was not the terror that had been described to us, even though we clearly had some work to do concerning his behavior. The following e-mail excerpt gives a glimpse into how things progressed after Ian came home.

Excerpt, June 11, 2007: *This is just a short note to let you know that Ian has arrived home safely and is doing great. We are just amazed, at this point, at how easily he is fitting into our family. He definitely seems to be used to ruling the roost and having everything he demands, and he has tried a few of his tricks on us when we wouldn't give him what he demanded. So far he has relented very quickly in the face of our firm resolve not to back down with him. He is charming and a very easy-to-love little boy with a good sense of humor and what appears to be a genuine hunger for love and clearly defined discipline. He is responding so beautifully to our boundaries and the consequences when he doesn't follow these rules, and he is also soaking up and joining in the fun and laughter with his siblings. He seems to be tender and sensitive toward Kathryn and desirous of pleasing us. It is an understatement to say that he is active, and we still watch him constantly, as he has so much to learn. Because of this, we are pretty exhausted, but it's a good – and even happy – kind of tired, and we are blessed beyond our expectations by his presence in our home. He seems to absolutely love this big, loud family and is already showing signs of thriving under our care. The other children have been great about the amount of time and attention we have been required to give to Ian, and they have so wholeheartedly welcomed him into their hearts that it has brought tears to our eyes to watch it unfold in front of us.*

We were taken by surprise, once again, that a child had entered our family through the path of a dissolved adoption and had slipped so easily into just being a Rosenow.

Kristen and Greg, after much deliberation, had scheduled their wedding for July 14. Early in June, almost immediately after Ian came home, all of the guys in the family had to assemble at the tuxedo store to be fitted for tuxes for the wedding. We wonder what Ian thought of all of this because, even though he seemed to take it all in stride, he didn't share any of his thoughts or feelings about the fact that it must have seemed like a strange thing to be doing with this new family.

No rest for the weary

Caelyn was still recovering from the loss of her Malone, which had happened at the end of May, and she seemed to be suffering a physical malaise whose cause we couldn't identify. Her appetite was down, her energy level was pretty well gone, and she just didn't seem to feel well. On top of that, she began leaking urine from her Mitrofanoff, which is not supposed to happen, ever. It got to the point that every morning, her sheets would be soaked, and sometimes we even had to change her saturated sheets during the night, only to get up and change them again in the morning. The urology team, after a number of tests, determined that she had a stone in her bladder. Her doctor told us that the stone would have to be removed surgically, but that it would be done on an outpatient basis.

So, here we were, trudging through the month of June, trying to juggle the demands of having a new child in the home, while also planning for a wedding that would involve virtually everyone in the family, and trying at the same time to take care of Caelyn, who seemed to be getting sicker all the time and whose regimen grew more and more demanding.

On June 21, Caelyn went in for outpatient surgery to have her bladder stone removed. The procedure was brief, and the surgeon reported afterward that he had successfully removed all of the stone. We all anticipated that Caelyn's symptoms would begin to subside and that she would soon be, once again, her normal self. Unfortunately this turned out not to be the case. Her Mitrofanoff continued to leak profusely, and as the weeks passed, we did not see her return to health as we had all hoped.

Wedding

Greg and Kristen had chosen a Renaissance theme for their wedding, and we had managed to find a local seamstress who helped create unique Renaissance-style dresses for all of the girls. On July 14, 2007, all of the Rosenow children donned their wedding togs and headed to our home church. It pretty much goes without saying that trying to get a family of sixteen—including eleven under the age of twelve—ready for a wedding is a pretty big deal. And when all sixteen of us are in the wedding, it gets even bigger. We were up at the crack of dawn, getting kids fed, getting dresses and tuxedos on, doing head after head of beautiful hair, feeding all of the little kids a snack, trying not to get any of the clothes dirty, and somehow finally loading everyone into three vehicles to leave for the church so we could be there early.

The wedding processional was memorable. Kathryn was in a wheelchair, Caelyn was able to walk only using forearm crutches, and because of Colin's blindness, some accommodations had to be made for him. Nathan pushed Kathryn's wheelchair for her, and Carlin guided Colin down the aisle under the ruse that he was escorting her. Colin held his white cane in one hand and held onto Carlin's arm with the other. Stephen escorted Caelyn down the aisle and carried the basket of flower petals for her. Periodically during their march, he would pause so that she could stop, lean on her crutches, and reach into the basket to pull out some petals and drop them on the floor. It was very sweet.

The wedding ceremony was beautiful. Greg and Kristen wrote their own vows and exchanged them with love and commitment radiating from their eyes. They both desired that their wedding ceremony, as the moment that would begin the rest of their lives together, should be very God-centered and symbolic—and it was. It was a meaningful event for all of us. At the end of the day, Kristen and Greg headed off to honeymoon at a cabin in Tennessee, and we set about getting back to normal life.

Caelyn

"Normal life," though, was complicated, since Caelyn was still having so much trouble with her Mitrofanoff. The continuous leaking of urine plagued her and made any excursions outside of home challenging for her. As we moved toward the end of July, we grew more and more concerned about Caelyn and the way she was deteriorating in front of us.

Just before the end of July, Caelyn began running a fever with no other symptoms. This went on for several days, at times running as high as 103 degrees (Fahrenheit). On August 2, she had a formal urodynamics study done at Children's Hospital. This was a scheduled test as part of the monitoring of her systems, both because of the damage done by the spina bifida and because of the reconstructive surgery she had had. The test revealed that her bladder was losing its elasticity, which was an indication that she might require bladder augmentation.

Caelyn's surgeon had told us that among children whose bladders are reconstructed but not augmented, about half of them require augmentation later on down the road — and that those who will require augmentation show it within the first year after reconstruction. So we were not completely surprised at this development, but we were deeply disappointed. This would mean another grueling surgery and recovery for Caelyn, as well as the increased risk for complications later in life.

On August 6, Caelyn was admitted to Children's because her persistent fever would not respond to oral antibiotics. The urology doctors suspected a kidney infection and wanted to administer intravenous antibiotics to treat it proactively while they ran tests to confirm it. The first thing they did was perform an ultrasonic evaluation of Caelyn's urologic system to check for damage to the kidneys. Fortunately, no damage was evident, though all of the floor nurses got pretty excited when Caelyn's temperature spiked to just over 106 degrees that day.

While we were with Caelyn in radiology for the ultrasound, we got a phone call from Guatemala with some amazing news. As of that day, we had a new son! The adoption of Ethan Alexander Rosenow had been approved and made official in Guatemala City, bringing our number of adopted children to an even dozen. The elation we felt was enormous, partly because we had protected our hearts from believing that this could really happen. After so many recent disappointments and frustrations, our spirits were lifted into the clouds at this news. We quickly had to return to earth and present reality, though, because Caelyn was so sick.

Caelyn stayed in the hospital for a few days while the doctors tried to battle her mysterious condition. Her primary specialist was in India during this time, but the fellows[38] and other partners did a great job taking care of Caelyn, and we remain grateful to the urology department at Children's for the care they have always provided. They did determine via renal scan that Caelyn had a kidney infection, and so they knew they were on the right track with the IV antibiotics. Within a few days, she had responded to the treatments and seemed to be recovering much of the vigor that had been missing for several months.

Finances

Jesus said, "Do not store up for yourselves treasures on earth, where moth and rust destroy, and where thieves break in and steal. But store up for yourselves treasures in heaven, where neither moth nor rust destroys, and where thieves do not break in or steal; for where your treasure is, there your heart will be also." (Matt. 6:19–21) There are times when it almost seems like He is making sure we take this to heart, and He does so by ensuring that we have no treasure on earth to store up.

While all of these events were going on in late summer, TSC found itself in serious financial difficulties. The ministry's finances, which were always borderline at best, had slipped into the critical sphere. We were facing the very real possibility that the ministry would have to fold and I would have to find another job to support the family.

On the personal front, our family's finances were also taking a beating. We had gotten the amazingly good news that Ethan's adoption was finished and we would be traveling soon to bring him home, but we didn't have the travel funds for us to go get him. Then, late in August, the air conditioner in our home died. It just quit working. This was especially frustrating to us because we had just replaced it three years earlier, and we had been forced to pay for a major repair on it earlier in August. We had no money to pay for a complete replacement.

A few years earlier we had taken out a home equity line of credit to pay for adoption expenses for Caelyn and to cover re-adoption expenses and some major automobile repairs. Just a couple of weeks earlier we had drawn more against this line of credit to pay the attorney fees for Ethan's adoption. Now we determined that we could add a little bit more to this line of credit, to pay for the replacement air conditioner, without exceeding the maximum we could borrow against that line—but we were pretty certain that it wouldn't be enough. On August 24, the day the unit died, the temperature hit 103 degrees in Cincinnati, and inside the house it rose to 93 degrees. We called a repair company, but their estimator couldn't come out to the house till 7:00 that evening. So we spent the day trying to stay cool—as cool as possible—and we prayed that God would provide a way for us to pay for the air conditioner.

The estimator showed up on time and spent about half an hour examining our system and estimating the replacement cost. The initial estimate was so high it caused us to gasp, but he reminded us that we had a discount because of the work done earlier in the month. After the discount, the estimate was still about $300 above what we could borrow against the home equity loan. He then shocked us by telling us that he was going to give us an additional discount, as he said, ". . . just because I think you guys deserve a break for all you are doing for these kids." This additional discount brought the estimate down to $400 *less* than we would be able to borrow.

We praised God and told the estimator to have someone come do the work the next day. Once again, God was reminding us of His unfailing provision—that He was still completely in control of everything, including our accumulating debt, even though we couldn't understand why He sometimes remained silent when we cried out for help. We prayed that He would increase our faith to be able to leave even our debt in His hands, and to be able to continue trusting Him to provide for us daily and eventually to make a way for us to pay off this debt.

Around this same time, Caelyn's urologist returned from India and we met with him to discuss the plans for Caelyn's future. He determined that her bladder had become noncompliant[39] and she would thus require augmentation surgery.

Ethan

As August gave way to September, we were finalizing details for a trip to Guatemala to bring home our new son, we were still grappling with the financial crisis in the ministry, and we were now making plans for another major surgery for Caelyn. Based on what the doctors were telling us, combined with Caelyn's strong desire, we decided to include another attempt at the Malone along with the bladder augmentation procedure. We weren't exactly sure when the surgery would take place, but we knew that it couldn't be until after the first of the year. And so we shifted our attention to our trip to Guatemala.

On September 9, Kathy and I flew to Guatemala City, along with Kathryn and Ryan. We had been praying for quite a while about whether or not we should take Kathryn along with us for the quick trip to get Ethan. At just three years old, she still did not typically do well when both Kathy and I were away, and she had been showing a lot of suspicious, seizure-like behavior over the last few weeks. We were concerned that the stress of both of us being away might induce a full-blown seizure, and we were torn between worrying about her possibly having a seizure in Guatemala, so far away from her doctors, and worrying about the possibility of her having a seizure at home while we were so far away from her. An organization, at the last minute, awarded us an adoption grant to help with expenses, and this seemed to us to be confirmation that our tentative plans for taking Kathryn along were being blessed by God. We felt that removing the stress of being separated from us might well reduce the risk of her having a seizure during our trip. We decided to take Ryan, too, because we knew we would need extra help dealing with both Kathryn and Ethan and that some of the time would include visits with Shannen, too. Ryan was almost eighteen and a senior in high school, and because we home-school it would be easy for him

The trip was a whirlwind of activity, including a visit to a number of facilities there that care for special-needs orphans. We were combining our trip to get Ethan with some TSC-related business, gathering information for ministry opportunities in the future. One of the facilities we visited is called *Obras Sociales Hermano Pedro Hospital*, located in the city of Antigua. This is a facility founded and operated by the Franciscan Order of the Roman Catholic Church, and it houses as many as four hundred patients ranging in age from a few days to more than ninety years. Most of the residents have some form of disability, such as cerebral palsy, muscular dystrophy, and mental retardation, and most reside permanently in the facility.

Our hearts broke as we walked through the children's wards of Hermano Pedro, seeing the many orphans languishing in cribs and beds. The work this facility does is important, and it is certainly a better life than its residents would face without it: without Hermano Pedro, most of the inhabitants would be forced to beg for daily sustenance, living in the streets—and dying there at an early age. But still, the life experienced by the inmates is, in most cases, bleak and colorless. We had been told that this was the very facility that Kathyrn would have been sent to had she not been adopted. We shuddered as we thought about our precious little girl spending day after day in a stainless steel crib, staring blankly into space, drifting further and further into a world of darkness and silence and isolation. We became even more determined, if possible, to serve as God's agents in finding homes for special-needs kids from anywhere on earth, for as long as He chooses to use us.

We, unfortunately, were not able to visit with Shannen as we had hoped, because Ethan had a terrible cold and we didn't want to chance exposing Shannen to illness. This was disappointing, but we knew it was best. We did, however, have the opportunity to visit Lauren's grave and show Ryan and Kathryn where their baby sister was buried. It was bittersweet to walk through the deserted cemetery again, purchase flowers for her little grave, and then stand before the "Wall of Babies," staring at the crypt that held our precious daughter's remains. The memories were still vivid and painful and brought fresh tears, but we were so grateful to have had the chance to visit there again. It made us wish we could find a way to bring all of our children there to see where Lauren had been buried.

At the end of this quick five-day trip, we brought home the newest little Rosenow child. Ethan was a mere thirteen months old, and he was one of the cutest little babies we had ever seen—and that's saying something. Once we got him home, we began the battery of tests, examinations, and evaluations necessary to ascertain his overall condition and to determine what we needed to address most urgently. An MRI we had done in October revealed, to our utter surprise, that he had schizencephaly, the same condition Kathryn has. Ethan's was a much milder form than Kathryn's, but it was schizencephaly just the same. Whereas Kathryn's was bilateral (on both sides of the brain), open- and closed-lip schizencephaly, Ethan's was unilateral (on only one side of the brain), closed-lip only. The differences between the open-lip and closed-lip forms remain something of a mystery to us, except that we have been told consistently that the former is more serious than the latter.

Finishing out the year

In October, Shannen's case moved into PGN. This was no small feat, since we had come almost to the conclusion that this beautiful child would never come home to us. After our confrontation with the attorney on our earlier trip to Guatemala, we feared that this attorney would refuse to do anything for Shannen, just out of spite toward us. And we did, in fact, have to continue badgering and cajoling her via e-mail throughout the month of October. Finally, late in the month, we received word from Guatemala that Shannen's case had entered PGN, and the end truly was in sight. Barring unforeseen complications, we envisioned being able to travel sometime in January to bring her home.

Early in December, Ian entered Children's Hospital for surgery to remove a cholesteatoma from his left ear. This was a repeat of a surgery he had had while still with his first adoptive family. Our ENT told us that it was not uncommon for a cholesteatoma to return, owing to the nature of the cyst. He said that a mere solitary cell left behind during surgical removal can be enough to re-grow the cholesteatoma, and that was apparently what happened in Ian's case. The surgeon, following the procedure, told us that he had had to remove a considerable amount of mastoid bone to ensure complete removal of the cholesteatoma, and that all three ossicles[40] of the inner ear were gone, having been eaten away by either the first or the second cholesteatoma. Fortunately, this was an outpatient procedure, and Ian returned home late in the day.

We managed to finish out 2007 with quite a bang. On Thursday, December 20, the whole Rosenow family gathered once again in the old Butler county courthouse for an adoption proceeding. This time, we were finalizing the adoption of Ian, and we were readopting Ethan. Ian seemed to understand that this ceremony somehow made him officially a Rosenow, officially a part of this family — and he beamed characteristically throughout. Ethan didn't understand any of it, but he loved all of the attention, nonetheless. A reporter from a local newspaper attended the event with us, and then he and a photographer followed us home for some additional interviewing. He was preparing a story on our family and the ministry, to run on Christmas Day.

The exciting day was made magical when we arrived home and found an e-mail waiting for us, stating that Shannen's case had cleared PGN! We almost couldn't believe it, and the timing was priceless. Her adoption in Guatemala was final and she was now our thirteenth adopted child! After sixteen months of fighting and struggling against what seemed to be the forces of hell, we could proclaim to the world that this beautiful little girl was now officially Shannen Mariana Rosenow.

Just before the year ended, we were given another reason to celebrate when Greg and Kristen announced that their first baby was due to be born the next summer—just in time for their first anniversary. We were going to be grandparents, and we had several children of our own who weren't even potty-trained yet. We were awed by the blessings God was dropping into our strange and beautiful life.

The year 2007 ended somewhat similarly to many other years, in that there was still a Rosenow child out there waiting to come home to us. But it was different, too, in that we knew that this child was officially ours, and we were simply waiting for the paperwork to catch up so we could bring her home. Our hearts were also occupied with thoughts of Caelyn and the fact that we couldn't seem to get her restored to good health. We knew that a major surgery was ahead for her, in a little over a month, and while we prayed that this procedure would be the one to correct her physical problems and help her, finally, achieve social continence, we were also plagued with worries that her body might not be strong enough to withstand all that was about to be required of it. But even these concerns, as real and as looming as they were, could not succeed in dampening the joy we felt as the year drew to a close. The year 2007 had brought three new Rosenow children — although one was not yet within our four walls — and our hearts were full as we said goodbye to '07 and bid a warm and expectant welcome to 2008.

Sometimes it's best not to know what lies ahead.

Chapter 18

Barely Holding On, But Firmly Held

When we are assured that nothing which is
appointed by our Father can come to us wrongly,
our cup of suffering becomes a cup of love!

John MacDuff

Welcome, 2008

January found us facing more surgeries with our kids. Two were scheduled for early in February, and the third at the end of February. The first two were for Ian and Stephen, and the third was for Caelyn.

Ian was having a pharyngeal flap procedure, to reduce the amount of nasal bypass during speaking—a procedure Stephen had gone through a few years earlier. Stephen, who was now seven, was scheduled for a bone graft to close the remaining small opening in his palate, which had been left open intentionally when his palate was initially closed, to allow for growth. This is normal in cleft palate repairs.

Both surgeries went very well, and the boys were home recovering by the middle of the month. Stephen faced the longer recovery period: he was not allowed to engage in any contact sports or rough activities for six weeks, while the bone graft donor site at his hip healed completely. Neither of the recoveries, though, presented any major difficulties, and both boys were soon back on their feet and back to their normal routines.

We also received some joyous news. Our dear friend Alison, who was TSC's Medical Ministries Coordinator and Managing Family Coordinator, became engaged. During the years since Alison first came into our lives through Carlin's adoption from Romania, she had become more than just a close family friend, and the role she now filled was much more like an aunt to our children. She and her fiancé, Jason Weibert, were planning the wedding for mid-May, and Alison really wanted Caelyn and Carlin to serve as flower girls in her wedding – and she really wanted our entire family to be there to share this important day with her. We desperately wanted to be there, too, but the cost of getting the whole family from Cincinnati to San Diego appeared to be prohibitive. We took a look at what we thought our income tax refund would be, and we began praying.

The month of February brought us another significant encouragement. On the fourth of the month, Robyn sat with Kathy and me in our family room and told us that she was ready to become a Christian. As we always do, we asked her a lot of questions about what it means to become a Christian, how it's done, etc. In her typically quiet and shy way, nine-year-old Robyn expressed the deep things of God and His salvation using the thoughts and words of a child, but truly and accurately, nonetheless. After about an hour of talking, we all solemnly and joyfully bowed our heads, and Robyn asked Jesus to save her from her sins and make her a child of God. Oh, how we rejoiced, along with the Host of Heaven, that another little Rosenow had been adopted into the eternal family of the Lord of Creation!

Caelyn's surgery

On February 26, Caelyn once again entered Children's Hospital in Cincinnati to begin preparations for her major bladder reconstruction surgery, scheduled for two days later. The preparations were more difficult for her this time than they had been the first time around, and she had to deal with quite a bit of nausea and diarrhea this time. She was a trooper throughout, but it was hard on her.

The surgery was performed on Thursday, February 28, 2008. She went into surgery at 7:30 a.m., and they were finished eleven hours later, at about 6:30 p.m. It was a long day for Kathy and me in the waiting room, but it wasn't the longest we were to face in the week to come. Following the surgery, the staff immediately moved Caelyn into the pediatric intensive care unit (PICU), a normal happening after such a lengthy surgical procedure. They expected to move her from the PICU to a regular room sometime the next afternoon.

They were able to move Caelyn from the PICU to a regular room at around 3:30 on the afternoon of February 29. We were glad that we were through what we thought was the toughest part of the ordeal, and that now all we had to do was help Caelyn through the initial stages of healing. As we went through that second night, though, she began experiencing spasms of pain, requiring an increase in the amount of Morphine she was receiving on a continual basis. And then, in the wee hours of the morning, her blood oxygen saturation levels, or sats, began to fall. The urology doctors wanted to maintain Caelyn's sats above ninety-two percent, but by around 5:00 a.m. she was having difficulty maintaining them at ninety percent, and often they would fall into the eighties.

Out of the frying pan and into the fire

Caelyn continued to deteriorate over the next half hour or so. As we would give her instructions on what to do to breathe more deeply and try to clear out the congestion that had begun to accumulate in her lungs, she would bravely do everything we asked of her. She was fighting so hard – in fact, harder than any of us knew at the time. Each time, her sats would rise briefly into the low nineties and then almost immediately begin falling again, now down into the seventies. The urology team was notified of what was going on and they ordered a chest x-ray. The floor nursing supervisor called in the Medical Response Team (MRT), a multi-disciplinary group of physicians, nurses, and technicians trained to respond to rapidly unfolding and challenging medical situations.

The chest x-ray indicated that Caelyn's right lung had collapsed completely, a condition called atelectasis. The MRT made the decision to move Caelyn back into the PICU immediately, and to administer continuous positive airway pressurization, or CPAP, to reinflate her collapsed lung. She was moved into the PICU at around 9:00 a.m. and the team quickly set up the CPAP and placed the breathing mask over Caelyn's face. Still the sats continued to drop, now into the forties. As they held the mask over Caelyn's face and told her to breathe deeply, her face began to betray the panic she was feeling as she experienced a form of suffocation. The team realized that she was in serious trouble and the ICU physician, who was part of the MRT, told us that she wanted to intubate Caelyn to get oxygen directly into her lungs via a ventilator.

E-mail excerpt from Kathy, March 1, 2008: *I will never, ever forget the look in Caelyn's eyes — the panic — as she looked up at me, trying to say something, through the tears and the gasping. I know now that she felt just as if we were holding her underwater. Even then, though, when I would lean close enough to whisper in her ear and try to help her calm down and breathe slowly, she would try with all her remaining strength to fight the panic and do what I asked. She actually slipped into unconsciousness just as they were starting the sedation before her intubation process. The nurses told us that this happened from the sheer exhaustion of trying to keep up the fight, and that her body wouldn't have been able to even try to breathe on its own from that point forward. They told us later that they had all underestimated just how much Caelyn was still fighting to breathe on her own at that point and just how severe her lung situation was, so that as soon as they sedated her, everything barreled toward coming to a stop.*

As she began slipping away, the ICU room exploded into noise and action, quickly filling up with the people who are trained to respond to such life-threatening situations. I had stepped out a few minutes earlier to make a phone call, to let the family know what was going on with Caelyn, and so Kathy was left alone while this intense portion of the drama began unfolding. She heard someone calling out, "Who has ears! Does anybody have ears?" while grabbing for a stethoscope and then shouting, "I can't hear anything!" Others shouted, "Get the crash cart!" or, "More epi. and more atropine!" or, "Conventional ain't gonna cut it here this time, folks!" Kathy was now as terrified as Caelyn had been, and Caelyn was by then unconscious.

I returned while this was still going on, and my mind raced as Kathy quickly filled me in on what had happened while I was gone, without ever taking her eyes off of Caelyn—or at least, as much as we could see of her through the gauntlet of nurses and doctors ministering to her as we stood in a corner of the room, out of the way. How could this be happening? Why had I stepped away, even for just a minute? Silently I prayed, "God, please protect our little girl. . . ."

It was only a short time afterward that the ICU doctor left the bedside briefly to tell us that Caelyn's immediate crisis was under control. Once they got her intubated, her right lung began to reinflate somewhat. As they were intubating, they extracted a mass of secretion that had been blocking the right lung, which they described as "lots and lots of very, very thick mucous." The doctor felt that Caelyn, who would remain heavily sedated for a couple of hours or so, would begin to do much better fairly quickly, now that they had cleared the blockage.

With that assurance, and once we managed almost completely to stop shaking, Kathy and I slipped down to the hospital cafeteria to grab a bite to eat while Caelyn slept. When we got back to the PICU, we found that the ICU doc had been looking for us. They were concerned because Caelyn's mean blood pressure (MBP) was too low. The MBP should be around sixty-five for a child Caelyn's age — seven years old — and hers was in the low fifties.

The doctor told us that he was going to have to insert a new central catheter into the internal jugular vein in Caelyn's neck. They would use this new central line to deliver strong blood pressure medication into Caelyn's heart, to try to elevate her MBP to an acceptable level. But, the doctor said, there was a down side: the blood pressure medication, dopamine, would somewhat impair the body's healing processes even while it was boosting Caelyn's blood pressure. He said that they would be walking something of a tightrope, fighting the low blood pressure which threatened Caelyn's health, on the one hand, and fighting to allow her body to heal itself following the surgery, on the other.

The PICU team surprised us again a little later when they told us that, in addition to the collapsed lung that morning and the low blood pressure they were currently battling, Caelyn was running a fever and had apparently contracted an infection of some sort. They didn't know where the infection resided, but they suspected the lungs. They began administering a broad-spectrum antibiotic while waiting for the results of lab tests to pinpoint the specific type and nature of the infection.

The ICU doctor made it clear to us that Caelyn had very nearly died that morning, and that they were all very relieved that all personnel involved — especially the floor nurses — had acted as quickly and positively as they had, but that Caelyn was not out of the woods yet. So, we thanked everyone involved, and then we sent e-mails to virtually everyone we knew, pleading for ardent prayer on behalf of our little girl.

Over the next few days, Caelyn continued struggling. She experienced some sort of psychotic reaction to the narcotics she was on, and it was all Kathy and I could do for a time to keep her in the bed and prevent her from pulling the tubes out of her body. In fact, they eventually had to use arm restraints for her own protection, which Caelyn found intensely distressing, even in her semi-conscious state. She was still running a fever, and the team couldn't seem to determine its source. They had a great deal of difficulty stabilizing her blood pressure, partly because of the large doses of medication they were giving her to fight the other issues she was dealing with.

Kathy discovered that the one thing that would most often keep Caelyn calm was hearing her special song. When we brought her home from China, we chose the Beatles' tune, "I Will" as her song. "Love you forever, and forever; Love you with all my heart. Love you whenever we're together, Love you when we're apart." Kathy searched the Internet and downloaded every version of this song she could find. We set up Kathy's computer close to Caelyn's bed so that Caelyn could hear her song playing over and over again throughout the long days. This music commingled with the beeps, clicks, and humming sounds of Caelyn's ICU equipment, as Kathy and I sat beside our daughter's bed for hours at a time, stroking her face and hands in our attempts to keep her calm. With memories of Lauren's death still so fresh in our minds, we begged God not to take another of our children Home, not yet.

In spite of a few setbacks and struggles, Caelyn did improve over the course of the next few days. Her surgery had been on Thursday, February 28. She had been moved back into the PICU on Saturday morning, March 1. She was released from the PICU and sent up to a regular room on Wednesday, March 5. She was still having problems with her nasogastric suction tube, but otherwise she was stable and doing quite well by then.

Once she got to the regular floor, she improved steadily and predictably. The doctors finally released Caelyn from the hospital on Friday, March 14, eighteen days after she had been admitted for pre-op preparations. Our frail little China doll had been to the brink of the abyss and had looked over the edge, but she had once again come home to us, praise God!

At one point during her struggles with the narcotics in the PICU, while Kathy and I were fighting to keep her calm and still, she would alternate between periods of giggly euphoria and intense sadness. As she was languishing in one of the emotional lows, she cried plaintively to Kathy, "Mommy, when can I see my kids? I just weally, weally, weally miss all my kids" (referring to all of her siblings). Now she was at home, surrounded by "her kids," barely able to lift a finger without somebody jumping up to get whatever it was she wanted. She still had three drains in her abdomen and a lot of things to deal with, but we had her home with us, and she was at least on the road to recovery.

Shannen

While we were living through the drama of Caelyn's time in the hospital, life in its other aspects was unfolding, too. Kathy and I continued wrestling with the powers-that-be in Guatemala to finalize Shannen's process. We once again had to spend several weeks expending precious energy and time to compel our attorney in Guatemala to complete the final piece in Shannen's adoption.

Once we managed to accomplish this, however, we ran into trouble with the immigrant visa section at the US Consulate, having to do with our form I-171H, one of the documents required for obtaining a US entry visa. While in the hospital with Caelyn, we had received a notice from the Consulate, telling us to submit a Form I-171H so they could process the case. We were confused by this notice until we learned that they had never received our I-171H for Shannen. Once again, our attorney, whose responsibility it was to submit this form, had neglected to do her job. Because of this, we were now unable to get a visa for our legally adopted daughter so that we could bring her home.

After several days and multiple complications, we managed to get a copy of our I-171H to the right people in Guatemala, only to be told that the document had expired several months earlier. We were going to have to come up with several hundred more dollars so that we could obtain new fingerprints and submit another application, so that we could try to get a new I-171H. This process can take several weeks to complete, and we couldn't bear the thought of this major setback in bringing Shannen home.

Kathy and I were able to contact our local CIS office and work with them to expedite the handling of our application and finger-printing. We submitted the paperwork late in March, praying that we could receive our approval in a matter of days rather than weeks. We later learned that, because of changes in US adoption laws and practices, the local CIS office here in Cincinnati would not accept any more applications for adoptions from Guatemala after April 1, 2008. Our paperwork landed on the CIS officer's desk on April 1.

We received our notice that our application had been approved and our I-171H had been issued on April 4. We praised God — and thanked our local CIS office — for this answer to many prayers. It once again looked like we could be traveling to get Shannen in a matter of a few weeks. On April 21, we finally got the notice of our visa appointment. It was done! We made our final plans to travel to Guatemala near the end of April to bring home our newest daughter.

Also while Caelyn was recovering in the hospital early in March, a development in The Shepherd's Crook came our way. One day, Greg and Kristen visited us at the hospital and said that they wanted to talk to us. They both knew how much we were strug-gling to do all of the work associated with running this ministry while also taking care of our unusual family. They knew that what we really needed was an administrative assistant to handle all of the routine and more mundane aspects of ministry operations, to free me up to do the tasks and responsibilities of Director. They also knew that we and TSC's Board of Trustees had been praying fervently, and for a long time, that God would bring the right person forward to meet this need — and that He would provide the means for TSC to pay this person's salary.

Greg then told us that he felt God leading him to step in and help. He had been working as a teacher, using the gifts and equipping the Lord had given him, but he really believed that God was now leading him to exercise some of those same gifts, along with some others that he had been given, to take over the tasks that an administrative assistant could do. His heart had become connected to the work of The Shepherd's Crook, and he really felt convicted that this step was something he needed to do. He and Kristen were committed to trusting God to provide for them, even if TSC were not able to provide a salary; they simply knew that they could depend on Him, and on Him alone, for their daily needs.

Kathy and I were floored, both at the timing of this and at the practical faith of our daughter and her new husband. After prayer and a lot of discussion, the Board decided to take Greg on as part-time Administrative Assistant, in April. Greg also took a job at Starbucks to supplement the meager salary TSC was able to pay him, until God made it possible for us to transition him to full-time later that year. Immediately, though, the work that Greg did proved to be a tremendous help to us. He is organized and efficient — qualities that are less fully developed in me — and I began very quickly to wonder how we, and the ministry, had gotten along without him. That sense of wonder, combined with gratitude to our Lord, has only increased since that time.

Kathryn

On April 3, while we were in the midst of wrestling through our immigration issues for Shannen, Kathryn had a number of seizures. This was a reality of life with schizencephaly that we had been prepared for, but knowing a thing may happen and seeing it happen are two very different situations.

Everyone has his or her own idea of what it means when someone says the word "seizure." The truth is, there are many different types of seizures, ranging from the severe tonic-clonic seizure — what used to be called grand mal — to the barely noticeable absence seizure — formerly called petit mal — both of which are known as generalized seizures, affecting the entire brain. There are also partial seizures, which affect only limited portions of the brain.

Kathryn's seizures are not the generalized tonic-clonic type, but manifest either as absence seizures, during which she sort of drifts off for a moment or two, or as prolonged episodes of uncontrollable crying, from which she cannot be consoled. She doesn't even respond to our voices during these crying seizures, which is highly unusual for Kathryn. The other thing that happens is that she is completely exhausted and lethargic after the seizure is finally over, sometimes even exhibiting temporary post-seizure symptoms, like weakness on one side of her body, or a "drooping" on one side of her face.

In response to this latest episode on April 3, Kathryn's neurologist increased the dosage of anti-seizure medication she was receiving daily and added a second medication, to be administered for only three days. This second medication was supposed to keep her calm and semi-sedated, to enable her body to rest and recover, and hopefully to get back to normal. After she finished her round with this second medication, she continued for several more days to seem sluggish and weak. Her doctor wasn't sure if we were seeing the lingering effects of the heavy medication or some long-term loss of function caused by the seizures.

Over the next couple of weeks, Kathryn gradually returned to her "normal" self. She regained all of the dexterity and coordination she had before the seizures—which, of course, were by no means considered normal for an almost-four-year-old. Still, we felt that we had gotten our Kathryn back, and we rejoiced that God had answered our prayers in this regard. We did, however, opt not to take Kathryn with us on our next trip to Guatemala. Because she was actively having seizures, we felt it was safest for her to stay close to her doctors while we made the trip there and back as quickly as we could.

At the end of April, Kathy and I traveled to Guatemala and, three days later, returned with Shannen. The trip was very quick and largely uneventful, but it was magical to have this child with us after fighting for almost two years to complete her adoption. We left Guatemala on April 30 and arrived back in Cincinnati late that evening. We praised God that Shannen would be able to celebrate her second birthday in a few months, with her family all around her. We couldn't stop marveling over the reality of her—the fact that she had actually come home to us. In fact, we have never lost sight of what a miracle it is that this little girl finally joined our family against so many impossible odds.

We learned, once we got home, that Kathryn had had another seizure. This seizure was a bit different than her previous ones. It lasted nearly ten minutes, and her head jerked rhythmically to one side the entire time. She also clawed at her face and mouth and cried uncontrollably. At the end, she just snapped out of it and returned instantly to her normal self, though she exhibited some lingering effects throughout the remainder of that evening. Her fragile system seemed to be showing more and more tendency to seizures and seizure activity, and we were getting worried about where things might go.

San Diego

After scraping together as much of our income tax refund as we could, and thanks to some help we received from some anonymous friends, we determined that, even though our whole family would not be able to travel to San Diego for Alison's wedding, at least some of us would make the trip. Caelyn and Carlin, of course, had to be there since they were in the wedding. We knew that Shannen needed to stay close to us during her initial adjustment into our family, and we felt strongly that Kathryn and Ethan would not do well away from us again so soon after our trip to Guatemala to get Shannen.

We also felt that this might be a once-in-a-lifetime experience for Colin, who was nine. He had never been to the ocean before, and because of his blindness he had no real concept of what it was. We wanted to give him the experience of standing in the sand, feeling the surf roll in and sweep under his feet and then roll out again.

We also knew that with Caelyn's limited ambulation, two strollers, Kathryn's wheelchair, and a blind son, we would need at least one helper. Kristen and Greg agreed to go along with us to help, and ten-year-old Nathan had recently been trained to serve as a sighted guide for Colin, so we opted to take him along as well.

So, in the end, eleven of us were able to make the trip. Allan and Ryan were able to arrange their schedules so that they could take care of the other children while we were gone. We so badly wished that we could have taken everyone, but that just wasn't possible. As it was, the eleven of us made quite a spectacle getting through the airports as we made our way out west, and then back again a few days later.

The wedding was beautiful, and the whole trip was something that those who made it will never forget, as we took part in the beginning of this dear friend's new direction in life. We did stand on the beach a couple of times, and Colin laughed as he felt the tug of the surf on his feet and experienced the size and power of the Pacific's waves, and as he tasted the surprising saltiness of the water. Parenting a blind child continually opens our own eyes to magical things in this world that we would so often miss otherwise.

Life

We returned from California and really hoped that things would settle down for a while. We soon realized, however, that that wasn't going to happen. On June 11, as we all celebrated Kathy's birthday together, we had one of those unexpected, nerve-wracking experiences that serve as exclamation points in the life of a brain-damaged child.

> **E-mail excerpt from Kathy, June 12, 2008:** *Very hard few days. Ended up in the ED at about 7:45 last night. They finally admitted Kathryn but have no idea what's going on. By the time she finally fell asleep at 1:30 this morning, she had been crying for eight straight hours with only two one-hour breaks — one at 6:00 p.m. and another at 10:00 p.m. And this was with her Keppra, Klonopin, Diastat, and Ativan all on board. We hope to get some answers this morning. . . . And yesterday was my birthday. The cake that Scott baked for me is still sitting on the table with the candles unlit — and the house is full of sad, worried children.*

The neurology doctors were a bit confused about what happened with Kathryn. She had begun crying uncontrollably just as the family was sitting down to Kathy's birthday dinner celebration, and nothing we did had any effect on her. She could not be consoled, and the crying at times reached almost-hysterical intensity. After about ten or fifteen minutes of this seizure, we administered the Diastat we had been given for such a situation, but it had absolutely no effect. We called Kathryn's neurologist's office and talked with a nurse, and together we determined that we needed to take her to the emergency room for treatment.

The emergency department staff were all wonderful and did a really good job trying to stop Kathryn's seizure, but in the end it simply had to run its course. As Kathy noted in her e-mail message, we had to sit and hold her, hour after hour, until it finally abated at around 1:30 in the morning, with Kathy curled around Kathryn's body in the hospital bed, holding her tightly, praying that God would intervene and bring Kathryn's suffering to an end. Once the crying stopped, we breathed a sigh of relief and wondered how much permanent damage might have been done to our sweet baby's brain. Afterward, as we shed a few tears ourselves and continued to pray for Kathryn, she slept a deep sleep, exhausted from her long ordeal. She was discharged from Children's later that day, after her EEG was completed. The staff neurologists told us that the EEG hadn't given them any useful information about what had caused the protracted seizure. They also couldn't yet tell whether or not it had caused any further brain damage. We took a very lethargic and emotionally disconnected Kathryn home and began watching to see if any lingering effects of the ordeal would persist.

Over time, she gradually returned to her normal self, though it took months. Her neurologist made periodic adjustments to her anti-seizure regimen until he felt he had her on the right dosage of the right medication. Her seizure activity eventually stopped altogether, and thanks in large part to her loving and dedicated physical-, occupational-, and speech therapists and a lot of hard work, all of her developmental achievements returned to their pre-seizure state. But as I said, this process took months.

Time for a new season

In mid-June, an amazing thing happened to Kathy and me. We became grandparents. On June 21, 2008, Josiah Christopher Godwin was born to Greg and Kristen. Suddenly, we had a household of sixteen aunts and uncles—and some of them were still in diapers! Kathy and I did not feel like grandparents, though we were full of joy at this new chapter in the life of our large family. We still felt relatively young, and the fact that we still had so many little children to take care of seemed to argue against the truth that we were now grandparents. But we very quickly adapted to this new reality, and it has been and remains a great source of joy in our lives.

Road trip for Carlin

Late in the summer, the Rosenow family again enjoyed a week of rest and relaxation—and swimming—at our friends' house while they traveled to Canada to visit family. The time was fun and refreshing, and way too short, but it helped us enter the end of summer/beginning of fall period with renewed energy, for which we were very grateful.

In September it became clear to us that Carlin was once again showing signs of tethered spinal cord syndrome and would have to have corrective surgery. The neurosurgeon who had done the previous releases on both Carlin and Caelyn was no longer at our Children's Hospital, having relocated to the Children's National Medical Center (CNMC) in Washington, D.C. For reasons that would be difficult to cover adequately, we made the decision that it would be in Carlin's best interests to have the same surgeon perform the operation again this time—which would mean a trip to our nation's capital. We spent a lot of time working on the details and logistics of such a trip, and in the end scheduled the surgery for Monday, November 17—which just happened to be Carlin's eighth birthday.

As we were wading through the difficult decisions and complicated plans for Carlin's surgery, two things happened in our family that served, once again, to put all of these things into their proper perspective and to give us renewed determination to keep doing this for as long as God sees fit. On September 13, Stephen accepted Christ as his Savior. Then, on October 2, Carlin followed suit and did the same thing. Our hearts were filled with joy at both of these momentous events. The instance of salvation is one of transformation, and that transformation was perhaps more outwardly obvious to us in Carlin's case than in Stephen's. Her story was so turbulent and her history so emotionally combative, and her transition into life as a child of God was both remarkable and metamorphic. These eternal decisions and their ongoing ramifications provide the reinforcement we sometimes need to buck us up when the trials of life threaten to drag us down. As the Apostle Paul said, "Rejoice in the Lord always; again I will say, rejoice!" (Phil. 4:4)

In mid-November, Kathy and I took Carlin to D.C. and had her admitted at the Children's National Medical Center. She had her surgery as scheduled on Monday, November 17, and everything went just beautifully. We checked her out of the hospital the following Friday and, after spending the weekend in D.C., had her post-operative check-up on Monday morning. By the end of the day we were all back at home, getting ready for Thanksgiving.

We closed out 2008 with somber reflections on some of the events of that year. We had had a few brushes with the darker side of parenting special-needs children, but the year had indeed been a good one, full of blessings from the hand of our Heavenly Father. The ministry was continuing to do the work God had called us to do, though at times we struggled with making ends meet and with some difficult decisions.

At the end of the year, we were able to proclaim, "God is good." But the beauty of that is that our saying it was not a consequence of the blessings God had showered us with during the year. God is good, period. Whatever seems to be going well in our lives and whatever seems to be going badly have no impact on the fact that God is good. Jesus even said at one point, "God alone is good." There is no good apart from God, and there is nothing but goodness in Him. We hope that we may never be misunderstood as saying that God is good *because* of the good things He does for us. We indeed praise Him when He blesses us with good things, but we praise Him, too, when things are not going so well. In Paul's first letter to the Thessalonians, he said, "Rejoice always; pray without ceasing; in everything give thanks, for this is God's will for you in Christ Jesus." (1 Thess. 5:16–18).

Praise God!

Epilogue

Not the End of the Story

We ourselves feel that what we are doing is just a drop in the
ocean, but if that drop was not in the ocean, I think the ocean
would be less because of that missing drop.

Mother Teresa

Still swaying

As we said in the Preface, this book represents a part of our
story. When we got to the end of 2008, where this book
ends, we marveled that God had taken us on such amazing adventures, the likes of which we could never have imagined ahead of
time. What we didn't know then was that He wasn't finished with
our wild ride yet; He had some other crazy-wild things ahead for
us. That portion of our journey will be covered in our next book,
still in progress, the title of which we're still discussing.

We still find ourselves swaying in the treetops, as we continue
listening for the voice of our Good Shepherd and following where
He leads. And we have discovered a few things along the way. One

of the striking things has to do with this figurative tree we've talked about. Though we know we are high up in the branches—and as we pointed out in the Preface, higher than when we started this journey—we see that the branches continue on above us, well beyond what we can now reach, or even see. There is no limit to the height of this tree.

Another thing we've seen—though we knew it all along—is that we are not alone up here. There are many, many of God's children climbing around in this tree. We recognize that we left some behind as we climbed higher, but we also see the feet of many saints[41] above us. In other words, we are not "there" yet. We still have so much to learn, and there are many brothers and sisters in Christ from whom we can learn. It is a delight to us to be here, right where we are, firmly held in the Master's hand—even though sometimes all we can sense is how shaky the branch is that we're perched upon. But we know that our job is merely to keep climbing, keep taking advantage of the light we're given along the way, and keep depending on God to lead us and support us as we go.

Forward and onward

We have been given privileges as redeemed children of God. One of these is the privilege of telling others the truth of the Gospel, "that Christ Jesus came into the world to save sinners." (1 Tim. 1:15) Another privilege we enjoy is to be used as His hands and feet in doing His work here on Earth, so long as He tarries. This work comes in many forms, many different descriptions. But each of us has work to do on the Lord's behalf. James 1:27 tells us that, among other things, the work that God has for us to do includes caring for the needy in real and tangible ways. These needy include the orphan, as numerous Scriptural references make clear.

We are inviting all of you who claim the name of Christ to pray for the orphan. Pray also that God would lead you into ways in which you, too, can minister to these special ones. You may be surprised at the number of ways available for you to get involved. The most obvious — and the biggest — is to adopt. As we have attempted to make clear throughout this book, adoption changes lives, both the life of the child adopted and the lives of the family into which this child comes. Those simple understatements do not and cannot do justice to the reality of such a momentous happening, but we hope that the stories we have presented have made it a little clearer.

Be advised, however, that this call is not for the timid or for those lacking conviction. This is a call to warriors — for it is indeed a battlefield, this world of adoption. The Scriptures make clear that we are engaged in warfare against an Enemy who refuses to admit his own defeat, whose entire being is bent toward the destruction of God's plans and God's servants. As Russell Moore has rightly observed,[42] the adoption landscape is rife with women heeding the call but woefully lacking in strong men with the same level of involvement. And men are needed, men whose warrior-hearts are engaged and committed, who will fight on behalf of the orphan. Join us in praying for this, too.

Other ways to get involved, short of actually adopting, include praying, both for the millions of orphans worldwide, and for the many thousands of families adopting. Pray especially for any families in your home church or your area who are adopting. Another need faced by most adopting families is for the funding required to bring home these special children. The cost of adoption, both private domestic (US) and international, is staggering. Wherever you can, please do whatever you can to support the financial needs of adopting families. This can be done either through direct donations to the families themselves,[43] or to non-profit organizations who provide financial assistance for adoption.

Look for other ways, too, to help families that are adopting orphans. As we have attempted to illustrate, the potential ways to help may be limited only by one's imagination. Little gifts of time and elbow grease, or encouraging notes or cards, or offers to provide childcare are all means of expressing support and the love of Christ to families who, because of their calling and differentness,[44] sometimes feel a bit isolated.

Please, please do not accept the widespread myth that there is nothing you, as an individual, can do about the overwhelming orphan problem in the world. You can do something to make a difference, even if only in the life of a single one of those orphans. But just imagine what a difference that one child would experience! Just imagine the impact that this one child's life would then have in all of the lives touched during his or her lifetime.

Every human is uniquely created in the image of God. Doing something consequential to change the life of one of these image bearers has eternal significance, and Scripture makes it clear that we are called by God to do something consequential.

Final thoughts

One of my all-time favorite musical artists is Rich Mullins. Rich brought us popular songs whose poetry and imagery were at times profound. And one of my favorite Rich Mullins songs is "If I Stand." It is a relatively simple song with deep truths in its words. "The stuff of earth competes for the allegiance I owe only to the Giver of all good things." Oh how true and how convicting

All of us who call on the name of Christ must admit that this earth is not our home, but is rather a temporary sojourn on our way to our final Home. We are strangers and aliens here, working in the service of the One who gave us life. C. S. Lewis said, "The greatest thing is to be found at one's post as a child of God, living each day as though it were our last, but planning as though our world might last a hundred years." The greatest thing! Lord, please sear that thought into our hearts and minds, that we would be found at our posts when the Lord returns or when He calls us home.

Soli Deo gloria!

Photographs

Kathy with her brother
Gary, ca. 1960

Kathy and Gary celebrating
their birthdays together, ca. 1975

Gary home on leave, Christmas
1976: the three of us and their
little sister, Rachel

Our wedding, June 1977

Early family photo with
Kristen and Erin, 1983

Family photo including
Allan, Christmas 1987

Family photo
including Ryan, 1997

Raiza arrives, summer 1997

Family outing, summer 1997

Meeting Nathan at his orphanage,
May 1998

In Mike & Kathleen's
home with our new son

Adoption finalization celebration dinner,
with Pablo & Christy, Kathleen, and
Sarah (with her baby, Sammy)

Nathan at home with his
brothers and sisters

The day Kathy met Meghan in
Changchun, October 1999

Sally, Kathy, and Meghan
shopping in Guangzhou

Meghan meeting her daddy for the
first time, at the airport

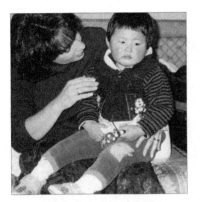

Our first meeting with Robyn in
Shenyang, October 2000

With Hannah and the police officers who
found Robyn the day she was abandoned

Robyn meeting her
family at the airport

Meeting Colin at his orphanage in
La Paz, November 2000.
Also pictured, Nathan with Maruja, his
caretaker when he was a baby

The day Colin came to stay with us at
Hotel Calacoto, telling his caretaker
Caridad good-bye

Colin playing with his new
brothers and sisters at our hotel

With Dean and Linda at Lake Titicaca

Home from Bolivia just in
time for Christmas, 2000

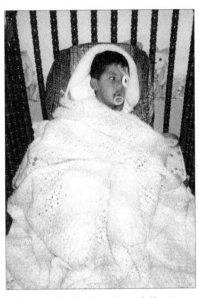

Stephen's adoption finalization, July 2002

Colin, as he had to sleep following
his eye surgery, February 2001

Stephen meeting the family
at the Dayton airport

Shopping in Wuhan

Kristen with Carlin in her foster home,
when she and Kathy traveled to
Romania to bring Carlin home,
December 2002

Carlin home in time
for Christmas, 2002

Flying home after meeting Madlin in
Miami, March 2003

Alison comes for a visit, spring 2003

Carlin's tethered spinal cord release, spring 2003

Our first triple-bunk bed, summer 2003

Trip to the zoo, fall 2003

Caelyn's adoption finalization in Xian, August 2004

Readoption ceremony,
November 2004

New pajamas for all our little ones,
Christmas 2004

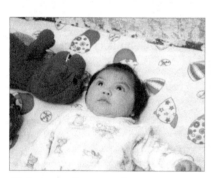

Kathryn as she was when we met her
in Guatemala, January 2005

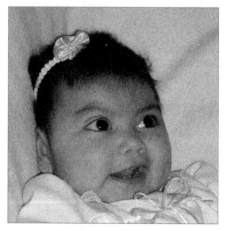

Kathryn after she began to
connect with us emotionally

Kathryn meeting her brothers and
sisters; we got home late at night and
woke them all up to meet her

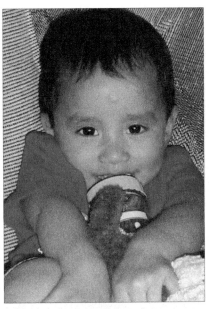

Braedan, our surprise
package, May 2005

Easter 2005

Our first family vacation at our
friends' house, summer 2005

Visiting Lauren and Evan in
Guatemala, March 2006

Visiting Evan again in August, 2006;
we didn't know that this was the last
time we would ever see him

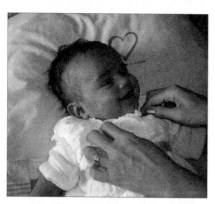

Lauren smiling and cooing at Kathy
right before her surgery in Guatemala,
August 2006

Lauren's headstone in Guatemala,
showing the name we would have
given her (first name misspelled)
when her adoption was complete

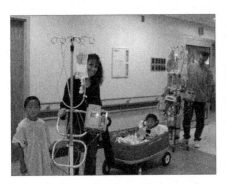

Out for a walk when Caelyn and
Stephen were in the hospital together,
October 2006

Ian comes home, June 2007

The younger boys headed to Greg &
Kristen's wedding, July 2007

Wedding Day for Greg and Kristen,
July 2007

Scott and Ryan, along with Kathryn and Ethan, while we were in Guatemala to bring Ethan home, September 2007

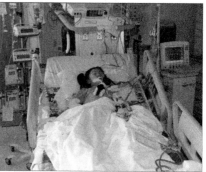

Caelyn in Intensive Care after we almost lost her, February 2008

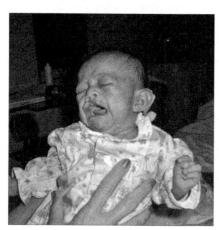

This was Shannen when we met her back in August, 2006

This was Shannen when we were finally able to bring her home, April 2008

Some of us in California for
Alison's wedding, May 2008

Our still-at-home kids, summer 2008

Christmas 2008. We didn't know, at the time this
book closed, that the mantle would grow even more
crowded with stockings in the coming years

Family photo with still-at-home kids, summer 2015 As you can see, our story continued after 2008, when this book closed. Stay tuned for the next part of this exciting saga, which we hope to publish soon.

About the Authors

Scott and Kathy Rosenow have been married for thirty-eight years. Many years ago, they committed themselves to following God's leading in their lives, no matter how crazy or impossible the journey might feel to them or look to those on the outside. At the time of this writing, they have four biological and eighteen adopted children, and they are the founders and directors of The Shepherd's Crook Orphan Ministry.

You can read more about the daily lives of the Rosenows at their family blog (wherelovelearnsitslessons.com), and you can read Kathy's blog (owningmynothingness.com) for insights into the heart and mind of a mother of twenty-two, many with medical and/or special needs.

To learn more about The Shepherd's Crook Orphan Ministry, visit tscorphans.org.

Notes

1 Genesis 32:22–31

2 Romans 8:28 (NASB)

3 Matthew 28:29, in which Jesus charges His followers to go "and make disciples of all the nations, baptizing them in the name of the Father and the Son and the Holy Spirit." (NASB)

4 Bolivia is, or was at that time, the second-poorest country in the Western Hemisphere

5 Matthew 10:37 (NIV)

6 Judges 7:12

7 Genesis 45:4–7

8 Genesis 50:19–20

9 For those not familiar with certain Southern dialects, "sho-nuff" is an expression derived from "sure enough," and it is roughly equivalent to saying, "really, really, really great!"

10 Ephesians 6:12

11 Jeremiah 29:11

12 This promise, like many of those found in Scripture, has two aspects of its realization. The first, often referred to as the "here and now," or temporal, portion, has to do with our life

here on earth. The second, often referred to as the "not yet," or eternal, portion, has to do with our life in Heaven with the Lord. It is usually the eternal portion of the promise that holds the greatest comfort and joy for the Believer, but the temporal portion, too, carries great assurance and comfort.

13 When we say "Communist-looking," we are referring to the type of austere construction characteristic of many of the buildings throughout Eastern Europe and China, with concrete block walls, unadorned windows and doors, and Spartan furnishings.

14 That is, until FY 2008, when adoptions in China fell to just under four thousand, for the first time in a decade.

15 This indiscriminate showing of affection is not uncommon for children who have never been genuinely and unconditionally loved as a parent loves a child, or who have never had the opportunity to bond or attach to anyone.

16 Many, if not most, of these maladaptive behaviors arise from attachment and bonding issues, and many resources are available to help understand children with such issues. One of the best is *The Connected Child*, by Dr. Karyn Purvis and Dr. David Cross.

17 This Pablo is the same Pablo we talked about in Chapters 3 and 4. We had met Pablo and Christy on our first trip to La Paz. Pablo worked with Mike Johnson in running RockSalt Ministries in Bolivia, and Christy was Mike's daughter. Mike and Kathleen were no longer living in Bolivia.

18 The "green card" is an identification card issued by our government for permanent-resident aliens residing in the United States. This card entitles the holder to work, as well as other privileges that accompany permanent-residency status—and it serves as a visa for re-entry to the States, should the holder travel out of the country.

19 I don't want to convey the mistaken impression that our entire time in La Paz was spent in depression, whining about not being able to leave on time, hating the opportunity God had given us. Quite the contrary. We did have some very low points, as I've described, but we also had a lot of rich, warm times, too. As I described earlier, our evenings were spent alone as a family, enjoying hot chocolate and The Chronicles of Narnia, and we were truly thankful for the amazing blessing God had given us in being able to make the trip together. We were continuing to bond with our two newest children, and we were quite simply basking in our special time in the beautiful country of Bolivia.

20 From a parable of Jesus, found in Matthew 13:24–30.

21 When I say that Colin's retina "lay down nicely," I mean nicely for a retina subjected to Stage V ROP. The damage done to Colin's eye by the ROP is such that his retina will never be smooth and flat against the back surface of the eye. Instead, the retina is very rippled and uneven. The optimal outcome would be for his damaged retina to relax and, for the most part, conform itself generally to the interior surface of the back of the eye.

22 Lin Hou was not this child's actual name. We have decided to assign him a fictitious name to preclude his identification.

23 Matthew 6:34.

24 The Mandarin word for mother sounds like ma-ma; the word for father sounds like ba-ba.

25 Revelation 21:27.

26 A state-run orphanage.

27 Microcephaly is a condition in which the size (circumference) of the head is significantly smaller than it should be.

28 Presidential Proclamation 5147 – National Sanctity of Human Life Day, 1984, signed January 13, 1984.

29 January 22, 1973 was the date on which the Supreme Court of the United States determined, in Roe v. Wade, that elective abortion could not be prohibited by the State up to the point of "viability" of the fetus, and that abortion after the point of viability could not be prohibited if it were deemed "necessary, in appropriate medical judgment, for the preservation of the life or health of the mother."

30 Mitrofanoff appendicovesicostomy, named for Paul Mitrofanoff, the French surgeon who developed the procedure in the early 1980s. This procedure uses the patient's appendix to create an organic conduit; one end of the conduit is inserted into the bladder and the other is connected to a stoma (a surface opening) formed in the abdominal wall. The patient empties the bladder periodically by inserting a catheter into the bladder via the stoma.

31 The Malone utilizes a conduit formed from the appendix to connect the cecum to an abdominal stoma, similar to the Mitrofanoff. In most cases, the Malone uses the entire appendix, but in Caelyn's case the appendix would be divided between the Malone and the Mitrofanoff.

32 We introduced Alison to you back in 2001, during her time as a missionary in Romania while we were adopting Carlin. Alison quickly came to play a critical role in The Shepherd's Crook, eventually serving as both our Medical Ministries Coordinator and our Managing Family Coordinator.

33 We later learned that the American Consulate in Guatemala eventually became so concerned about this attorney and her habitual practices that they black-listed her, refusing to process any visa request for an adoption in which she had played a part.

34 They have since changed their name to Show Hope.

35 Convention on Protection of Children and Co-operation in Respect of Inter-country Adoption, The Hague, May 29, 1993.

36 The Malone, sometimes referred to as a cecostomy, is a procedure in which the appendix is used to create a conduit or tube to connect the very end of the large intestine — the cecum — with an opening in the abdominal wall. This conduit is used to irrigate the large intestine daily via a catheter, permitting the patient to be free of soiling accidents.

37 In this case, "benign" means "not cancerous" rather than "kind and gracious" or "causing no harm." The tumorous

mass in the middle ear does cause harm, often destroying the ossicles and bony structures as it grows.

38 In this context, a fellow is a graduate physician who has completed his or her internship and residency and is now doing further study and research in a particular medical specialty — in this case, urology.

39 Noncompliant in this sense means that the bladder no longer functions the way a bladder is supposed to, expanding as it fills and contracting as it empties.

40 The ossicles are the three small bones in the inner ear, comprising the malleus, the incus, and the stapes.

41 The Bible refers to all Christians as saints, not just those who have been canonized through the official policies and practices of a particular church or denomination.

42 Dr. Russell Moore, "How the Orphan Care Movement Could Wreck Itself . . . and What's Needed to Avoid It," CAFO Summit 2015.

43 Such direct donations are generally not tax-deductible.

44 Yes, I looked this word up in the dictionary, and I used it because I think it well expresses what I was trying to say."

CPSIA information can be obtained
at www.ICGtesting.com
Printed in the USA
LVOW02s0848291115

464530LV00011B/317/P

9 781498 454735